D1083382

NISHIDA KITARŌ

NANZAN STUDIES IN RELIGION AND CULTURE

James W. Heisig, General Editor

Heinrich Dumoulin, *Zen Buddhism: A History. Vol. 1, India and China*. Trans. J. Heisig and Paul Knitter (New York: Macmillan, 1988)

Heinrich Dumoulin, *Zen Buddhism: A History. Vol. 2, Japan*. Trans. J. Heisig and Paul Knitter (New York: Macmillan, 1989)

Frederick Franck, ed., *The Buddha Eye: An Anthology of the Kyoto School* (New York: Crossroad, 1982)

Frederick Franck, *To Be Human Against All Odds* (Berkeley: Asian Humanities Press, 1991)

Winston L. King, *Death Was His Kōan: The Samurai-Zen of Suzuki Shōsan*, with a foreword by Nakamura Hajime (Berkeley: Asian Humanities Press, 1986)

Robert E. Morrell, *Early Kamakura Buddhism: A Minority Report* (Berkeley: Asian Humanities Press, 1987)

Nagao Gadjin, *The Foundational Standpoint of Mādhyamika Philosophy*. Trans. John Keenan (New York: SUNY, 1989)

Nishida Kitarō, *Intuition and Reflection in Self-Consciousness*. Trans. Valdo Viglielmo et al., with an introduction by Joseph O'Leary (New York: SUNY, 1987)

Nishitani Keiji, *Religion and Nothingness*. Trans. Jan Van Bragt with an introduction by Winston L. King (Berkeley: University of California Press, 1985)

Nishitani Keiji, *The Self-Overcoming of Nihilism*. Trans. G. Parkes and S. Aihara (New York: SUNY, 1990)

Paul Swanson, *Foundations of T'ien-T'ai Philosophy: The Flowering of the Two Truths Theory in Chinese Buddhism* (Berkeley: Asian Humanities Press, 1989)

Takeuchi Yoshinori, *The Heart of Buddhism: In Search of the Timeless Spirit of Primitive Buddhism*. Trans. with an introduction by J. Heisig and a foreword by Hans Küng (New York: Crossroad, 1983)

Tanabe Hajime, *Philosophy as Metanoetics*. Trans. Takeuchi Yoshinori et al., with an introduction by J. Heisig (Berkeley: University of California Press, 1987)

Taitetsu Unno, ed., *The Religious Philosophy of Nishitani Keiji: Encounter with Emptiness* (Berkeley: Asian Humanities Press, 1990)

Taitetsu Unno and James Heisig, ed., *The Religious Philosophy of Tanabe Hajime: The Metanoetic Imperative* (Berkeley: Asian Humanities Press, 1990)

Hans Waldenfels, *Absolute Nothingness: Foundations for a Buddhist-Christian Dialogue*. Trans. J. Heisig (New York: Paulist Press, 1980)

Nishida Kitarō

NISHITANI Keiji

Translated by
Yamamoto Seisaku & James W. Heisig

Introduction by D. S. Clarke, Jr.

UNIVERSITY OF CALIFORNIA PRESS
Berkeley · *Los Angeles* · *Oxford*

University of California Press
Berkeley and Los Angeles, California

University of California Press, Ltd.
Oxford, England

Library of Congress Cataloging-in-Publication Data

Nishitani, Keiji, 1900–1990
  [Nishida Kitarō. English]
  Nishida Kitarō / Nishitani Keiji ; translated by Yamamoto Seisaku
and James W. Heisig.
    p.   cm.   — (Nanzan studies in religion and culture)
  Translation of: Nishida Kitarō: sono hito to shisō.
  Includes bibliographical references and index.
  ISBN 0-520-07364-9
  1. Nishida, Kitarō, 1870–1945.   I. Title.   II. Series.
B5244.N554N5713   1991
181'.12 – dc20   90-23322
                                  CIP

Printed in the United States of America   ∞

1 2 3 4 5 6 7 8 9

Contents

Introduction

D. S. Clarke, Jr.

NISHIDA KITARŌ (1870–1945), Tanabe Hajime (1885–1962), and Nishitani Keiji (1900–1990) comprise the three most prominent members of what is referred to as the "Kyoto School" of Japanese philosophy, the philosophical movement centered at Kyoto University that assimilated Western philosophic and religious ideas and used them to reformulate religious and moral insights unique to the East Asian cultural tradition. Western readers are now fortunate to have translations of major works by all three philosophers and several studies setting forth their principal ideas and their historical derivations.[1] This present work adds to this corpus in a unique way the reflections of Nishitani as a contemporary representative of the Kyoto School on the life and thought of his teacher, Nishida, the school's founder and central figure. Also included are two lengthy essays summarizing what Nishitani regards

---

1. Nishida's works translated into English include *Intelligibility and the Philosophy of Nothingness*, trans. Robert Schinzinger (Westport, 1958); *An Inquiry into the Good*, trans. Masao ABE and Christopher Ives (New Haven, 1990); *Fundamental Problems of Philosophy*, trans. David Dilworth (Tokyo, 1970); *Art and Morality*, trans. D. Dilworth and Valdo Viglielmo (Honolulu, 1973); *Nothingness and the Religious World View*, trans. D. Dilworth (Honolulu: University Press of Hawaii, 1973), and by Michiko YUSA in *The Eastern Buddhist* 19/2 (1986): 1–29, 20/1 (1987): 81–119; and *Intuition and Reflection in Self-Consciousness*, trans. V. Viglielmo et al. (Albany, 1987). Also available are Tanabe's *Philosophy as Metanoetics*, trans. Takeuchi Yoshinori et al. (Berkeley, 1986) and Nishitani's *Religion and Nothingness*, trans. Jan Van Bragt (Berkeley, 1982). The introductions and accompanying essays in all translations provide valuable expositions and background material. Professor Van Bragt's translation includes also a useful glossary of the central philosophic terms employed by Nishitani. A glossary of terms used by Nishida in his later period appears in R. Schinzinger's translation of *Intelligibility and the Philosophy of Nothingness*.

as the principal similarities and differences between the views of Nishida and Tanabe. In the course of these pages Western readers are offered fascinating glimpses of Japanese attitudes towards philosophy and its relation to religion, the ambitions of a particular group of thinkers for making a unique contribution to world philosophy by synthesizing insights of East and West, and the persistence into the present of the traditional sage-disciple relation.

The biographical material in part 1 assumes a knowledge of Nishida's life that would have been shared by the Japanese audience for which the essays were originally intended. Nishida was born in the remote village of Unoge near the city of Kanazawa located on the northwest coast of Japan's main island of Honshū. He left the Kanazawa area to study at Tokyo University, but as punishment for having participated in student protests critical of the government while in high school he was forced to enroll as one of a group of "special students" denied some of the privileges of regular students. He graduated in 1894 and returned directly to Kanazawa to become first a junior high school teacher and then a high school teacher. In 1898 he was appointed to a post at what is now Kanazawa University,[2] remaining there for the next ten years. It was during this period that he recorded many of the early diary entries referred to by Nishitani in the first three essays of this collection.

Nishida's reading knowledge of English was superior to that of German in his earlier years, and this helped direct his study towards the British psychologists Alexander Bain and G. F. Stout, the writings of William James, and Josiah Royce's system of speculative metaphysics in *The World and the Individual*. This background is evident in his initial major work, *An Inquiry into the Good*, published in 1911. Here the term "pure experience" used by the nineteenth-century psychologists was introduced and given a novel interpretation in terms of a special kind of religious experience.

---

2. Referred to in chapter 1 as the Fourth Senior High School. Earlier Nishida had taught at Yamaguchi Senior High School, which was later to become Yamaguchi University. Nishitani's education was at the prestigious First High School, later to become part of Tokyo University. The Third High School became part of Kyoto University. The incorporation of several of what had been termed high schools within universities was brought about in 1946.

In 1909 he received an appointment at what later became Ga-kushūin University in Tokyo, and in 1910 was appointed associate professor at Kyoto University. Three years later he received his doctoral degree from Kyoto and was appointed full professor, the position he held until his retirement in 1928.

The intensity and eloquence of *An Inquiry into the Good*, coupled with its comprehensive assimilation of central ideas in Western philosophy, established the reputation of its author and helped attract gifted students like Nishitani to Kyoto. Thus was founded the Kyoto School of philosophy. In 1917 appeared Nishida's second systematic work, *Intuition and Reflection in Self-Consciousness*, followed by *The Problem of Consciousness* in 1920, *Art and Morality* in 1923, and *From Acting to Seeing* in 1927. These later works exhibit the growing influence of German philosophy on his thinking, beginning with Fichte, Schelling, and Hegel and continuing on through Heidegger into the twentieth century. Increasingly the orientation of Nishida's philosophy was to shift from psychological experiences unique to an individual to the perspective of a metaphysical system in which the individual is regarded as a part of a comprehensive whole. This change is reflected in his introduction in *From Acting to Seeing* of the concept of "place" (*basho*) as the "self-determination of absolute nothingness" and his preoccupation with dialectical relationships between individuals and the whole of which they are a part.

By 1930 the outlines of Nishida's system were in place and had secured for him the position of Japan's preeminent philosopher. By then he had established the terminology and concepts central to Japan's own modern philosophical movement, forcing other philosophers to define their own theories relative to his. The criticisms Nishitani outlines and replies to in the final two essays of this collection reflect the unique position he held in Japanese philosophy.

Tanabe Hajime's early career developed independently of Nishida's. He graduated from Tokyo University's Department of Philosophy in 1908, and began his university academic career as a lecturer at Tōhoku University in 1913. His early interest was in German neo-Kantian philosophers, and his writings on them attracted the attention of Nishida. The two men corresponded, and in 1919 Nishida helped secure an appointment for Tanabe in Kyoto University's Faculty of Arts and Letters.

In 1922 Tanabe traveled to Germany and came into contact with Husserl's phenomenology, but he was far more influenced by Heidegger's phenomenological existentialism. He returned to Kyoto in 1924. Though greatly influenced by Nishida, after his return Tanabe developed an increasingly independent stance, culminating during the early 1930s in the publication of "The Logic of Species and the World Scheme," in which he develops his social theory of the "logic of species," and "Looking to the Teachings of Nishida," where he criticizes Nishida's metaphysical system from the vantage point of this novel theory. These criticisms are discussed at the end of Nishitani's final essay. Relations between the men soured shortly afterwards to the extent of their breaking off all contact and even refusing to refer to each other by name in later publications.

Tanabe's social theory sought to redress what he regarded as an imbalance towards individualism in Nishida's philosophy. Nishida stressed the individual's self-discipline and achievement of inner harmony by a religious enlightenment (*satori*) consistent with the Zen Buddhist tradition. This inner harmony opened up personal relations to others, but was essentially an individual's quest and achievement. In contrast, Tanabe regarded the individual as defined by the community of which he or she is a part. The most immediate community he regarded as the "species," the racial community of which the individual is a member by birth. The wider community is the "genus," the world republic to which individuals are expected to contribute for the common benefit of humanity. The theory of species is regarded by many as having helped develop an intellectual climate supporting the feelings of racial superiority and the conception of a "manifest destiny" borrowed from Western colonialism that prevailed in Japan during the 1930s.

Whether Tanabe himself should be held partly responsible for the disastrous consequences of this conception has been a topic of a debate. (The debate extends also to Nishida, who because of the great prestige he enjoyed could have been an effective moral critic of militaristic policies.) His important later work, *Philosophy as*

Metanoetics (1946), expresses his feelings when faced with these consequences. In its preface he tells of the conflict between his desire to criticize his nation's policies and his feeling that

> there seemed something traitorous about expressing in time of war ideas that, while perfectly proper in time of peace, might end up causing divisions and conflicts among our people that would only further expose them to their enemies.[3]

This was the occasion for a personal "metanoesis" (*zange*), a feeling of "utter helplessness" and remorse leading to the experience of the saving grace of a divine "Other power." The contrast between this doctrine of grace and salvation, held by the Jōdo (or Pure Land) Sect of Buddhism, and Nishida's own emphasis on the intellectual discipline involved in attaining self-awareness is the topic of the next to last essay in this collection. In *Philosophy as Metanoetics* Tanabe calls on the Japanese people to repeat his own experience of "death and resurrection," to feel remorse over the past, and to experience a rebirth where "sorrow and lament are turned into joy, shame and disgrace into gratitude."[4]

Nishitani Keiji was born in the village of Ushizu in the same prefecture of Ishikawa where Nishida spent all but a few of his first forty years. As we learn in the first essay, their common origins were to help cement a natural bond between the two men. When he was seven years old, his family moved to Tokyo. There he attended the First High School where he decided in what he describes in chapter 1 as an act of "renunciation" to devote himself to philosophy. This resulted in his taking graduate work at Kyoto University to study under Nishida's tutelage, with graduation from its Philosophy Department coming in 1924, the year of Tanabe's return from Germany. Nishitani followed Tanabe's path to Germany and, like his elder colleague, came under the influence of Heidegger there. He returned two years later, in 1926, to assume a teaching post at Kyoto University and then in 1928 a concurrent lectureship at the Buddhist Ōtani University. In 1935 he was appointed professor of religion at Kyoto University and in

---

3. *Philosophy as Metanoetics*, 1.
4. *Philosophy as Metanoetics*, 1.

1955 headed its Department of Modern Philosophy, remaining there until his retirement in 1963.

Nishitani's background prior to taking up philosophy was very different from that of Nishida and Tanabe, both of whom had seriously considered careers in mathematics in their early years and were well versed in the natural sciences. Nishitani's early interests, in contrast, were directed more towards literature. This background undoubtedly influenced the aspects of Nishida's philosophy selected for attention in this present work, leading him, for example, to devote relatively little attention to Nishida's development of a "logic of predicates" and much more attention to the religious implications of his philosophy. Of chief concern for him are tensions within our individual emotional lives, not issues of abstract dialectical logic. This background may also explain the strong interest he developed in existentialist philosophers and writers such as Kierkegaard, Nietzsche, Dostoevsky, and Sartre, and his use of their ideas to explain in direct, forceful language what is distinct in the Zen Buddhist approach towards religion.

Nishitani's unique contribution to the development of Japanese philosophy has its origins in his analysis of what he refers to as the "nihilism" arrived at concurrently by the empiricist tradition in Western philosophy and by existentialist writers. Nihilism arose, Nishitani claims, through the breakdown of Christian natural theology's distinction between a universal spirit or mind (God) and the physical universe as the object of scientific study, the dualist distinction between mind and matter. Nishitani endorses the collapse of this theological tradition. But he rejects the skepticism of the empiricists, the atheism of Nietzsche and Sartre, and the materialism of many scientifically minded philosophers. In their place he proposes in his major work, *Religion and Nothingness*, a new type of religious faith based on Nishida's philosophy, arguing that since Nishida rejects the dualistic assumptions of traditional theology and emphasizes the facts of direct experience, his thought is not vulnerable to the same criticisms. In this way the wisdom of the East as represented by Zen Buddhism can help resolve an impasse created by an untenable framework developed in the West. This thesis is stated in a variety of ways throughout this present work, but perhaps most explicitly in chapters 2, 4, and 5.

Besides Tanabe and Nishitani, a number of other distinguished philosophers can be regarded as members of the Kyoto School, sharing the basic assumptions of Nishida and employing the philosophical vocabulary he had developed, but disagreeing on significant issues. Among them is the neo-Hegelian Yamanouchi Tokuryū, whose criticisms of Nishida's concept of "place" as neglecting the aspect of temporal, historical development are discussed by Nishitani in chapter 10. (Takahashi Satomi, whose criticisms are also considered in this essay, is excluded from the school by geography, if not philosophical orientation: he was a professor of philosophy at Tōhoku University in Sendai.) Other prominent members include Takeuchi Yoshinori, Ueda Shizuteru, and Abe Masao.[5]

MANY WESTERN READERS—certainly those with backgrounds in analytic philosophy—will at first be puzzled when they encounter the method of philosophizing characteristic of the Kyoto School. Absent is any sustained discussion of the issues of epistemology and ethics defined by Descartes, Locke, Hume, Kant, and Mill that have dominated philosophic discussion in the West. When Western philosophy is referred to, more expressive and speculative writers such as Plotinus, Hegel, Heidegger, or Sartre usually figure most prominently. What are the reasons for such selectivity? And what is the underlying conception of philosophy that is responsible for it?

---

5. See Takeuchi Yoshinori, *The Heart of Buddhism*, trans. James Heisig (New York, 1983). See also the collection edited by Frederick Franck, *The Buddha Eye: An Anthology of the Kyoto School* (New York, 1982). In addition to the introductory essays accompanying the translations listed in note 1 above, further information on the Kyoto School is available in Hans Waldenfels, *Absolute Nothingness* (New York, 1980); Matao NODA, "East-West Synthesis in K. Nishida," *Philosophy East and West* 4 (1955): 345–59; Takeuchi Yoshinori, "The Philosophy of Nishida: An Interpretation," *Japanese Religions* 3/4 (1963): 1–32; D. Dilworth, "Nishida Kitarō: Nothingness as the Negative Space of Experiential Immediacy," *International Philosophical Quarterly* 13/4 (1973): 463–83; J. W. Heisig, "The Religious Philosophy of the Kyoto School: An Overview," *Japanese Journal of Religious Studies* 17/1 (1990): 51–81; *The Religious Philosophy of Tanabe Hajime*, ed. T. Unno and J. Heisig (Berkeley, 1990); and *The Religious Philosophy of Nishitani Keiji*, ed. T. Unno (Berkeley, 1990).

Perhaps the best clues are provided by chapter 2 of this collection. There Nishitani outlines the main features of Western philosophy and contrasts them with those of the Eastern tradition. He notes the inquiring spirit of the Platonic dialogues, where there is no given starting point, all theses are open to question, and agreement is reached only by rational consensus. Philosophy conducted in this spirit is associated with science, at least to the extent of insisting on the use of an explicit method in the formulation of issues and in attempts to solve them. The methods used in Western philosophy are well known. They include Descartes' method of logical derivation from self-evident propositions, Locke's "new way of ideas" for describing ideas and mental operations as developed later by Berkeley and Hume, and Kant's method of deriving the categories by means of transcendental deductions. More recently, the method employed has been one of describing the uses of various forms of language, whether the more specialized forms employed in the sciences or the ordinary language of everyday communication. The success of a method is judged by the extent to which it avoids the difficulties of the method it was designed to replace, by the extent to which significant issues are raised or reformulated, and by its success in enabling cooperating inquirers to reach consensus on a range of issues and to use this as a basis for further development. Those employing a successful method thus arrive at some degree of that "objectivity and universality" that Nishitani sees as characteristic of Western philosophy and science. One employing an accepted philosophic method would not think of himself as engaging in "Western philosophy" any more than a French biologist would think of himself as a "Western biologist" or a Chinese physicist as an "Eastern physicist." Sharing a common method unites inquirers across all national and cultural boundaries.

Nishitani characterizes East Asian philosophy in very different terms. It is, he says, "intuitive and practical," with its emphasis on religious aspects of experience not lending themselves readily to theoretical description. True wisdom is to be distinguished from intellectual understanding of the kind appropriate to the sciences. The "appropriation" of Nishida's thought, Nishitani emphasizes, "embraces difficulties entirely different from those of intellectual understanding" (p. 102). And those who "pretend to understand much but do not really understand, no matter how much they intellectually understand" are the object of his scorn. That "intellectual understanding" is not appropriate is evident from the paradoxes the reader is asked to accept. These are especially evident in chapter 10, where we are told by Nishitani and Nishida that the world "must be simultaneously subjective and objective, simultaneously inside and outside" (p. 194), that "'one' equals 'many,' and 'many' equals 'one,'" that "to be immanent equals being transcendent, and to be transcendent equals being immanent," that the dialectical universal is the universal "negating and at the same time affirming independent individuals," and that religious experiences are those in which "motion equals standstill, and standstill equals motion."

But what is perhaps most distinctive of Eastern philosophy — and the element that may explain its apparent irrationality — is the role of "personality," which is the topic of Nishitani's preface and guides the overall organization of *Nishida Kitarō*. The sage-philosopher of the Oriental tradition is one who wrestles with the conflicting emotions and attitudes that afflict all humans and after a period of struggle attains a kind of inner harmony and serenity that balances opposing forces. His philosophy then becomes a testimony to this conflict and his personal resolution of it, but expressed in a way that will aid others in achieving their own inner harmony. For his immediate disciples he is an inspiring example; as a writer he expresses to others more distant the conflicts they themselves experience and provides hints of a kind of "peace that passeth all understanding." Each philosopher regards himself as a link in an unbroken chain extending back to a remote past where his predecessors left records of their own struggles and resolutions.

Of course, the philosopher of contemporary times must do more than harmonize the inner life. He or she must also arrive at some resolution of the conflicting attitudes that prevail within the wider society, attitudes that represent the perspective of the scientific community, as well as the ideals and aspirations of the artistic, literary community. But philosophers of the Kyoto School consider these conflicts of attitudes in terms of the model of conflicting personal emotions, not as theoretical issues to be resolved by a method pursued by cooperating inquirers. From this follows their emphasis on paradox and their lack of sympathy for the rigor and logical consistency characteristic of contemporary analytic philosophy. Emotions are, after all, inconsistent: we can love and hate another at the same time; and we can both want and not want a certain state of affairs to be brought about. Nor are the attitudes essential for our personal well-being entirely consistent. We must be fully involved in those affairs that concern us deeply, but at the same time we must often exercise a degree of detachment in order to maintain mental balance when subject to destructive passions. We must strive to attain those things we want that are within our control but be fatalistic towards matters beyond our power, somehow preserving the attitudes of both the libertarian and the determinist. Each of us realizes how insignificant and dispensable we are in the larger order of things, but must feel our efforts to be of importance in order to justify making them. We must be at times selfish, at others altruistic. Our mistakes require from us remorse, but future productive activity requires hope that we can avoid making similar mistakes.

Nishida, Tanabe, and Nishitani are chiefly concerned with such tensions between fundamental life attitudes. Given this concern it is natural for them to employ the language of German idealism and existentialism to express these tensions, in particular the language of Hegelian dialectics with its oppositions between "being" and "non-being," "thesis" and "antithesis," and so forth and its "mediation" between them. Moreover, the ambiguity of such language, its susceptibility to a variety of interpretations, makes it admirably suited for expressing attitudes, allowing readers to relate its abstractions to their own innermost feelings in a way impossible for the more precise language of technical philosophy. This may partly explain the wide popularity of the writings of the Kyoto School in Japan, especially those of Nishida, and the fact that they have gained an audience far beyond academic circles. Though perhaps often daunted by their difficulty and obscurity, most educated readers can appreciate and be moved by the many passages that help focus and enhance feelings shared by all.

THE RELIGIOUS attitude of reverence towards some inclusive whole of which we are a part dominates the writings of the Kyoto School. It is expressed in a variety of ways throughout this present work, perhaps most eloquently by Nishitani in chapter 1.

> Each of us is one of the focal points for the world's creative self-awareness. In giving birth to an infinite number of such focal points of self-awareness, the world reflects itself through them and becomes creative in the process. . . . That we exist as self-conscious individuals independent of one another, and that we live and act as such, is the world's reflection of itself in us as its foci of self-awareness. We are what Leibniz called "living mirrors of the universe."

Nishida uses the term "self-identity of absolute contradictories" to describe the fact that independent individuals can also be focal points in which "the world reflects itself." If this religious intuition is never questioned by the Kyoto School, neither is it explicitly argued for. Atheism is never a serious philosophic alternative; materialism, though also inconsistent with dualism and the "two worlds" theory, is rejected principally on the grounds of conflicting with the central religious intuition. The intuition itself is characterized as "pure experience" in Nishida's *An Inquiry into the Good*. In later writings it is described as "action-intuition," a state of self-forgetfulness occurring when we become the "self of no-self" and when "subject and object become one," a state of total absorption in our present activity and at one with all around us.

The whole with which we feel united in such an experience is described in a variety of ways. In the passage just quoted it is referred to as the "world." It is alternatively described in other places throughout the work as "reality," the "law of the universe," the "One," "God," and Hegel's "concrete universal." It is also described as the "unifying force" (*tōitsu ryoku*) of all things, a force that Nishida, the "man of passion" described in the first essay, seems to regard as primarily volitional, a cosmic impulse or desire in which all participate, perhaps what the poet Emerson had in mind when he wrote:

> O what are heroes, prophets, men,
> But pipes through which the breath of Pan doth blow
> A momentary music.

This religious intuition is articulated by means of a metaphysical theory in which the term "nothingness" is substituted for the "being" of Western classical philosophy and the systems of Hegel and Heidegger as the theory's central term. Understanding the reasons for a substitution at this level of generality poses a formidable problem to the interpreter of Nishida's thought, and controversy on this elusive subject is perhaps inevitable. The most plausible solution in the view of this writer is obtained by interpreting the substitution of "nothingness" for "being" to be derived from differences between the "emanation" theory originating with Plotinus and the conceptual framework of Mahāyāna Buddhism from which Zen Buddhism was derived.

The emanation theory has strongly influenced Christian theology and has persisted into the present in a variety of guises. Its main features are familiar. We finite individuals, according to it, have been generated by a primordial overflowing of, or emanation from, the One as the source of all being, a process producing first the intellectual realm of ideas, then the realm of souls, and finally the material world that includes our bodies. Each successive stage is more remote from the original source and to that extent suffers from a greater degree of imperfection, with the material world the final stage and hence most imperfect of all. Each individual as isolated and finite yearns for union with Being, the eternal One, as a means of release from the bondage and suffering of the material world. Mystical experiences were described through the Middle Ages as humans' achievement of such a union, an achievement possible only after great efforts to "purify" the imperfections of the body.

Western speculative metaphysicians and theologians, beginning with the Scholastics of the late Middle Ages and continuing on through the twentieth century, have carried out a series of transformations of the theory. First, they eliminated from it references to a personal "God" and anthropomorphic features attached to it by Augustine. Later, they abandoned the dualistic mind-matter framework within which it was originally formulated. But they retained, though in different ways, the fundamental notion of what Hegel terms a "diremption," a separation of parts from the whole, as the ground of the antithesis between "Being," the primordial source, and "Non-Being," that which is further removed from this source.

The basic lot of humankind as a result of this fundamental separation is to lead an "inauthentic existence," the vague awareness of which produces the feeling of alienation and the emotional response of anxiety or *Angst*. The religious life is depicted as one that attempts to overcome this separation and isolation and to regain, if only partially, aspects of a primordial existence predating the "fall." The basic features of the emanation theory, the feelings of alienation and loneliness it expresses, and the hopes for release from these feelings it arouses have thus persisted into the present as a part of the Western religious heritage.

Nishida's alternative may be metaphorically termed the "condensation" theory, though no single term can adequately convey its fundamental contrast to the model dominating much of Western religious thought. According to this theory, each individual is like a condensation point within a boundless, unlimited medium, a determination in space and time of what is itself indeterminate. This indeterminate, boundless medium Nishida denotes by his term "absolute nothingness." As Schinzinger expresses it in his introduction to *Intelligibility and the Philosophy of Nothingness*, for Nishida "all being is a self-unfolding of the eternal, formless nothingness; all finite forms are shadows of the formless." There is no separation of finite individuals from some primordial Being, nor is there alienation due to a turning away from Being towards Non-Being. Instead, each individual is simply a particular determination of the indeterminate. The religious life is depicted as a progression by means of mediation and self-discipline to a realization of this fundamental aspect of our existence.

This is a difficult notion to grasp as a metaphysical abstraction. Fortunately examples in the areas of aesthetics, logic, and physics are available that illustrate it in different ways. Western art emphasizes form in both painting and music. A painter covers the entire canvas with color; from the beginning to the end of a piece of music, the composer provides a melody and accompanying harmonizing chords. Oriental art characteristically emphasizes the contrast between form and a neutral background. In *sumi* painting the blankness of the white rice paper is pervasive; the black brush strokes mark sharp contrasts with this background. In seeing what the artist has formed one is aware at the same time of the blankness it interrupts. Similarly, what pervades much flute and koto music is silence. The sounds produced by the performers are sudden interruptions of this silence; to listen is to listen to a contrast. Perhaps the most famous of all Japanese *haiku* poems is Bashō's description of the sound of a frog jumping into a pond, a sound also breaking a pervasive silence. The characteristic aesthetic experience is thus the perception of the formless, the indeterminate, out of which brush strokes and sounds are like condensations or crystallizations at specific points in time and space.

"Negation" is a logical term and can only be explained by linguistic illustrations of logical principles. Suppose we are describing a collection of objects, say swatches of cloth, all of which are assumed to be some shade of red. For me to describe a particular swatch as "pink" is to mark a contrast between it and those that are "not pink," namely those we would describe by a range of predicates including "crimson," "magenta," and "scarlet." To be "not pink" is to be one of the alternative shades of red within this range. The meaning of "pink" is defined by its position in this range of incompatible alternatives. Similarly, "red" marks a contrast to what is "not red," namely to those colors we describe as "yellow," "orange," "blue," "violet," etc.; its meaning is also defined by its position within a range exhausted by such specifications of color. The term "color," in turn, acquires meaning by contrast to "not colored," for example, "black," "gray," or "white." But this process of forming progressively more inclusive incompatibility ranges of predicates must eventually terminate. "Absolute negation," at least according to one interpretation, stands for that which contrasts to the most inclusive of such ranges, and therefore for that which cannot in principle be exhausted by further specifications. As the totally indeterminate, it stands in contrast to every determination of meaning, no matter how specific or general.

The third illustration of absolute nothingness is one Nishida often employs: he compares the idea to Plato's conception of a "receptacle" in the *Timaeus*, the indeterminate "potentiality" from which every individual thing as substance with form is an "actualization." In contemporary physics this conception can be interpreted as being reintroduced in the form of the medium or "carrier" of the waves correlated to subatomic particles. Such particles can be interpreted as "wave packets," overlapping waves whose coincidence constitutes the particles out of which all other material things are formed as their combinations. But what is the medium or "carrier" through which the waves travel? It is the absolute indeterminate lying at the base of all determinate matter whose "form" is described in terms of the particles' charge, spin, charm, and so forth.

Of course, these are only illustrations of what Nishida means by "absolute nothingness." As we have seen, for him the nature of the whole seems to be primarily volitional and what is referred to as the "self" as part of this whole is that particular locus of wants and desires that characterizes each individual. Within this framework the fundamental religious intuition becomes that of realizing that this particular locus or "place" is the determination or "condensation" of the force animating all living things. With this realization the "self," with its specific goals and projects for wealth, fame, and success, becomes the "no-self" identifying itself with that of which it is a partial expression.

The form-background, positive-negative, and substratum-form contrasts in art, logic, and physics are all but indications within various aspects of our thought and experience of this more fundamental type of determination. In contrast, the emanation theory focuses on the emotions of "anxiety" or *Angst* that are outcomes of the primordial "diremption." The fundamental desire shared by all, though not necessarily in a self-conscious way, is for union with the One, an object of desire replacing for the religious the more specific objects of everyday life. It is by formulating a theory providing a framework in which very different emotions and attitudes are given expression—ones that seem to many of us more positive and "healthy minded," to use Nishitani's phrase, than those emphasized by its Western alternative—that Nishida has made his own unique contribution to religious thought. To the other members of the Kyoto School that followed him all students of philosophy and religion owe a debt of gratitude for preserving and reinterpreting this contribution and on occasion for criticizing his formulations of it.

Translators' Note

THE PRESENT VOLUME is based on a work published in 1985 under the title 西田幾多郎—その人と思想 by Chikuma Shobō of Tokyo. As indicated in an author's preface written especially for this collection, the essays gathered together here span the period from 1936 to 1968. The work is presented here in its entirety save for one chapter on Nishida's diaries. This latter, composed as an afterword to the diaries themselves, was felt to break the unity of the work and to require too great a familiarity with the contents of the diaries. It has been omitted with the consent of the author.

Together with two essays on the philosophy of Tanabe Hajime (also omitted from this translation), the entire work was reprinted in volume 9 of the *Collected Writings of Nishitani Keiji* (Tokyo, 1987). The original Japanese titles and relevant bibliographical information for each of the chapters translated here are as follows:

1. わが師西田幾多郎先生を語る，社会思想研究会『わが師を語る』，1951.
2. 西田先生の人格と思想，西田幾多郎先生頌徳記念会『西田先生とその哲学』，1949.
3. 西田先生の日記について，「東海人」，『西田幾多郎全集』 vol. 15, 月報，岩波書店，1948.
4. 哲学が日本に根を下ろすために，『西田幾多郎全集』，全集再刊パンフレット，岩波書店，1965.
5. 西田哲学，『哲学講座』，vol. 2, 筑摩書房，1950.
6-8. 『善の研究』について，現代日本思想大系，vol. 22, 『西田幾多郎』，1968.
9. 西田哲学と田辺哲学，『田辺哲学』，弘文堂，1951.
10. 西田哲学をめぐる論点，『思想』，1936.

xxiv / TRANSLATORS' NOTE

The footnotes are almost exclusively the additions of the translators and have been kept to a minimum. Only references to the Japanese original of *An Inquiry into the Good* (volume 1 of Nishida's *Collected Works*) have been inserted into the text itself. A draft of a much needed new translation of the book by Abe Masao and Christopher Ives was consulted, but at the time our own work was being completed the final text had not appeared in print. In deference to the coordination of philosophical terms throughout this work, the translations of citations from this work are therefore our own.

Chinese characters for names and technical terms, when not given in the notes, can be found in the Index. The names of Japanese persons cited in the translation are given in their normal order, that is, family name followed by personal name. In the case of works published in the West in which the order has been reversed, the family name has been set in capital letters to avoid ambiguity.

THE TRANSLATORS would like to express their gratitude to Professor Clarke both for providing an introduction to the translation and for the considerable effort he put into a stylistic revision of an earlier draft of the work. Thanks are also due to Sadako Clarke for her many valued suggestions and to Katherine Clarke for typing the earlier draft. Finally, we would like to acknowledge the painstaking assistance of Jan Van Bragt, a seasoned translator of Nishitani's work who has once again brought his skills to bear on our efforts.

Preface

THE MATERIAL brought together in this book represents a scatter-
ing of essays written in reply to requests from various quarters. As
such they constitute less an academic elucidation of the system of
thought of the great philosopher Nishida Kitarō than a collation
of altogether personal and subjective impressions and reflections
on the man who was my teacher. This is not to say, of course, that
I have not wanted to examine his thought objectively and purely
as thought. But so many factors have intervened to obstruct that
intention, and meantime so many others have begun to take up
this kind of research, that I have not had the opportunity to pursue this path myself. I can only hope that the articles included here
may serve as some small compensation for my failure in this regard. If these pages can but mark a milestone on the difficult road
to a proper study of Nishida's philosophy, I shall consider my
modest labors to have been more than rewarded.

When these labors are set against the wider background of
our times, however, it is clear that much more is involved than
presenting the thought of one particular philosopher. A glance at
the present world situation shows us that in the economic and political realms the world is already being transformed into "one
world" in the true sense of the term. As international exchange
between East and West grows deeper, exchange at the level of intellectual culture has increased dramatically. More than ever before, our age has seen the tides of history swell pregnant with great
changes propelling us into a new future. The current diffusion of
interest in Nishida's philosophy among Europeans and Americans
seems to be in keeping with this general temper. A number of his
works, beginning with *An Inquiry into the Good,* have already been
translated, and other translations are now in progress. The uni-

versal mood of interchange in the realm of intellectual culture —
perhaps as yet little known in Japan — is so deeply rooted in historical necessity that it can only develop still more rapidly with the
passage of time. And with it, interest in Nishida's philosophy will
also advance. In this context, an intensification of serious work on
his philosophy in Japan will be an important task for the future.

I HAVE SAID that the pieces included in this volume reflect merely
my own impressions, but there is another element here on which
I will touch from time to time in these pages. Simply put, my
chance encounter with certain of Nishida's writings affected the
entire course of my later life. I cannot imagine what my life would
have been like, or even what I myself would be like now, had it not
been for *An Inquiry into the Good* and the man who wrote it. When I
say the entire course of my life was altered, I am not referring to
the posts I would hold or the work I would do to earn a living. I
mean that I was shown a way I could make my own to face the
problem of whether my life had any meaning. I was given the basic
strength to live life. Here again, to say that Nishida's writings
pointed the way does not mean that they inspired me to a lifelong
interest in the philosophical disciplines, let alone to a career in
philosophy. Mine was the prior problem of personal survival itself:
it was a question of "to be or not to be." The locus of my doubts was
pre-philosophical. In this sense, it was through the encounter with
Nishida the person, prior to the encounter with Nishida's thought,
that I was shown the way.

Given the circumstances under which I became his student,
even when I read Nishida's writings, I had the sense that in understanding his thought I was coming in touch with the man. Instead
of falling into the common heresy of blending one's own feelings
into what one is understanding, I believe that this recognition
helped me better to appreciate the ideas of my teacher. This may
be part of the reason why what I have to say about Nishida naturally turns into personal memories and reflections.

Understanding thought of any kind, and philosophical thought
in particular, has its own sorts of problems. Among them is the
problem we just noted: in the course of struggling to understand

a philosopher, one's own views are often mixed in. It is only natural to try to be objective in grasping the meaning of another's ideas, but the attempt is no guarantee that problems will not arise. The very attempt to conform to another's thought in a purely objective fashion easily turns it into what we in our contemporary world call information, the mere transfer of cumulative knowledge. Where this happens, the person of the philosopher out of which ideas are born falls away like a cicada's shell. This is a difficulty inherent in the objective approach. In the case of philosophical thought, the person of the philosopher, the basic formative dynamism, houses the very spirit and life of the ideas. In this way philosophical thought and ideas are communicated from person to person (or from mind to mind). From the start the matter of philosophical thought is inseparably bound up with the person of the philosopher.

This approach has problems of its own. Granted that in some broad sense philosophical ideas entail as their formative dynamism the person of the thinker and that the two are inseparable for understanding a philosophy, nevertheless the idea that there is a spirit or life to thought seems too vague and ambiguous. Philosophy is already a discipline, and philosophical knowledge needs to be seen as a kind of scientific knowledge. The idea that philosophy contains as its basic dynamism something less than transparent, something dark and impenetrable to the eye, seems to run counter to its very nature.

Such objections have already been raised in the discussion of whether the essence of philosophy is to be sought in philosophy as science or in philosophy as life. Without wishing to enter into this difficult question here, I would only note that from a perspective that sees philosophy as an academic discipline, the question of the person that arises in philosophy as life probably falls outside the philosophical frame of reference, left over from an objective comprehension of the content of the thought. Even so, we cannot fail to see the person of one who philosophizes expressing itself as a basic dynamism. Obviously the person can be understood through its self-expression in thought, but at the same time an understanding of thought emerges from an understanding of the person behind it.

For those who see philosophy as a science, the reciprocal relation of person to thought and thought to thinker is a post-philosophical afterthought, something outside the pale of the primary task of the student of philosophy. The person's relationship to the thought surfaces only in hazy ideas of a sense of "life" or an indwelling "spirit" floating about in the ideas. In the end, the matter of the thinker as a person has no place in the elucidation of ideas.

From the opposite perspective that sees thought and person as inseparable, it is precisely spirit or life that permeates the two and binds them to one another. One gets a good sense of the soul and vitality of ideas through the person of the thinker. What is *post*-philosophical from the standpoint of philosophy as science becomes post-*philosophical* from the standpoint of philosophy as life; what lies outside the framework of philosophy becomes the very cornerstone of philosophy. It is present in the philosophizing person and also in thought, where it appears as the basic dynamism of thought and as fundamental subjectivity. The self as subject is an important part of the content of thought. It may be likened to the halo with which holy figures are depicted in religious art. Insofar as the ambiguity referred to above points to something essentially ambiguous, resistant to any final clear and distinct analysis or quantification, inexhaustibly open to discrimination of any sort, we can only accept it from the outset just as it is. The way to clear understanding can only begin in this mode of ambiguity. This is the starting point for a proper understanding of philosophical thought.

The eighth century Chinese Zen master Shih-t'ou Hsi-ch'ien writes in his *Ts'an-t'ung-chi*: "The darkness is in the middle of the light—you cannot find it in its darkness."[1] The point is that one does not need to shun clear and distinct places and deliberately grope around for inscrutable mysteries. From a standpoint that is all light, the darkness may only look like ambiguity, but in fact the truly mysterious and mystical is there. At the same time, the encounter with the mystical cannot take place in mere darkness, cut

---

1. Shih-t'ou Hsi-ch'ien (700–91) was father of one of the two main lines of Chinese Zen.

off from all light. Just as a merely surface rationalism is lacking in true reason, the arationality of a deep mysticism prevents us from encountering what is truly mystical. Shih-t'ou Hsi-ch'ien adds later in the same work: "The light is in the middle of the darkness—you cannot see it in its brightness." What is the light in the very middle of the truly mystical? To see it, he says, we cannot look only at its bright side, turning the light of reason on it.

Without our going into too much detail here, a first reading of these two short lines of an ancient writer suffices to reveal a complex structural relation between the elements, here given as light and darkness, that rule the interiority of things themselves. There is a dialectical logic at work in the development of this idea that includes contradictories like affirmation and negation and the negation of negation. The problems of the person of the thinker referred to above and of the transmission of thought are also woven into the working of this logic. In addition, different readers find different meanings in these lines. The passage winds up in a sort of conclusion with these words: "Light and darkness face each other—like footsteps following one after the other." Light and darkness are relative and yet move as one body, as when we shift our weight from the back foot to the front in walking. In the words of the Zen saying, "Light and darkness, at bottom a pair."[2] All of this may help in some way to understand the method and content of Nishida's philosophy.

The foregoing is all related to the fact that although I am one of Nishida's disciples, the essays that make up this book do not in the main represent the results of an objective study based on the subject matter of his thought so much as my own experiences and impressions of Nishida as a person as well as my own feelings. At my first meeting with Nishida I came into contact not with the discipline of philosophy but only with the "person." The pre-philosophical locus of this meeting becomes a kind of post-philosophical locus in the present book, written as one who has engaged with Nishida's thought as a student of philosophy. And yet even in my

---

2. These words appear in the opening commentary to case 51 of the classic Zen text of Sung China, *Pi-yen lu* (*Blue Cliff Record*).

pre-philosophical contact with him there was an orientation towards the discipline of philosophy. The *pre*-philosophical was at the same time pre-*philosophical*.

In the same way, I consider what is *post*-philosophical in these essays to be post-*philosophical*. Insofar as I speak as one of Nishida's disciples about his person, I am dealing with something outside the framework of philosophy, something left over after the study of his ideas. And yet at the same time, insofar as the person of the philosopher belongs inseparably to the matter of his or her ideas, what pertains to the person reverts to our understanding of the thought. This is why I speak of it as post-*philosophical*. For myself, it is possible also to relate this post-*philosophical* personal question to the personal aspect of what I called my pre-*philosophical* period. In other words, my relationship to Nishida is part of the total horizon of my life.

THIS BOOK represents a record of personal sentiments covering a period of nearly three decades, from 1936 to 1968. The period of personal confusion that forms a backdrop to these years has been detailed in two essays entitled "My Youth" and "My Philosophical Starting Point," both of which are contained in *The Mind of the Wind.*[3]

I owe the preparation of this volume entirely to the labors of Sasaki Tōru, who edited and arranged the material here, as he had with *The Mind of the Wind*, and to Ōnishi Atsushi, one of the editors of the Chikuma Publishing House. To both of them I wish to express my deepest appreciation.

Nishitani Keiji
Kyoto
1 May 1980

---

3. 風のこころ (Tokyo, 1980). For English translations of these essays, see "The Days of My Youth: An Autobiographical Sketch," *FAS Society Journal* (Winter 1985–86): 25–30; "The Starting Point of My Philosophy," *FAS Society Journal* (Spring 1986): 24–29. Concerning the latter, see also the opening pages of Jan Van Bragt, "Nishitani on Japanese Religiosity," *Japanese Religiosity*, ed. J. Spae (Tokyo, 1971), pp. 271–84.

Part 1

Nishida, the Person

1 Nishida, My Teacher

SO MANY have written about Nishida that I doubt there is anything left for me to add. At best what I have to say will be fragmentary — like picking scales off a dragon — but I trust it will serve some wider purpose for me to commit my thoughts to paper. To begin with, I would like to say something of why I felt moved to go to Kyoto and to study under Nishida. In so doing, I am speaking not so much of my teacher as of myself. Still, the place Nishida held in the soul of a simple student like me seems to mirror on a broader scale the position he has held in the post-Meiji Japanese mind.

Reading Nishida's *Thinking and Experience* set the direction for the rest of my life. While a student at First High School, I was invited to spend the summer vacation after my first year (at that time, school began in September) at the home of Usui Jishō in Nagano prefecture. On my way back to Tokyo after vacation, Nishida's book caught my eye at a bookstore in Yotsuya Shiomachi. I think it was only after the publication of Kurata Hyakuzō's *Beginning from Love and Knowledge*[1] that Nishida's name first attracted national attention, but Kurata's book had not yet appeared nor, do I believe, had the Iwanami edition of Nishida's *An Inquiry into the Good*. In any case, his name was not widely known, and certainly I had never heard of him. I bought his book only because it was the kind of title that appealed to a high school student. The first part of this book was made up of purely philosophical articles such as "Understanding Logic and Mathematics." Once I got home and

---

1. Kurata Hyakuzō (1891–1943). His novel, published in Tokyo in 1921, was a minor classic for the generation of youth who grew up with its vision of love, sex, and religion. His play 出家とその弟子 [The Monk and His Disciples] has been hailed by Romain Rolland as one of the greatest twentieth-century works of religious literature.

started making my way through them, I found that it was all rather over my head, since I had never read this sort of book before.

At the same time, I was deeply impressed by the various lighter essays that made up the last part of the book. Not only did I feel a greater affinity to these than to anything I had read previously, but I also felt the presence of something qualitatively different. I felt as if what I was reading had emerged from the recesses of my own soul. Of course, I do not mean that I could have written them myself, only that I did not feel that someone else had written them. When I look back on what I have produced myself since I began writing, I have to admit that not everything gives me the same feeling of intimacy that I had at that time towards Nishida's writings.

This may sound odd, but on reflection it seems to me altogether natural. It is no easy matter for one to be oneself authentically, and it is in fact altogether possible for somebody else to be closer to one than one is to oneself. To have been given the opportunity as a young man to encounter someone nearer to me than I was to myself I consider one of the greatest blessings and joys of my life. Such an experience brings one to an awareness of oneself by reflecting onto an external mirror an image of oneself elevated far above one's actual self. To be sure, such a lofty self-image is no more than a possibility whose realization is beset with difficulties. Still, when one has not been given the opportunity to encounter someone in whom this loftier self can be reflected, life tends to wear itself out in comings and goings on the flatlands without ever venturing up the hills and mountains, and indeed this is the case for a great many people. For them, life comes to an end without their having realized this vertical dimension. To meet a teacher in the genuine sense of the word — one who invites you to ascend the mountain path that turns out to be the way that leads you to yourself — is rare good fortune. I am deeply convinced that this is just what happened when I picked up Nishida's *Thinking and Experience*.

I had of course been influenced by other books before that. I still recall how taken I was by Kunikida Doppo's novel *Musashino*,[2]

---

2. 武蔵野. Kunikida Doppo (1871–1908). His story, published in Tokyo in 1901, is full of the poetic descriptions of natural beauty for which Kunikida is remembered. As a student at Waseda University, he was baptized a Christian.

which I read in the early years of junior high school at the recommendation of a friend who spent a lot of time reading Doppo's novels. (My friend committed suicide just before graduation from junior high.) As an upper-class student I grew fond of Natsume Sōseki's novels, and indeed Sōseki's impact on me at the time was as decisive as Nishida's was to prove later on.[3] For me it was a time laden with extreme difficulties because of a variety of external events. A sense of despair had settled inside me from which I was unable to shake free. It made everything look empty and vain; it felt like an endless desolate wind blowing through my inner parts.

In these straits, the voices of suffering I heard in the novels of Sōseki reverberated within me, and I felt as if inwardly attuned to the very shuddering of nerves of which he wrote. I was also learning, without being aware of it, that the only way to overcome such suffering and despair was to transcend the world. And since this lesson took the form of a philosophical posture or a Zen state of mind in Sōseki, I was drawn spontaneously to these things. It was this encounter with Sōseki that prepared the way for my meeting with Nishida two or three years later.

The main thing I learned from Sōseki was the true meaning of courage: to be truly serious about the most important things in life, never to forget that the self is always the self, never to forfeit one's personal independence and freedom. Heartened by the lesson, I found that I was able to hold on without giving in to despair, however far my spiritual state may have deteriorated. In short, Sōseki showed me the way to a higher world of interiority.

It was my great fortune to have learned about profound health in the midst of distress, or perhaps I should say a healthy way to accept suffering, at a time when I was leaving my boyhood behind but was burdened with afflictions too great for a young soul to shoulder. Because of my newfound health, I was able not only to resist the evil and unhappy events that nature and humanity threw up at me from their depths, but also in the long run to overcome them. That is, I gradually came to regard the events that

---

3. Natsume Sōseki (1867–1916) was a major figure in modern Japanese literature. Sōseki had an immense influence on Japanese intellectuals caught between the excitement of modernization and the apprehension of losing touch with traditional values. Translations of his major works are now available in English.

6 / NISHIDA, THE PERSON

befell me as ineluctable elements in the course of my own small history. I was able to see the blessing in them without having to sanction the evil and unhappiness they contained. As things that had happened to me, they were fortuitous; but as manifestations of the essence of nature and humanity, there was something necessary about them. This was the source of the unredeemable despair they left in their wake. Such despair—what the ancients called *avidyā* (the darkness of ignorance) or original sin—is overcome by transforming it into the destiny of the "self" in the sense just referred to. Later on, I had a chance to read what Nietzsche had to say about *amor fati*, which I interpreted in terms of the course I myself had begun to set out on and whose first steps I owe to the inspiration of Sōseki.

Soon after I enrolled in the First Senior High School in 1917, I learned of *The Diary of Santarō*.[4] At the time the book had just begun to attract a wide audience of young students, and in fact I came to know of it at a presentation by a third-year student on campus who spoke of how the book was everything for him at present. I rushed to buy a copy and read it. Around the same time I also devoured several books of Watsuji Tetsurō,[5] including his *Restoration of the Idols* and his studies on Kierkegaard and Nietzsche. After securing some command of German, I read Nietzsche's *Thus Spoke Zarathustra*—over and over. Although I had no hope at the time of fathoming the depths of Nietzsche's thought, something in the book resonated ineffably with my current state of mind, which my own personal problems had rendered progressively more painful and desperate. Throughout my three years of high school I read voraciously, including whatever Russian and northern European literature I could get my hands on. While few Japanese translations were available, I was fortunate to be able to read Eng-

---

4. 三太郎の日記. The book was written by Abe Jirō (1883–1959) and published in Tokyo in 1916. Although Abe was a serious philosopher (he is credited with having introduced neo-Kantian thought into Japan), he was also a devotee of Natsume Sōseki. *The Diary of Santarō*, actually a collection of his own diaries, essays, and short stories, was extremely popular among young people at the time.

5. Watsuji Tetsurō (1889–1960). *Restoration of the Idols* (Tokyo, 1918) is a collection of essays written in his late twenties that deal with his growing interest in Buddhist aesthetics and Japanese culture. His studies on Nietzsche and Kierkegaard preceded this work in 1913 and 1915 respectively.

lish rather fluently, and thus many of these books were accessible to me. Ibsen and Strindberg I read in German translation. Even today I recall vividly staying behind in the dormitory and skipping lectures in order to immerse myself in Tolstoy's *War and Peace* and *Anna Karenina*. It was in such circumstances that I picked up Nishida's *Thinking and Experience*.

MY SITUATION at the time was the typical psychological state of young people—awakening to themselves and at the same time running up against the problems of life, struggling to deepen their own self-awareness and at the same time to understand what it means to be alive. It also seems to me to reflect the particular stage in Japanese intellectual history that began with the Meiji era. But in addition to all of that, my own personal state came into the picture: a personal sense of despair had worked its way into the problems of life and troubled me day and night. While these three currents flowed together, I was not then aware of the particular spiritual and intellectual stage of history in which I was caught up.

Distinctive to that period of history was the emergence, for the first time since the Meiji era, of an awareness of the individual. The importation of Western civilization began with things institutional and industrial but gradually spread into art, thought, science, and morality. Pursued vigorously, this trend could only lead to the individual's inner self-awareness, to the consciousness of ego. This stage of awareness of the individual, mediated by the Western spirit, set the stage for the appearance of *The Diary of Santarō*.

It was not a question here of the former problem of the freedom of the individual in society, which had to do with practical issues like the freedom and rights of the people, but with the problem of the inner freedom of the individual as individual. It did not show up as a critique of society, but took the negative form of throwing one's view of life and of the world into doubt and the positive form of an awareness of the moral person. What was sought was a cultivation of art, history, and philosophy that would embrace this doubt and this ethic—a refinement that would maintain the possibility of a way to individual self-awareness and self-assurance. This was why Japan opened its arms widely to German philosophy, which was representative in the West of just such a standpoint of inner self-awareness. Although Karaki Junzō[6] was critical of this climate of what he dubbed "cultivationists" (in contrast to the "cultured" or "intelligentsia" who would follow later), it must be said that these cultivationists were in search of the independence of the inner self and saw the need for morality in the wide sense of the term.

The pursuit of the self we see in thinkers like Sōseki and Nishida differed from that of the generation that followed them. Theirs was a quest for the self that began from itself as center and reached outwards instead of simply turning further inwards in search of itself. For them, the more one probes the interior of the self, the more one fails to understand the self. It is something like a road that begins wide but branches off in all directions the further one advances on it and finally ends up in a swamp or disappears into the underbrush. Following such a path is liable to land one in nihilism, or at least to incapacitate one from overcoming nihilism.

Sōseki and Nishida both set out in search of the self from the exact opposite direction. For them, one begins from the self as center and sets out ahead in search of something beyond the self, something normative for the self, and in this way tries to find the self. In other words, the self breaks through itself and looks for its source in a deeper interiority beyond the self. It is a matter not only of cultivation and refinement but of religious passion; it is a matter not only of knowledge but more deeply of will. This attitude, prevalent in the generation of Sōseki and Nishida, probably arose from the fact that those who embraced it still had the tradition of the spirit of the East as their base. And it was probably by aligning itself forcefully with the spirit of the West that had been flowing into the country from abroad that the concern of this spirit with securing the self in the individual — one of the fundamental issues ever since the beginning of the Meiji era — came to flower. If this is in fact the case, there seems to be a great gap between their generation and the one that followed.

---

6. Karaki Junzō (1904–80) graduated from Kyoto University in 1927 and later became a professor at Meiji University in Tokyo.

Be that as it may, having fallen early into a nihilistic frame of mind, I found that first Sōseki and then Nishida inspired me with the strength to resist my nihilism. I found in them a signpost to the only path I could follow.

Still, until the last moment I could not make up my mind about studying philosophy, mainly because I was altogether lacking in self-confidence and moreover had the idea that philosophizing was halfway the same as forsaking the world. During a farewell party held at an inn on Hongō Street, one of my friends said to me, "You really made up your mind to *entsagen*, didn't you!" And in fact the sense of a kind of renunciation was very much a part of my decision at the time to major in philosophy.

I was also worried about leaving Tokyo, where I had lived from the time I was a young child, and moving to a place I was not used to. It seemed as if I was running away on my own from the big city into the country. One day I met my ethics and psychology teacher at the First Senior High School, Mr. Hayami Akira, in the administration office. He asked me what I planned to do, and I replied that I would go to Kyoto University to take up philosophy. He gave me the name of someone who had already left Tokyo for Kyoto. I did not pay much attention to it at the time I left. Only later did I realize that the name he had mentioned was that of Miki Kiyoshi.[7]

AS A STUDENT at Kyoto University, I came into contact with Nishida three times a week. In our day he always appeared in class wearing a kimono and low-cut shoes. Having never seen such a combination before, we found it strange. (Later on, he switched to straw sandals.) The first thing to strike one about him was his incomparably high forehead. I had never seen such a high forehead on anyone else. It looked almost as if it did not belong to his face at all but had an independent existence all its own. Another conspicuous trait was the way the top of his head projected upwards

---

7. Miki Kiyoshi (1897–1945) introduced Marxist thought to the philosophical circles of Japan. He was arrested during World War II on a charge of subverting public order and died in prison.

so as to give the impression that his ears were much lower than they actually were. His ears, nose, and mouth were all large and strong. He was so nearsighted that he could not read a book without holding it right up to his face. His sharp, piercing eyes bespoke a depth rarely seen in the world today.

I used to look at his face and think to myself: When nature breathed life into his body, its breath must have been stronger than usual and must have let up only just before disrupting the organic balance of his body. That was why his skull had risen so abnormally, why his ears and nose had become so strong and large, and why his already delicate eyesight, unable to bear the force emanating from his life, had suffered a functional breakdown — much like Beethoven's hearing had. Of course, this was no more than my private fantasy, but it came to me one day when I heard him say that in his youth he had once had to go a year without reading because of an eye affliction. After that, I was unable to look at him without that thought returning to mind.

His personal appearance gave one the sense that life had embodied itself a stage further in him than in others and that through him it pressed more forcefully on us. But this impression came from more than his personal appearance alone. His manner, the tone of his voice, and the working of his mind all gave the impression of something keen and overflowing with vigor. Even when he talked to us at his home his words were full of energy and often uttered with a voice so deep and low that they seemed to rise up from the pit of his stomach. His bearing was usually calm but would often overflow in a burst of rhythmic energy, giving him a strong and stately appearance.

Nishida was shorter than average and appeared to be round-shouldered, the upper part of his body being bent rather far forward. Not that he looked unstable or weak; on the contrary, his posture made one feel that this was just his body's way of holding itself together and in balance around its own center of gravity. To see him walk confirmed the impression. Every part of him moved briskly, his shoulders relaxing so that his arms could swing freely in time with his brusque gait. The whole of his body seemed to work in perfect harmony, and never more than when he was pacing to and fro on the dais during his lectures. This physical vigor seemed to lend special vitality to his words.

This was particularly true for his special lectures, which were delivered every Saturday afternoon in a tiered classroom in the Faculty of Law and Economics. A mixed audience of students from various departments and Kyoto University graduates came to the lectures. Nishida usually walked into the room thirty minutes late. He stood on the platform, mumbled for a while in a low voice, and then began to walk to and fro. When he grew excited about the subject, he became quite oblivious of his pace, gestures, and facial expression. The words flowed out of him as if charged with electricity and occasionally erupted into flashes of lightning.

His lectures were not what one would normally call well organized. His strategy was not to construct a lecture by following a single thread of logical connections and presenting his thought as a unified and well-articulated whole. It was as if all sorts of ideas inside him were jostling against one another and rushing to the exit at the same time. One sentence might not even be completed before another began. This made it altogether impossible to take notes; instead, the listener was stirred almost without knowing it. To me it felt like listening to a great piece of music—at times feeling struck by something in my innermost being, at times wafted into flight as on the wings of a bird. His lectures truly touched the spirit.

Sitting in the lecture hall I sometimes had the sense that I had grasped the whole of his thought intuitively, much as if the night sky had for a fleeting moment been illuminated by a bolt of lightning. This is not to say that I would have had an easy time articulating what I saw; in fact, I probably did not grasp it as completely as I thought I did. Surely no one left the classroom without having had the mind's eye opened to something beyond words. Such were Nishida's lectures.

When I entered university, Nishida was using Hegel's *Enzyklopädie der philosophischen Wissenschaften* as a text, a carryover from the previous year. His seminar took place in a small classroom located in a wooden building that has since disappeared. As I recall, there were fewer than twenty participants. I remember the sedate mood of the class with a sense of nostalgia. A number of people dressed in suits and somewhat older than ourselves attended, including Mutai Risaku[8] and Miki Kiyoshi. The seminar had been organized for students in the second year and above, but I was allowed to participate along with Tosaka Jun,[9] a First Senior High School graduate like myself.

Professor Nishida usually arrived at the seminar looking tired. He appeared to be bored while the students were busy translating and looked out of the window, occasionally giving way to a gaping yawn. Once a paragraph had been translated, he explained it. Because his explanations were always lengthy, he was in the habit of pacing back and forth on the platform. Although not as exciting as the lectures on his own thought that he delivered for philosophy majors, these seminars were animated and rich in content, perhaps because he found Hegel so congenial. Enthralled by what he was saying, I was occasionally embarrassed by the sudden realization that he had been talking with his gaze fixed on me. He had the habit of coming to a stop from time to time and looking directly at the first face he saw looking his way. Later, in our second and third years, he took as texts Aristotle's *Metaphysics* and Husserl's *Logische Untersuchungen*. The year after I entered university, enrollment increased sharply, and a larger classroom had to be used. As a result — or perhaps it was because of the texts we were studying — his seminars seemed to me to lose some of the tense yet friendly atmosphere of that first year.

His general lectures seemed to me the least exciting. As they were open to students not majoring in philosophy, he seemed to lower the level to make the content more intelligible, although his material was better organized. The rumor among the students was that his lectures were the same every year and that he even cracked the same jokes at the same places. In any case, his lectures for philosophy majors were the most dynamic.

---

8. Mutai Risaku (1890–1974) majored in philosophy at Kyoto University. A disciple of Nishida, he went on to develop his own philosophy of a "Third Humanism."

9. Tosaka Jun (1900–1945) studied philosophy at Kyoto University. He was arrested during the war in connection with the publication of a journal begun in 1932 under the title *Studies in Materialism*. He died in prison.

NISHIDA'S personality and spirit transmitted an undeniable sense of strength and vigor, and yet not as a force he wielded consciously. Like a volcanic flame erupting from beneath the earth's crust, his was a strength that emerged from the inner nature of Nishida the man. This lent a kind of unself-conscious dignity to his presence. One felt that his conscious activities of speaking and thinking were not taking place merely within the framework of the conscious, reflective ego, as is the case with ordinary people, but that they welled up from recesses far beyond the boundaries of the ego. His vitality had something deeply impulsive, something inexhaustibly creative that he himself often spoke of in his early writings as "spontaneous and self-unfolding." It was the feeling of "life" in the most profound sense of the word. Both what he said and how he said it had a severity and a directness that went right to the heart of the matter — all of which his quiet manner of speaking belied.

Perhaps it was this strength of spirit that propelled his thought to such fearlessness and power. Beginning with *An Inquiry into the Good*, Nishida's thinking became an expression of his own awareness of a spontaneous and self-unfolding process within him. This is not to say that his ideas were no more than subjective opinions, but rather that they were the self-expression of the reality that he himself was. In any event, the very fact that during the ten years he spent as a teacher at a senior high school in a provincial city far from the main circles of academia, Nishida was able to produce for Japan's as yet undeveloped world of philosophy an original system of thought of such international stature as *An Inquiry into the Good* attests to his strength of spirit. This spirit shines through even more in his *Intuition and Reflection in Self-Consciousness*, a concerted effort to transcend the system he had already constructed. In his case, transcending a system of thinking that represented the crystallization of years of intellectual activity, and had its roots deep in his own inner parts, was no easy matter. It required the resolution and strength to crash into a wall at top speed. Little wonder that he himself described his *Intuition and Reflection in Self-Consciousness* as "a document of a hard-fought battle of thought."[10]

10. Nishida Kitarō, *Intuition and Reflection in Self-Consciousness*, trans. Valdo Viglielmo et al. (New York, 1987), xxiii.

We may have no way to know what he meant without being forced into the same situation ourselves, and no doubt the same holds true in the worlds of art and business. Later, Nishida's thinking was to undergo this self-transcendence or metamorphosis many times over, but I am sure that on each occasion he must have experienced a struggle similar to, if not quite so desperate as, what he went through in *Intuition and Reflection in Self-Consciousness*. When he stepped down from his chair at the university, having reached the age of retirement, he composed this verse:

> Like the sun that sets over Mount Atago
> To blaze red for the time that remains.

I shall never forget how moved I was the first time I saw these lines on a hanging scroll at Professor Tanabe Hajime's home in Kyoto — a true tribute to the spirit that burned ardently in Nishida.

Whence came a temperament so fierce and a spiritual energy so indomitable? Surely much is due to native character, but much also to rigorous self-discipline. As Nishida once remarked at table, "There is something in a family line that moves continuously in the same direction in search of something. It surfaces in certain members of the family and then perishes. But it can also happen that it erupts abruptly in a single individual, gushing forth like a fountain." I took it that he was referring to himself.

Although I lack adequate details of his genealogy, it was said that his grandfather had also been an avid reader, so addicted to books that he paused only for meals, driving his relatives to murmur, "What is to become of him if he carries on this way!" In one place Nishida writes that as a child he was fond of paging through the Chinese books his grandfather had left behind in the upper room of the family storehouse.

Nishida's father was a skilled calligrapher. His mother, to quote from a book by Nishida's eldest daughter, Ueda Yayoi, "though she did not consider herself an academic, felt there was no greater treasure under heaven than a scholar, and used to enjoy thinking all sorts of things out on her own." Her grandmother, she goes on, had courage of steel, like a man, and it was her determination that enabled Nishida to study at Tokyo University. Nishida's lasting affection for his mother is evident in the verse he penned about her:

> Even now I can't forget
> The image of my aged mother
> Standing at the gate
> To see me off.

He comments:

> While my mother was alive, I used to go home to Kanazawa once or twice a year. Her advanced age made it difficult for her to walk, but she would always come out to see me off, leaning against the gate.

One of Nishida's sisters was also given to study. All of this leads us to assume a reflective disposition and fondness for academic work on both sides of his family.

But one senses something else extraordinary in the blood that flowed through Nishida's veins. He once remarked that he was half-mad, although I should think that whatever madness there was at work in him was functioning at a very high level, outside of the framework of the everyday. When I lived in Germany, I was on friendly terms for two years with the late Takahashi Fumi, Nishida's niece, whom he had asked me to keep an eye on. "At bottom she's a good and simple-minded person," he told me, "but her man-like temperament tends to drive her to eccentricities." It was just as he had said. She was a bold and free spirit, undaunted by anything, oblivious of what others might say about her; but at the same time she had a tender humanness about her, a warm and womanly affection. I also saw in her a quality that set her apart from others—something *ausserordentlich* that Nietzsche would have called "a mind out of the ordinary." In no sense do I mean to compare her to Nishida, only to record my impression that she had certain natural endowments in common with her uncle. Might there not have been an extraordinary temperament flowing in the family line that erupted in the person of Nishida?

Simply by itself, a temperament out of the ordinary only produces an abnormal individual. Even if such a temperament turned out to be the source of an intuitive capacity far surpassing that of ordinary people, what is to keep those powers of intuition from falling prey to narrow, dogmatic prejudices? In Nishida's case, however, joined to his extraordinary temperament was a self-awareness that drew its strength from a larger whole—a kind of universe, a world—that lay somewhere beyond the confines of the ordinary, beyond the framework of the ego of reflective consciousness.

An entry in his diary dated May 1901 reads:

> Why go to all the trouble of right-following? Right-thinking, as in the axioms of mathematics, is the great law of the universe. Try to bend it if you will—it does not bend.

Such phrases as *right-thinking* and *great law of the universe* make one think of Zen, which Nishida was practicing earnestly at the time. They also smack of Oriental mathematics in the broad sense of the term, including Confucian thought. Since he had studied the Chinese classics in his boyhood and later retained an affection for Zen literature and Chinese classical works, we may suppose that these influences surfaced spontaneously in his diaries. His interest in mathematics dated back to his youth. In an essay entitled "Conic Sections," he noted that seeing complicated geometrical problems in such a way that various curves are all described in terms of quadratic equations "had stimulated in me an interest in theories." Or again, informed by a teacher of physics that a curve produced by a capillary attraction is a hyperbola, he records that he "was struck deeply by a sense of the exquisiteness of nature." This interest in the axioms of mathematics seems to point to the influence of philosophy in the sense that it is a form of Western "science." But a closer look beneath the surface suggests a more immediate intuition rooted in his soul.

Nishida himself tells us that from his early years he felt that reality, as it is, is absolute. Hence the undercurrent in his diary of a profound feeling of reality as something actualized in the deepest part of the self and going beyond the ordinary confines of the ego, a feeling that seemed to embody his very soul and give his self-awareness its content. Might it not be, too, that his understanding of the spirit of Oriental mathematics was modeled after this same self-awareness and in turn helped to illuminate it? The vital energy that flowed through the inner recesses of Nishida's personality had affinities with both the dark forces of nature and the conscious will to follow the great law of the universe. This, it seems to me, was the source of the harsh self-discipline he exacted from himself and of his consuming desire to elucidate and purify his self-awareness.

The impulsive element in his personality took the form of powerful desires and harsh sentiments, which he made strenuous efforts to rein in and to purify. Few people I know had passions so strong, melancholy, grief, or anger so profound. Time and again we find such phrases in his diaries around 1897 as "something disquieting within me," "unable to find peace of heart," "in the grip of feelings," and "getting angrier and angrier," "a foment of spirit," and so forth. As a teacher at the Fourth Senior High School in Kanazawa,[11] he earned the nickname *Denken-Schrecken*.[12] Even when I entered Kyoto University he cut the gloomy and unapproachable figure of a "thinker." To put it simply, as a teacher he was distant.

The first time I visited him at his home behind the Seifu Villa was at the end of my first year. I found him sitting at his desk in the corner of an upstairs room. Books were piled high along the wall on the tatami that had parched red with age. The electric light burned dimly, giving a rather gloomy effect to the surroundings. We sat on the floor facing each other, with a hibachi between us. He sat there grim and taciturn. Asked a question, he answered curtly and then relapsed into silence. Feeling at a loss, I quickly asked him what books I might consult on the problem of evil and then beat a hasty retreat. I was so discouraged that I never visited him again during my undergraduate years, although I occasionally went to his office to have him sign a release for me to check books out of the library. I was always awestruck by his pale and

11. The Fourth Senior High School was the predecessor of the present Kanazawa University.

12. A not-quite-idiomatic German combination, clearly formed by Japanese grammar, meaning "to think-to-scare." The idea was to give a harsh-sounding name in a philosophical language to someone who was a Scary Thinker.

gloomy face and by his eyes piercing out through the thick lenses of glasses.

AFTER GRADUATION examinations, I visited him at his home in Tanaka Kasugai-chō and was welcomed warmly. When he found out I came from Noto, he inquired further of the precise place in Noto. Thinking him unfamiliar with the geography of the place, I replied that I came from a place beyond Nanao. Growing impatient, he asked me to specify further the place beyond Nanao. When I told him that the name of the place was Udetsu, he told me that he had once spent a night there. I was taken by surprise. Only then did I learn that he had taught at a middle school in Nanao soon after graduation from Tokyo University. He told me that he had made a trip around the Okunoto area to recruit students. I remember him reminiscing about a visit to Sōji-ji, a main temple of the Sōtō Zen then located in Monzen, and telling me how a long time ago Ōtomo no Yakamochi had held a post for many years in northern Japan and composed a poem about Lake Tamasu in Okunoto.[13] I also learned that Nishida had been born in Unoge, which was on the way to Nanao if one took the Nanao National Railway from Kanazawa station. I had passed it every time I went home! Riding that train always gave me the feeling of entering a remote region, so desolate and sparsely populated. Even the dialect of the passengers boarding there was different. Only when I had transferred to the Nanao line did I feel I had come home.

When he told me he was born in Unoge, I felt a sense of familiarity enter the conversation. He talked on about his boyhood days when he had walked on the sand and played in the pine groves, about how blue the sea had been. Recently I found an account in his diary of the day of my visit, mentioning that a student coming from Noto had reminded him of the old days.

On a visit to Nanao three or four years ago, I chanced to meet a relative who told me of a story he had heard from an old lady

13. Ōtomo no Yakamochi (718–85), a poet and son of one of the influential families of Japan. His poems were later taken up in the *Man'yōshū*.

called him, was a peculiar man, she had said. He used to go every day to the beach and stand for a long time staring out at the sea. "On one occasion," she went on, "I asked him what he was thinking about. He told me he was thinking about the world and how strange it all is. I thought to myself, What peculiar things this fellow says."

The next time I paid a visit to Nishida at night, I walked in on a terrible scene. A visitor was there who seemed to have just graduated from the faculty of law or economics at Kyoto University and was calling on Nishida for the first time. Some time before my arrival, Nishida seemed to have blown up at him, and now he just sat there silently with a look of extreme displeasure on his face. At each remark the visitor made, Nishida lashed back angrily. Everything the fellow said seemed to be off the mark. Undaunted, the guest kept on. "What direction do you think is suited to me?" Nishida got excited and cried aloud, "How should I know!" To which the visitor retorted, "But you talk so much about intuition, I thought you would have plenty of it." Unable to contain himself any longer, Nishida exploded again. His rage flaring and about to drive him up off the floor, he retorted, "I was not talking about that kind of intuition. What you need is a fortune-teller. I know one in Tokyo. His name is Takashima something-or-other." Then turning toward me, he said, "Something like that, isn't it?" I couldn't find anything to say and just kept silent. Then, in an evident attempt to restrain his mood, Nishida proceeded to explain in a more subdued tone what he meant by intuition. As he went on, though, he grew progressively more agitated. The scene was repeated several times. Never again did I see my teacher as angry as he was that night, nor indeed have I ever seen anyone in my whole life so enraged. I felt myself in the presence of something daemonic.

I have heard of several similar outbursts by Nishida, but only rarely have I heard of him scolding his disciples. Nishida tended to let most things pass unnoticed. After Miki Kiyoshi had returned from Europe, a group of us, including Tosaka Jun, Kanba Toshio,[14]

---

14. Kanba Toshio (1904–80) studied philosophy at Kyoto University and later taught sociology and philosophy at Chūō University.

Kojima Takehiko,[15] and the late Toda Saburō[16] used to meet at Miki's apartment to read Aristotle. At the time all of us felt something new and fresh about this man who had been with Heidegger. During this period Miki was summoned by Nishida and scolded about something or other that sent him dashing off pale-faced to a friend's house afterwards. From that time on Miki often spoke ill of Nishida at our meetings, drew closer to Marxist thought, and finally left for Tokyo.

Several years later I myself was in for a scolding. In those days I was a lecturer at the Third Senior High School.[17] I once skipped out early from a meeting for correcting exams and went to the library to read. Everything that had anything to do with me was already finished, and the meeting was dragging on interminably. My absence was the main problem. First I was called in by Professor Tanabe, informed of the problem, and told to see Professor Nishida. Having seen him angry before, I crossed the threshold of his house as if walking on thin ice. In fact, I got no more than a mild scolding, delivered with a look of displeasure. He told me in a low tone of voice that there are duties I have to perform as I make my way in this world, and that my negligence would not be tolerated. Needless to say, I had nothing to say in my defense, but as I looked at his face—which was hard to please even apart from such circumstances—the words seemed to freeze in my mouth, try as I might to get them out. Self-willed sort that I am, I rarely felt afraid of anything, but even though I had not received a particularly stern dressing-down, I can still remember cowering with fear before him that day.

The blood that flowed in Nishida's veins was quick to boil and erupt, but such outbursts usually drove his feelings into a dark mood of unrest. Nonetheless, he attempted to keep his strong emotions in check and to restrain his extraordinary wrath, and in

---

15. Kojima Takehiko (1903–) graduated from Kyoto University in 1930 and later taught philosophy at the Fifth Senior High School, predecessor of what is now Kumamoto University. He was a disciple of Nishida and a leading figure in the International Association of Philosophy.

16. Toda Saburō (1901–37) graduated from Kyoto University's department of philosophy in 1926.

17. The predecessor of the present Kyoto University.

his diaries he clearly expresses himself to this effect. Frequently he warns himself to guard against personal desires and self-interest. In a 1901 entry, for example, he writes:

> When I am reading I often get impetuous, and a thirst for fame makes me restless. I need to reflect seriously on this. It happens because of a contemptible drive for success. Why can't I just stop making such a fuss about Nishida and stop trying to be so stylish?

Or again we have statements like these: "At times like this I tend to get ugly"; "My mind clouds and I can't make up my mind about anything"; and "When I sit up straight and think about it, I grow deeply ashamed of how much selfishness there is in my heart."

The efforts Nishida made to submit his passions and desires to right-thinking, to "go to the trouble of right-following," seemed to take two forms. The first was to actualize right-thinking in his own person, which was to take the form of the practice of Zen. The second was to seek in right-thinking, "as in the axioms of mathematics, the great law of the universe." And here his study of philosophy came in. Clearly these two paths needed to be kept distinct if they were to be followed; to run them together would only lead to a standstill. In his diary Nishida reminds himself that Zen must not be practiced for the sake of academic work. When I myself took up Zen, he admonished me to keep it distinct from my study of philosophy and to beware of a careless conflation of the two. The advice may be correct, but it is clear that in Nishida's case the two derived from the same internal source. At bottom, the quest of the great law of the universe was transformed for him into the search for the self through Zen, and Zen in turn provided the key to his philosophical research. Nishida himself seemed to have anticipated this mutuality. In a diary entry dated 1901 he writes:

> Surely in all things I must not turn to others but must rely solely on my own efforts. As for my philosophical studies, I must break away from any abject quest for fame, begin from a serene self, pursue my studies quietly, unify my thoughts, and integrate everything with tranquility at home.

The following year he noted in the same vein:

Scholarship is after all pursued for the sake of *life* [Nishida used the English word]. *Life* holds first place. Without *life*, scholarship is useless.

From 1907 on all allusions to Zen cease in his diary. This does not imply that he gave up its practice, but only that as his philosophical ideas slowly began to take shape, Zen was fused into philosophy and the practice of Zen had become a recourse for everyday life.

NISHIDA IS SAID to have been introduced to the practice of Zen by his teacher Hojō Tokitaka. In reading his diary one can hardly fail to be impressed by the zeal of his search for the Way, beginning from the time of his teaching at the Fourth Senior High School (1896–97), then at Yamaguchi Senior High School,[18] and carrying on to his term as professor at the Fourth Senior High School (from 1898). At first he sat in daily meditation from after dark until midnight; later on he used to wake up at five or six o'clock in the morning to meditate. Here I can only reiterate what has already been written by Shimomura Toratarō in his book *The Young Nishida Kitarō*[19] and Kōsaka Masaaki in his *Life and Thought of Nishida*.[20] In the beginning he met personally with Tekisui, a well-known monk at Tenryū-ji, for guidance. When Nishida later wrote a letter asking for a point of clarification, Tekisui replied that he would never again permit a *mondō* (question-and-answer session) through correspondence and penned a large 無 , the glyph for *nothingness*. Nishida kept the letter and had it mounted, and was once kind enough to show it to me. He told me that when Tekisui, who usually looked like just an old man, came into the room for an interview, it was as if a tiger had walked in.

---

18. The predecessor of the present Yamaguchi University.

19. Shimomura Toratarō (1902–) has been one of the best-known interpreters of Nishida's thought. An English translation of his essay, "Nishida Kitarō and Some Aspects of His Philosophical Thought" was included in Valdo Viglielmo's translation of *A Study of Good* (Tokyo, 1960), 191–217. In the text, Nishitani has apparently misquoted the title of his work on Nishida; it has been adjusted accordingly.

20. Kōsaka Masaaki (1900–1969). His book appeared in 1948 and was later included in vol. 8 of his *Collected Writings* 高坂正顕著作集(Tokyo, 1965).

He practiced Zen mainly under the monks Setsumon and Kō-shū.[21] Setsumon guided his meditation at Senshin-an in Kanazawa and gave him the name of Sunshin-koji. Kōshū directed his meditation at Daitoku-ji, where Nishida concentrated on the *kōan* of the single character *mu*, or nothingness.[22] He seems to have thrown himself into his practice with a passion. He used to laugh and say how little good it did him to go to a mountain and spend the night sitting on a rock. The fervor of Nishida's practice may have had something to do with the sheer overflow of vital energy in him, but it may also be that his vigor was purified in the process and tempered into a "finely honed will."

In this regard I am reminded of a trivial incident that took place once on a visit to his home. On that occasion — I don't remember exactly when it was — I took out a pencil to write down the title of a book. It was a short stub of a pencil that I used to carry around with me for emergencies, not because I was particularly fond of using short pencils. Catching sight of it, Nishida handed me one of his pencils with the remark that mine was pretty useless. His was a long and well-sharpened pencil with a good lead in it. I felt as if something inside him were thrusting itself out at me. The image of Nishida handing me that pencil and the vivid expression on his face still come back to me from time to time.

In conversations at his house he often spoke to us of Zen, and from time to time he brought along books to help him explain things. It was from him that I learned about the *Oxherding Pictures*.[23] I can still see him tracing his finger across the text and its accompanying verses as he explained its meaning to us. At such times he uttered all sorts of Zen-like sayings himself. One that I recall particularly well because he repeated it so often was this: "If you only see what your teacher sees, you diminish the teacher's

---

21. Kōshū Sōtaku (1840–1907) was head of Daitoku-ji in Kyoto. Setsumon Genshō (1850–1915) practiced at Shōkoku-ji in Kyoto and later became chief priest at Kokutai-ji in Etchū. In 1893 he retired to Senshin-an in Kanazawa, where he directed Nishida in Zen.

22. See case 1 of the *Mumonkan*.

23. There are numerous translations of this book, including one by D. T. Suzuki in *Essays in Zen Buddhism–I* (London, 1927) and H. Buechner and K. Tsuchimura, *The Ox and His Herdsman* (Tokyo, 1969).

merit by half." He was trying to tell us that we should learn to think by ourselves and that merely to imitate the opinions of one's teachers is to pare away half of the teacher's achievement. Another phrase we heard often around the time of my graduation was that "Good children do not use their father's money." For someone like me, who had worked hard to absorb my teacher's point of view, such phrases were strong medicine. That Nishida spoke in these terms made it clear that he aimed to inspire an independent spirit in his students so that they might go their own ways and not be fettered to their teacher's ideas. One hears frequently of Nishida's broad-mindedness in allowing his disciples to pursue their own courses of study. Here, too, the same aim was at work — and I think the same spirit of Zen. Of course, he himself maintained a radical independence in his own work, as a verse of his bears witness:

> Let others do as they will,
> I am who I am.
> At any rate I will walk the way
> That I make my own.

Nishida gave this spirit full rein by encouraging his students to this same independence rather than keeping them tethered to his own way of thinking. As a way of cultivating the person, Nishida's approach seemed to have affinities with that of Zen. What is more, his attitude was a boon not only to his disciples but also to him, especially in his last years. Even though the uniqueness of his thinking developed out of his own experience, in many ways he was stimulated by the various efforts of his disciples.

I should think that one of the greatest effects that Zen had on Nishida was to give him the courage to follow an independent course in his thought. Perhaps that courage was already inherent in him, but surely Zen helped to temper it. A framed calligraphy of Nishida's that hangs in the home of Kōsaka Masaaki reads 乾一坤擲, meaning "To risk everything, win or lose." Nishida's thought was rooted in strong determination and courage, and there it shows the spirit of Zen. In fact, his thinking was a continuation of his Zen meditation, which for him meant the quest for the self or enlightenment. He once told us, "I realized what sort of a thing that self is when I was writing the final part of *Intuition and Reflec-*

NISHIDA, MY TEACHER / 25

tion in Self-Consciousness that deals with the will of absolute freedom." On the inside back cover of the copy of *Philosophical Essays* that I received from Nishida, he had penned the enlightenment verse of Hottō Kokushi:[24]

> Mind is Buddha and Buddha is mind.
> Mind and Buddha are the same both past and present.

Nishida had previously recorded this text in his diary on 1 January 1905, and I am sure the state to which the verse refers had become clear in his heart in 1935 when he published that first collection of essays.

From this time on, Nishida gradually stopped talking about Zen, and topics associated with Zen ceased to appear in his writings. For one thing, his thought had taken a turn towards regarding the historical world as the most concrete world, bringing him into touch with a realm of meaning not usually included in the world of Zen. For another, he seems to have felt that his thought was philosophical through and through and not to be reduced to Zen and its traditional views. He would not have been happy to have his own novel originality accord with ancient Zen such as it was. At the same time, I should think that he maintained to the last the conviction that his own philosophy was an unfolding of Zen within himself, a new manifestation of the Zen spirit. He once wrote me in a letter that he had differentiated his philosophy from Zen to avoid being misunderstood. Nevertheless, the spirit of Zen was surely alive in Nishida's philosophy, which he himself characterized as a radical realism or a radical positivism.

As his own philosophy came to take shape, he gave up Zen meditation. On one hand, it fused into his philosophy; on the other, it became a kind of "recourse in the midst of activity" for everyday life. This amalgamation of Zen into his life and thought may have been the source of the absolute realism that marked the basic nature of Nishida's philosophical activities from the time of *An Inquiry into the Good*. As far as Nishida's Zen side is concerned, his closest associates were D. T. Suzuki and Hisamatsu Shin'ichi. I

---

24. Hottō Enmyō Kokushi, the posthumous name of Shinchi Kakushin (d. 1298), as founder of the Hattō Branch of Rinzai Buddhism.

recall being at Nishida's house once with Suzuki. At one point in the conversation Suzuki began rattling the table in front of him to illustrate what Zen was all about. Referring back to this incident at a later date, Nishida looked over my way to say, "You know about this because you were there," and then began to rattle the table, telling the others present, "As Suzuki said once, this is what Zen is all about." This is not my only memory of such incidents.

Here we see something of Nishida's philosophy of absolute realism. His way of looking at things in terms of "poesis," "action-intuition," "the historical body," or "the self as the self-awareness of the historical world" derived from this source. In addition, Nishida often used to take walks. It was of course good for his health, but clearly these walks were also meant as a kind of retreat in the midst of activity, as a time of meditative exercise or *kinhin*. No doubt, too, these walks gave him new ideas, the sort of ideas that the body grasps better than the brain. This was what Nishida's thought was like. Even in the ordinary things of life, which for him revolved around logical and systematic thinking, the occasional flash of Zen-like illumination broke through. Relatively late in life he once drew in his diary with a red pencil a picture of something that looked like a sun radiating light. It seems that there was some special reflective insight on that day. It is not hard to imagine that these inner experiences flowed into his philosophical reflections so that the two deepened each another.

This is not to say, of course, that Nishida's interests stopped at Zen. For example, he had extremely high respect for the *Tannishō*.[25] His friends have recorded his remarks that if all other books were to disappear, one could get by with only the *Rinzai-roku*[26] and the *Tannishō*, and that there are sections in the *Tannishō* that show the thrust of a master swordsman. It is also clear from entries in his diary during his time in Kanazawa that Nishida had

---

25. The *Tannishō* is a collection of the sayings of Shinran (1173–1262), the founder of the Pure Land Shin Sect of Buddhism, recorded by his disciple Yuien. An English translation has been issued recently by Taitetsu Unno (Kyoto, 1988).

26. The *Rinzairoku* comprises the recorded sayings of the Chinese monk Lin-chi, founder of the Rinzai tradition in Chinese and Japanese Zen. An English translation under the title *Record of Lin-chi: The Recorded Sayings of Ch'an Master Lin-chi Hui-chao of Chen Prefecture* was published by Ruth Fuller Sasaki (Kyoto, 1975).

an interest in Christianity from quite early on. Later he read widely in the new theology. He was particularly fond of Augustine, of whom he once said that the hot blood of Africa coursed through his veins. When I read the verses of Browning translated in *Thinking and Experience*, the images of the blood-red glow of the setting sun, the flaming tide, the stars shining in the African sky, and so forth I got some sense of what fascinated him about Augustine.

ZEN TAMED the fierce life-force that raged within Nishida and made it into a finely honed will. Moreover, it brought to the light of self-awareness the right law of the universe that is met at the fountainhead of that energy, at a point beyond the narrow framework of ego. In short, Zen was what tempered his will so that it might meet the right law of the universe; or, put the other way around, it was what united him to the great law of the universe by purifying his self through will. Nishida always took as his starting place the point within himself at which self and the law of the universe came together. And for him this always meant a serious struggle. No doubt for people of intense vital energy like Nishida, it is no easy matter to direct their passions and desires. He may have felt a profound antagonism between the impulsive energy within him and the principles of the universe, but I think the very force of this antagonism would have brought him to a deeper awareness of the point at which self and universe come together. Surely no one could come in contact with Nishida without feeling that there was something daemonic or deeply karmic in him, and yet at the same time a severity of will intent on overcoming it. This severity of will showed up in the demands he made on himself and others for uncompromising honesty and sincerity. He hated nothing so much as falsehood and insincerity, and yet his awareness of his own weaknesses and errors made him uncommonly tolerant and compassionate towards the failings of others. A gentle humanity lay hidden in the shadows of those fiercely penetrating eyes and did not surface in his features. Nishida was first and foremost a man not of intellect but of heart.

It was probably his basic uncertainty regarding the opposition or unity of the self and the right law of the universe that spurred him towards Zen and towards seeing philosophical research as its continuation. Moreover, his zeal in the practice of Zen and the study of philosophy seems to have come from the ferocity of his vital energy and from the rigorous obligation he felt to follow the principles of the universe. It was precisely because the opposition between the two was so intense that their unity was so deep, and indeed the attempt to resolve this conflict runs like a leitmotif throughout his philosophy. In other words, it was a question for him of the relation between the self and the world that envelops it; or in a more internalized idiom, between the individual and the transindividual, between the particular and the universal.

For Nishida the problems of knowledge, reality, and praxis all start from here. Early works like *An Inquiry into the Good* place less emphasis on the direction of the opposition between the individual and the universal than on their unity. His aim was to treat all problems — knowledge, reality, morality, religion, and so forth — in terms of immediate experience prior to the split between subject and object. From this standpoint, experience develops as a kind of spontaneous self-unfolding of the universal. In *Intuition and Reflection in Self-Consciousness,* he presents the "will of absolute freedom" as the unifying element among the countless systems of experience, as the point at which infinite reality achieves unity, as an "a priori of all a priori." He argues further that the working of this will *is* our present reality, and that within this reality there is a true self, beyond the individual self, that unifies the whole of the real world. As his thinking developed, however, Nishida came to see a profound contradiction, even a negative relationship, between the self and the wider world of the universal enveloping it, between the particular and the universal, yet he continued to think of a deep unity between them. It was, we might say, a deepening of the self-awareness of individual and world.

Nishida's concern here was larger than the task that nature imposes on us at birth and which all human beings bear within them. Fate imposed many afflictions of its own on him. Some arose, no doubt, from his extraordinarily severe disposition. For example, he was in difficult straits for some time because of his decision to drop out of the Fourth Senior High School before graduation and enroll as a special student at Tokyo University. He often spoke to us of the miserable treatment and humiliation meted out to special students in those days and even wrote of it later in an essay. His written remarks make it clear that he tried to rise above this indisposition and arouse a sense of self-reliance. His diaries show that he went through similar struggles during the long period he spent buried in the countryside. He once remarked, obviously deeply moved, that Bergson had also taught high school in the provinces for a long time.

Nor was Nishida's family life without its share of bitterness. One of his daughters, Shizuko, spoke of the insufferably gloomy atmosphere that pervaded the home when she was growing up. Might this not have something to do with Nishida's fierce disposition? Takahashi Fumi, whom (as I mentioned earlier) I came to know in Berlin, criticized her uncle roundly, saying that however good a scholar he was, he had made life at home thoroughly unhappy and was not much of a human being at all. I remember arguing with her that although I did not know anything of his family life, her criticisms seemed to me to exhibit a narrow-minded, woman's way of looking at things and that she had better look at things with a more tolerant eye. (After this incident Fumi's outlook changed, and she even took up my suggestion to translate some of her uncle's essays into German. She was a talented and spirited woman, and also kind at heart. She suffered from tuberculosis in Germany, and died after returning to Japan. As I said, her personality had something in common with my teacher's, and her passing was a loss.)

Retirement from Kyoto University was a great turning point in Nishida's life. The undiminished enthusiasm he showed for carrying on his research after being freed from academic obligations surfaced in the verse cited earlier on the sun setting over Mount Atago. Yet I remember him saying, "Now I am ready to die." Against this backdrop of ambivalent feelings he immersed himself in thought more deeply than ever. With the death of his wife, his house had taken on a most desolate mood. His manner had something dark and melancholy about it. And even his thought seemed to have shut itself up in a dense forest of contemplation just prior to the publication of his *Philosophical Essays*. Marxism was on the rise. I used to go to Nishida's house with Tosaka Jun and others for discussions, usually staying until midnight or one o'clock in the morning. Through it all, Nishida kept quiet for the most part. During this period he wrote the verse:

> It is because of Marx
> That sleep comes hard to me.

Nishida did his best to drive his own thinking deeper and deeper, without concern for the intellectual currents of the time, which in any case were far removed from his own thought. He occasionally held a series of extracurricular classes to talk about new developments in his thought. On one occasion his class overlapped with a lecture by Miki, who during his time in Tokyo had swung towards Marxism. Rather few students went to Nishida's lecture, leaving the large classroom far from full. He carried on in a quiet, almost lonely tone. During the class a storm of applause erupted from the neighboring lecture hall. He looked puzzled for a moment and then continued speaking.

I recall another incident that took place around the same time. Many of the young lecturers at the Third Senior High School, where I was teaching then, pooled our resources to subscribe to a number of magazines, which usually lay in disarray on a large table in the faculty lounge. The current issue of a leftist magazine called *Senki* (War Banner) ran a lead essay that opened with the courageous claim that the time was finally coming around for us to pulverize Nishida's philosophy theoretically (or was it practically?). As it happened, Nishida had some business that took him to the teachers' lounge where he chanced to pick up the magazine. I sat quietly nearby, watching with a mixture of curiosity and apprehension. Turning the pages, he came to the essay in question, read a little of it and threw it aside. His face showed no expression whatsoever.

At such moments there seemed to be something in him that said, as I quoted earlier, "Let others do as they will / I am who I am." Whatever it was, it was cultivated in his perseverance against adversity from his time as a special student to his period of seclusion as a country high school teacher, in his overcoming the moods of depression and irritation, and in his self-purification through scholarship. His posture was tempered especially by Zen and philosophy. It enabled him to endure great family tragedy, to transcend the currents of the age, and to chart his own course between Scylla and Charybdis.[27] At the same time, these external events gave his solitary way a certain undeniable sense of desolation. A dark, depressing air hung about his house, and even his appearance projected a gloomy shadow, as of one who had cut himself off from the world and sunk into himself.

After the fall lectures that the Kyoto Philosophical Society used to hold in those days, a group of us living in Kyoto and some friends from outside—sometimes as many as ten persons—made a habit of calling on Nishida at his home in the evening. On one such occasion, perhaps the first, we met Nishida in one of the Japanese-style rooms of the house rather than in his study. The color had faded from his cheeks and he looked despondent as he sat behind a small table on the tatami. Even the lights seemed to dim with his mood. When some inquired after his health he replied, "I feel these days as if I were in the middle of a deep forest." All of this left a deep but inexplicable impression on me. It was a mixture of loneliness, melancholy, and a kind of pensive inwardness. In fact, one of the reasons we arranged those annual get-togethers was to try to cheer him up. Later we learned how much he looked forward to our visits, for which he used to treat us to *shiruko*.[28] At any rate, it was during this period that Nishida seemed most turned in on himself in terms of both his thinking and family matters.

Nishida remarried in 1931, and after that the atmosphere in his house gradually brightened and things began to fall into place for him. I first learned of his plans to remarry during an evening stroll around Ogawa-chō area with Iwanami Shigeo.[29] I remember how taken aback I felt and how Iwanami laughed and said, "Oh, but your teacher is a man of passion!"

---

27. The phrase Nishitani uses, 白道, refers to a famous parable in the 観無量寿経疏, a commentary on the *Meditation Sūtra* composed by the Chinese Pure Land Buddhist, Zendō (613–81). The allusion is to the narrow "white path" bounded on one side by fire and on the other by water, which the sojourner en route to the Pure Land must follow.

28. A kind of red-bean soup with glutinous rice dumplings.

29. Iwanami Shigeo (1881–1946) was the founder of Japan's most prestigious publishing house, Iwanami Shoten.

Having finally and after long reflection fixed the basic standpoint of what he called the "logic of place," Nishida turned, in a surprising burst of new energy, to develop a new set of ideas on these foundations. With Marxism on the wane and the new vogue of "Japanism" not yet having taken root, there was something of a lull in popular currents of thought.

Apart from the final year or two of his life, when the tides of war had turned against Japan, Nishida's late years seem to have been his happiest. His thinking had come to its proper resting place in the notions of the world as "dialectical universal" and as the "self-identity of absolute contradictories." What followed was the pure creative activity of refining and deepening this standpoint and using it to resolve a number of different problems. In this way he broke free of his tribulations and found a second wind that seemed to sweep away the darkness from his visage and fill him with bright life. The oppressive air of severity that used to frighten us had lifted from him, and his sharpness had mellowed without losing any of its keenness. The harsh, chilling winds of autumn had passed and in their place the bright skies of spring shone gently about his person.

Within this gentleness, however, Nishida had attained a lofty inner state. On my departure for Europe in 1937, he presented me with a number of *shikishi* plaques[30] on which he had inscribed the Japanese verse:

> When the flowers bloom,
> Think of what spring is like
> In your Yamato home of Yoshida.

And on another the Chinese poem:

> Though apart ten thousand miles
> We see the crescent moon over Ch'ang-an.

On two others he wrote:

> Nan-ch'üan says the everyday mind is the Way.

---

30. *Shikishi* 色紙 are stiff paper plaques about 12 inches square used to inscribe greetings.

and

> Speak to heaven silently,
> Silently walk with heaven.

I suppose he chose these last two verses intending them to be maxims for me during my time in foreign lands. But as I think back on them now, they also seem to illumine the spirit of his own philosophy. The idea that the everyday mind, in its various words and deeds, is silently speaking and walking with heaven accords well with the way Nishida's thinking was invigorated by the presence of what he called the historical world.

In fact, Nishida's thought opened the way to a fundamentally new philosophical standpoint that could not have appeared within the tradition of Western philosophy. Here is not the place to embark on a detailed discussion, but the following remarks may give some hint of what I mean. In Western philosophy the speculative standpoint, which reached its peak in the thought of Hegel, was dominant. Empiricism and materialism, although not without meaning in their own right, fall short of satisfying the deepest aspects of the philosophical quest, and in the modern world they tend rather to be reduced to sciences, from physics to psychology. For a philosophy set up in opposition to the speculative standpoint we must turn to the existential philosophies that begin with thinkers like Kierkegaard. Although it is only in existential philosophy that subjectivity has to some extent come into its own, this philosophy has had a hard time including the objectivity inherent in nature, human society, and history—that is to say, the subject matter of the natural sciences and the humanities as well as the content of speculative philosophies. Hence the demand at present for a sublation (*Aufhebung*) of subjectivity and objectivity, of existential reality and speculative thought. In the West such a standpoint may not yet be clearly in evidence, but this was precisely the point from which Nishida's philosophy began.

The "pure experience" he spoke of in *An Inquiry into the Good* was entirely subjective and as such was qualitatively different from the treatment of experience in previous empirical philosophies. He understood experience in terms of what Hegel called the spontaneous self-unfolding of the concrete universal, at the root of whose self-awareness it became one with the reason of the universe. To think about experience in terms of the dichotomy of subject and object or of mind and matter already presupposes a reflective standpoint. It is not a straightforward grasp of experience in its pure form. Pure experience comes about rather at a point prior to the differentiation of subject and object. It is the same whatever we do, whenever we feel something or desire something. But pure experience does not emerge from some "thing" encompassed by the framework of an "ego." The framework is added later through reflection, but experience itself is an unfolding of the universal out of itself prior to such a framework. Nor is it merely a matter of some objective process. The unfolding of the universal out of itself is as such the original form of the self. In other words, it is the manifestation of the very self that is originally one with the great principle of the universe.

This standpoint of *An Inquiry into the Good* restores unity at a deeper and more basic level to the standpoints of speculation, experience, and Existenz that have become cut off from one another in Western philosophy. Such was the unique starting point of Nishida's philosophy, in which, as I have said, we can see reflected Nishida's own individuality. Moreover, we may see at work in this conscious transformation of person into standpoint the orientation of an Oriental spirit at work, specifically the power of Zen. At any rate, new foundations were laid for the Western philosophical tradition that could not have been laid in the West. Nishida's final years were devoted to deepening and broadening these foundations and at the same time to developing more fully the substance of his philosophical system.

To this end Nishida tried to keep abreast of new advances in virtually every field of learning. For example, in his attempt to come to terms with the deep paradox involved in the constitution of the individual as it was presented in the form of the "I and Thou," we see the influence of Kierkegaard and dialectical theology. Or again, we see the impact of Ranke and Marx on Nishida's idea of the shaping of history as a transition "from the created to the creating" (from the conditioning of individuals by their environment to their conditioning of that environment) or on his idea of the historical body. We may also detect the influence of the new physics with its theories of relativity and quantum mechanics, of mathematical set theory, and of Holden's work in biology. Far from simply accepting new ideas passively, Nishida was stimulated by them to develop his own thought further. This motivation may seem rather a matter of course, but it is surprising to see the lengths he went to in order to take in new ideas and through them to develop his unique thought.

The development of Nishida's philosophical system is treated in the books of Kōsaka and others referred to earlier. To put it briefly, there is no difference between the basic character of his system and the character of *An Inquiry into the Good* referred to above, although the two differ as greatly as the visage of a mellow old man and that of a beardless youth. To put it somewhat crudely, the speculations in *The Self-Conscious Determination of Nothingness* attempted to burrow deep into the interiority of phenomena and the self. His standpoint is that of someone looking out from within. It all has an air of introverted submersion. However broad and deep his outlook on the world and inner self, dim traces of the self submerged in its own depths remain in the background; the shadow of the immediately intuited self lingers.

With the *Philosophical Essays*, Nishida switched from seeing things from the perspective of the self to seeing them from the perspective of the world. With this shift, the return to the outermost realm became a return to what was innermost. It was as if in digging a tunnel he had suddenly returned to an expansive world of light. His thinking sets its feet firmly on a mode of reality that in some sense is the most outward—a mode that one might characterize as fact determining fact, as reality determining reality, as historical body, or as *poiēsis* (activity at work). At the same time, this mode of reality is a manifestation of the dialectical "world" that always includes an infinite past and future in each moment like a vast, fathomless, billowing sea. It is the self-determination and self-manifestation of the world. Nishida never gave up asking questions like: What sort of a thing is knowing? What about thinking? Working? Making?

The strength of his thinking, which essentially meant a return to what is simplest and clearest, showed in his way of putting questions. Needless to say, appeals to the ability of human reason and will or to the exercise of brain cells did nothing to answer such questions and amounted to no more than an *ignotum per ignotius*. The point is to explain what these activities are and why they take place (in the world) in the first place. With this end in mind, we have to begin by asking what sort of thing it is to know.

Knowing is the essence of the ability to know, but this is no explanation of what knowing is. It is first necessary to explain what it is like to know and what it means that something like knowing takes place in the world; and this explanation begins from basic grounds or first principles. A first principle is something that emerges by itself and is self-evident. In Nishida's philosophy knowing entails a description of the world as a self-identity of absolute contradictories. In the activity of knowing, this world reflects itself within itself. In other words, knowing is the self-expression of the world. When we know, the world becomes self-conscious.

What is more, since each act of our knowing belongs to our life activity, as an historically creative activity, the self-expression of the world becomes at once the creative activity of the world. Each of us is one of the focal points for the world's creative self-awareness. In giving birth to an infinite number of such focal points of self-awareness, the world reflects itself in them and becomes creative in the process. We do not of course reflect the world by standing outside the world, independent of it. To say that we reflect the world means that we exist as self-conscious beings, that we live and act. This is not to deny ourselves independence. That we exist as self-conscious individuals independent of one another, and that we live and act as such, *is* the world's reflection of itself in us as its foci of self-awareness. We are what Leibniz called "living mirrors of the universe." The very activity of our living and acting is a reflection of the world and at the same time the world's reflection of itself. The world seen in terms of an infinite number of such self-conscious foci is the historical world in the most basic sense of the word. And it is this world that Nishida describes as an absolute self-identity of contradictories.

During these later years Nishida used to leave Kamakura twice each year, in spring and autumn, to return to Kyoto. When word came, a number of us arranged a time to meet him at his residence and hear what he had to say about the newest development in his thinking. At these gatherings he talked as if one possessed by ideas. His whole body came to life and the words flowed out of him in an endless stream. After a long talk, there was time for questions and discussion which later blossomed into light conversation on current affairs and a variety of other topics. It was always around midnight before things wound up.

The reason Nishida called us together to share his thought, as he told us on more than one occasion, was that he felt the general public was liable to misunderstand, and he wanted to make himself understood at least by a small circle. As the war hastened its approach, Nishida's pen accelerated, too. The writings of his final years are his most mature.

He died on 7 June 1945, just before the end of the war. In April he had published an essay tying his thought together under the title "The Logic of Place and a Religious World View." One can only marvel at a spiritual fortitude able to engage itself in such powerful thought when the country was under the constant fury of bombing raids and one city after the other was going up in flames. When his diary and letters from those days are published,[31] they will show how deep was his daily anxiety for the outcome of the war and the future of the country. As he told his friends at the time, he wrote with a feeling of "do or die."

Earlier I noted Nishida's remark upon retirement from the university that the time had come for him to prepare for death, but at the same time he also remarked that being free from official duties would enable him to do a lot of writing. No doubt he did bear these opposing sentiments within himself. This is not to say that they were necessarily contradictory. Or perhaps we should say that they were able to come together completely in their very contradiction. Indeed, his idea of a world of the self-identity of contradictories belonged to a way of life deep enough to harbor these sorts of opposing sentiments. Might we not see in Nishida a state of

---

31. Nishida's diaries were published in the same year that Nishitani wrote these lines, 1951. The letters followed in 1953, but were updated in a later edition of Nishida's *Collected Works*.

mind similar to that of Bashō who, although so absorbed in the writing of *haiku* poems that he wandered around barren fields in his dreams, said that every line he wrote was like a farewell verse to life? Nishida's late remark about the do or die mood of his writing near the end of the war and before he died seems to show a sense of this taking leave of life, a feeling at once deep within him and far beyond him. The dedication of his entire life to creative activity *was* Nishida's preparation for death. It was a lifestyle forged through long discipline, not easily come by. In his later years he was fond of quoting Daitō Kokushi's words:

> To be apart from one another for millions of eons and
> not to be distant for a single moment,
> To be together all day long and not together for a single
> instant.[32]

Comparing this to the similar verse, "Though apart ten thousand miles / We see the crescent moon over Ch'ang-an," which he had presented to me some ten years before when I was about to depart for Europe, one remarks a deepening in his state of mind, a profound grasp of life that is very hard for modern Japanese to see and understand.

---

32. Daitō Kokushi, the posthumous title of Shūhō Myōchō (1282–1337), was the founder of Daitoku-ji in Kyoto and a member of the Rinzai sect of Japanese Zen.

2 Nishida's Personality and Thought

As ANYONE who has read Nishida knows, his thought is extremely difficult to understand and hence equally difficult to put in simple terms. Here I should like to sketch a rough picture of one of its basic points, namely the way he tended to think about things.[1]

Nishida's thought is deserving of world status. A number of great thinkers have appeared in the course of Japanese history who can hold their own anywhere in the world, and I consider Nishida to be among them. Furthermore, in one respect his thought differs greatly from that of his predecessors, and that is, of course, that the base of his thought is worldwide in scope. Nishida thought on common ground with Western thinkers, and this was something that had not happened before. His thought was the outcome of a most profound study of Western philosophy, which is very different in character from traditional Eastern thought. In so doing he ranged widely from ancient to modern thought, leaving virtually no stone unturned in his research.

He had an eye for new ideas from abroad, in some cases ideas not yet given much attention outside Japan. The sheer range of things he thought about seems to have sharpened his eye — or perhaps better, his powers of intuition — for critical reading and made it possible for him to introduce to Japanese academia one new idea after another from the West.

---

1. The reader is referred to a short introduction Nishitani wrote to a selection of Nishida's diaries and published in Kyoto University's *Philosophical Studies* 哲学研究. Nishitani also wrote the afterword to vol. 17 of Nishida's *Collected Works*, which contains the diaries. This essay, included in the original of the present book, has not been reproduced in the translation.

But there is more. We must not overlook the fact that Nishida's thought was grounded deeply in the Eastern, and in particular Buddhist, intellectual spirit. Looking at the diary entries dating from the time he was teaching at the Fourth Senior High School, we find him practicing Zen with great dedication. He used to sit in meditation every day for several hours and of course participate in formal meditation sessions as well. Entries inscribed during vacation were often no more than the simplest of phrases such as "Sitting in the morning, sitting at noon, sitting in the evening," indicating that he had spent the whole day meditating. And even when school was in full session he practiced Zen meditation whenever he could find the time. During one vacation, for instance, he stayed at the hermitage of the Zen master Setsumon on Mount Utatsu for New Year's Eve and New Year's Day. I do not think he ever celebrated these events at home in those days, such was the fervor of his devotion to Zen.

His books show us one whose eyes have been opened by Zen meditation, and this influence may be one reason his thought is as difficult to understand as it is. For he looked at things from a completely different angle, one that turned our ordinary way of seeing inside out. At the same time, this way of seeing is one of the things that draws us most powerfully to his thought and leaves such a deep impression. His way of seeing was in the spirit of Buddhism — or more particularly, Zen — and so altogether different from our normal way of seeing as to turn it on its head. The difficulty is not that all of us lack this power, but only that we may not awaken to it within ourselves. It is because it is so different that it is so very hard to understand, and yet it moves our hearts. This side of Nishida's thought I attribute to the Eastern, Zen Buddhist standpoint that forms the bedrock of his philosophy.

Nishida studied Western thought seriously, then, and in the process pioneered a new standpoint very different from that of Western thought until then. This was possible because, although he was rooted in the spirit of the East, he took a position different from that of ancient Buddhism and other forms of Oriental thought, one that shared the same foundations as Western thought. The novelty that resulted in his thinking may be considered either in terms of an Eastern way of seeing renewed by Western thought or of a Western way of thinking renewed by an Eastern way of seeing. One finds in Nishida's thought both Western thought and a modernization of the Eastern spirit.

This seems to me the route that Japanese culture has to take as it makes its way into the future. For all the splendors of the intellectual history of the East, the present asks something more of us, and in any event there is no way simply to resurrect ideas from the past for a life in the present. A basic acceptance of Western thought, and perhaps even culture, is required. But merely to follow in the footsteps of the West will never lay the foundations for a contribution to world culture, no matter how long we keep at it. Nevertheless, we find ourselves truly in a culturally advantageous position in the world in the sense that we bear a tradition deeply rooted in an Eastern spirit and Eastern culture that people of the West do not have. One way or another, we must find a way to bring it back to life. Left in its time-worn form it is of no use. And the right way to go, in my view, is to resurrect the culture of the East through the culture of the West—in the form of a rebirth through Western culture, if you will, or of a new development of Western culture.

In the world of literature, for example, writers after the Meiji Restoration like Natsume Sōseki and Mori Ōgai pursued just such a course. So deeply did they cast themselves into Western literature that they became almost Westernized, and yet out of their efforts something Eastern emerged. As radically as their work differed from what was formerly seen as Eastern, it kept something of the vital Eastern spirit through ties with its own tradition at the same time as it shared common ground with the culture and thought of the West. In a sense one finds in their work what may be called a living unity of East and West. This quality is also to be seen in Nishida's thought.

TO PURSUE the point a little further, let me begin by touching on the characteristic feature of Western thought. The question is difficult in the extreme, but roughly comes down to this: Western thought is primarily rational, or we might say, logical.

The thought of the West has its foundations in science — which includes the natural sciences, the human sciences, and so forth — and philosophy. Both of them belong to the world of "learning." The East of course had its own words for learned inquiry, but I think it safe to say that it did not have a term for learning that would include, as it did in the West, both science and philosophy.[2] The Western notion of learning begins with the Greeks. This spirit of learning was assimilated into Western culture and eventually built up a unique spirit to be found nowhere else in history. As difficult as it is to say in simple terms just what this spirit is, an example may help.

Among the philosophers of Greece was a certain Plato who, as everyone knows, was the single greatest source for Greek philosophy and science. It is no exaggeration to say that Plato and his disciple Aristotle laid the foundations for Western science and philosophy. Incidentally, Plato presented his philosophy in the form of dialogues, usually by having his ideas worked out in the conversations of various people with his own teacher, Socrates. I find this a matter of great interest and significance. Dialogue is a disputation that takes place when I and someone else — self and other — stand on common ground. What common ground? Ultimately, that of reason.

I recently heard of a Shin Buddhist temple somewhere or other in Hakui (Ishikawa Prefecture) that has the custom of gathering its members together once a year to hold dialogues.[3] In fact dialogues in the East go back to ancient times, usually within a fixed setting. In the case of Shin Buddhism, for instance, the setting revolves around Pure Land's "faith" and the aim of the dialogue is to grasp correctly what this faith means. Within a given pattern, then, upon foundations from which one is not permitted to stray, dialogue takes place. This form of dialogue was also common in medieval Christianity.

---

2. The translation of Nishitani's terms related to learning, knowledge, scholarship, and science presents problems for English that would not apply, for example, to German. In order to make his sense as transparent as possible, the word *learning* has been kept in place of more ordinary but complex English equivalents for the Japanese 学 *gaku*.

3. The word used here, *mondō*, means literally question-and-answer. It is the same word that is used for a dialogue between a Zen master and disciple.

What sets Plato's dialogues apart is precisely that they lack such a fixed framework or pattern. They are no different from ordinary discussions: if I see the sense in what another is saying, or the other in what I am saying, and consider it reasonable and accept it as a matter of course, the discussion continues. Unlike dialogues in the Eastern style, these have no fixed patterns; the discussion simply advances on its own without the need for one. As for what the whole discussion rests on, where its standards for certitude lie, the answer lies in — logic. By setting our feet squarely on the sorts of things that anyone can recognize, on the common ground of "I see, . . . but of course, . . . it only stands to reason . . . ," we are able to walk one step at a time. In other words, reason is the ground of dialogue, and apart from reason there is no other framework. Thus everyone carries on thinking logically, or perhaps we might say, according to the laws of theory.

There is no resisting this way of reason; we cannot but follow it. To acknowledge reason and yet cling to one's own opinion because one hates to lose an argument is to stop arguing. There is nothing left to discuss. One has really turned against oneself. Not to insist on the "I" but to follow what is reasonable is to find within oneself a standpoint common to self and other, common to people everywhere: the standpoint of reason. In other words, reason is a standpoint of universality and objectivity. Dialogue begins, therefore, not from an undisputed object of faith, not from any central dogma or "I," but from a letting go of the ego and a submission to reasonableness, from an ascent from a standpoint of ego to a standpoint of reason.

In this regard, we may add that dialogue in the above sense is always and everywhere a quest. Its spirit is the spirit of inquiry and discovery. This spirit is something that Eastern dialogue by and large lacks. It is not altogether absent. True faith in the sense that Shin Buddhism speaks of it, for example, may also be called a quest. But the sense of quest I have in mind, as it appears for instance in Plato's dialogues, entails a spirit of inquiry aimed at the gradual discovery through dialogue of something new, something not yet known to the participants. This spirit appears at the standpoint of pure reason that seeks to uncover something new and completely unknown, to discover according to the laws of logic.

Simply put, in the spirit of dialogue the standpoint of reason becomes conscious within self and other in the very give-and-take that goes on at the standpoint of reason. It is an upbringing, a making, of the human being on the standpoint of reason. This is the educational significance of dialogue. At the same time it is extremely creative and revealing.

The spirit of the West, as I said at the outset, is rational — the spirit of rationality and logic. Its meaning, as we have just seen, is to be seen in the gradual, rational creation of the human, in the quest and discovery of novelty through that spirit. This represents an important element of the Western spirit that strikes me as very different from the spirit of the East. The science and philosophy of the West have developed as a learning not to be found in the East, one whose essence is reasonable, rational, creative, and revealing.

There is another element to be considered here: the essential role that method plays in learning for the West. In both its science and its philosophy, the problem of method is much discussed. But when philosophy asks what method is, it lands in every sort of difficulty. To take one example, the geometry now taught in our schools is said to have been established and extensively developed in Plato's academy. But what is the standpoint of this geometry? Geometry talks about circles, when in fact there are no such things anywhere in the world we live in — only lots of circular things.

We might say, for example, that the watch I am wearing is circular, but we do not mean thereby that it forms a true, absolute circle. It is, in fact, a misshapen circle. The reason we speak of it as a circle is that we carry within us the idea of an absolute, perfectly shaped circle, by rough comparison with which my watch is circular. Yet there is nothing anywhere corresponding to an absolute circle. No matter how precise we try to make a circle, there is no avoiding some distortion. Still, we can try to approach absolute circularity by making things as round as we can. Simply because there are no absolute circles at all in the visible world does not mean that the absolute circle is an empty fantasy. It is very real for science. We draw circles on paper when we study geometry, but those circles are not the problem. The problem lies in the invisible circle that the visible circle leads us to talk about — namely, the pure spatial form made by a trail of points equidistant from a central point. This is the absolute circularity in terms of which we think of circles. Once we understand what a circle is, we can proceed to draw one. We simply hold one leg of a compass steady while we let the other rotate and trace a line on the paper, thus fulfilling the definition. To know a circle is to be able to make one. In other words, by knowing what an absolute circle is, we are thereby empowered to use that knowledge to construct circles. Thus learned inquiry incorporates method; learning comes about as an amalgam of knowledge and method.

Or take the example of chemistry. Knowing that water is H_2O, a compound made up of two parts hydrogen and one part oxygen, we can break water up into its component parts and also bring them together again to make water. As with the circle, we do not stop short at the water we can see directly with our eyes, but we dissolve it into its elements, hydrogen and oxygen, or take the further step to resynthesize the elements back into water. The ability to do this is what makes chemistry a learned inquiry with a method. That is to say, chemistry is knowledge in which things are known rationally. There is method in the power of knowledge to analyze, synthesize, and produce. And if any knowledge is to be called methodical, it is of course the knowledge gained by the natural sciences, but even in the humanities and philosophy I should think that this aspect of method is fundamental. As both the natural sciences and branches of the liberal arts like law and economics show, knowledge is directly tied to technology and production (for example, in the form of a system of law or a form of government). This is not the case with knowledge in the East. In short, the spirit of what the West calls "learning" is at once rational and logical as well as inquisitive, revealing, and creative; and it is in method that this spirit shows up concretely.

One final consideration regarding the thought and cultural spirit of the West has to do with their historical and social nature, which follows as a matter of course from what we have been saying. Method entails knowledge. Because the method is objective, anyone who knows it can gain the knowledge. In the East one finds a great deal of the arcane, or what is called "transmission from mind to mind", which is not accessible to everyone. Something in this kind of knowledge prohibits development. In the communication of knowledge from A to B, B must always start from the same point at which A started. While knowledge acquired in this way always has the merit of coming from a deep source, it is weak developmentally. In the West, anyone who has the method can use it to attain the knowledge that it brings. And once acquired, this knowledge forms a stepping-stone for others to carry on and make new discoveries. In this way the past becomes the foundation for an ongoing advance; science, thought, and culture continue to develop historically. This capacity for development represents one of the basic features of Western philosophy and science. The East has had no such historicity, at least not in the sense of a body of knowledge grounded in method and continually growing and changing through the discovery of new methods.

The social quality present in Western culture derives, of course, from the same source. We have seen this social element in the Western style of dialogue. Learned inquiry, as we have used the term, is open to anyone who has a proper grasp of the method. It also provides a common ground for research. Western scholarship is communal in the broad sense of the term. From quite early on, in fact, joint research was carried on in institutes. The ancient academies of Plato and Aristotle, for example, represent a kind of collaborative research institute. Even research carried on individually, rather than cooperatively, exhibits this element of the communal or social in the broad sense. This is why historical and social consciousness developed so quickly in the West and why theories of history and society are so advanced.

The rational, inquisitive, methodical, historical, and social dimensions of the Western spirit are joined together, we might say, at the roots. To speak of the logical is at the same time to speak of the inquisitive and the discovering. All of them share the quality of a quest for novelty, out of which historicity emerges to forge the various facets of the Western spirit into a single whole. I have drawn my examples from science, but the point is much broader. Even in the talk of democracy, of which one hears a great deal nowadays, the spirit of the West is present. Roughly speaking, democracy is a form of government in which the entire population of a country constitute the agent of government. In reality, a limited number of persons take charge of government as representatives of the whole, as a minority that reflects the will of the majority and embodies it in the conduct of government. The nature of this relationship has been the subject of debate in the West from ancient times. Philosophers as early as Plato and Aristotle discussed social structures. Distinguishing between autocracy, oligarchy, and democracy, they argued the relative merits of each and examined their successes and failures. But this entire debate seems to me to come down to the problem of the one and the many.

We always think of societies in terms of unified bodies of individuals. If the accent is placed on the many, the individuals that make it up become disparate and the society dissolves and collapses. To avoid this, the one must always be set up in opposition to the many. If, however, the one is overemphasized, we end up with despotic, totalitarian government—hardly what we call "good government." The basis for thinking about government, therefore, is the question regarding what form government is to take in order to preserve a proper relationship between the one and the many. The logical question involved has to do with the relationship among the individual, the many, and the one—the form in which many individuals are gathered into one. This is the sort of question that comes up in the first pages of logic books and indeed belongs to the framework within which all of us operate when we think about things.

Thinking about things is what logic calls judgment. For example, if I say that my watch is made in Japan, I am passing a judgment on my watch, or what is called a singular judgment. But if I say that only some watches are made in Japan, I imply that watches are also made in other countries, which is what logic calls a plural judgment. If I were to claim further that all watches are made in Japan, I would be making a universal judgment, which in this case is patently false. The example may be altogether too simple, but at least it shows how we think about things and about whether our thoughts are right or wrong. In this way logic begins and ends with talk about the individual, the many, and the one.

The case of the watch is simple and falls within the compass of formal logic, but logic can also be much more difficult, as the following fictitious example shows. South of Greece lies an island called Crete whose inhabitants are so given to lying that it is said,

"All Cretans are liars." Here we have a universal proposition. Now one of those Cretans is heard to say, "All Cretans are liars." What has happened logically? On one hand, if the fellow were not himself a liar, his judgment would clearly be a lie. Conversely, if what he said was not a lie, then this very fact would make him a liar. We are caught in a contradiction. On the other hand, if the Cretan is in fact a liar, for him to say that all Cretans are liars must also be a lie. Whichever way we look at it, we land in contradiction; there appears to be no good way out.[4]

This may seem to be no more than a logical game, but in fact this is the way all facts are established. Facts are laden with relationships that cannot be embraced by formal logic. In the example of politics discussed above, we found a contradictory relationship between the one or the whole and the individuals that make it up. If we are to think about the relationship we need a logic other than formal logic. Formal logic eludes the problem, saying we cannot think about it because it is a contradiction. But reality, it may be said, contains contradiction by nature.

All sorts of things have been said of late about the Japanese being no good at anything. If a Japanese says it, how can we trust the statement itself as being any good? The contradiction is plain. Is it merely an irate remark that all Japanese except me are no good? Or is it an act of self-reproach in which I recognize myself as a no-good Japanese? In either case, it is all Japanese who are said to be no good. If those who say so are Japanese, they are among the no-good. But if they speak out of anger or self-reproach, they have reached a self-awareness that has taken them a step away from the current condition of the Japanese. They have set their sights away from what is no good, turning away from the present state of affairs and eager to take a step in the other direction. It means that there is a dynamic, three-dimensional relationship at work within the actual state of the Japanese.

The contradictions referred to above also stem from just such a growing and working relationship. Here we may think in terms of a three-dimensional logic of relationships, or what is often

---

4. The reference is, of course, to the famous logical puzzle in classical Greek philosophy, posed by Epimenides the Cretan.

called a dialectical logic. That is to say, a certain condition is negated and a new situation unfolds in its place. Once this new situation becomes stable, another new situation emerges to negate it and go beyond it. Within one and the same thing we see a developmental or dynamic power advancing from one new position to another by a series of self-negations, and this process leads us to think in terms of a logic for such things. The relationship involves the individuals and the one, in the sense not of a two-dimensional relationship but rather of a developmental, working, three-dimensional one, and logic must follow suit. Thus we can think of the logical structure inherent in things like history, society, spirit, and culture. In the last analysis, the logic in terms of which the West is said to be logical or methodical or historical turns out to be a logic and a method suited to things that work and develop and make history. Hegel in particular made a profound attempt to unify the rational and the historical from the standpoint of this dialectical logic, to show that reason is historical and that history is reasonable. This ability to take the one and the many into account from a logical and historical standpoint has yet to make itself manifest in the Eastern spirit. Clear consideration for history and method have been wanting.

THE EASTERN SPIRIT has a form very different from the Western spirit as we have been speaking of it. Rather than logical, rational, and methodical, it has been extremely intuitive. When it looks at water, for instance, it does not think in terms of the analysis or synthesis of its composite elements of hydrogen and oxygen, but takes hold of it in a straightforward manner. The Eastern spirit tends to think of water in its actual form. As the Zen saying has it, "Hot and cold one knows oneself." One does not step away from oneself to look at things, but looks at things from a point where one is united with them. Conversely, one does not step away from things to look at oneself; one looks at oneself from a point where things are one with oneself. The Eastern spirit is thus intuitive as well as active. This is the standpoint of nothingness or emptiness. Nishida's philosophy was also based on the standpoint of an absolute nothingness, but here nothingness and emptiness do not mean that there is nothing. On the contrary, nothingness is the "actual form of all dharmas." It is the appearance of all things in their actual form, each in its own place and station. But the point at which the actual form of something becomes visible as such, the point at which what is real comes into reality is—in nothingness.

In order to grasp something in its actual form, we must distance ourselves from the discriminating, relativizing self. The term "conscious self" often appears in Nishida's books. For him, the standpoint of the conscious self consists in setting up an opposition between the self and things, so that we have a self on the one hand and things existing apart from the self on the other. It means thinking in terms of an opposition of subject and object, setting up a relative world in which the inner and the outer are opposed. This way of thinking, which we are to transcend, is one we all know from the ordinary, everyday way in which we look at things and think about them. Hence the standpoint that transcends it is called nothingness or no-ego. It is not a discriminating consciousness that sets self and things against one another, but rather goes beyond to a standpoint where it is possible for one to think in terms of becoming one with things and also to act at one with things. As Nishida often said, "becoming a thing, think it; becoming a thing, do it." When we become what we think and do, we can no longer think in terms of a self within the confines of a conscious self. The standpoint of no-ego is one that smashes that pattern we call self to become one with the Life of the universe, of nature. When one stands there, all things, just as they are, become the actual form and actual reality that they are—the truth of their "suchness."

This is very different from materialism, which is not a standpoint that thinks things by becoming them. The critical term here is *becoming*. Materialism—which sees us also as things—begins by looking at us, then looks at the material world, and then concludes that we, too, are matter. This view resides, or perhaps we should say hides, at the foundations of materialism. At any rate, it is very different from the view of becoming things in order to think and act on those things. This latter is the great standpoint of the true self, the standpoint of no-ego, of the Life of the universe, where we may speak of becoming one with things. And this very union with the Life of the universe through which all things live and have their being is absolute nothingness. Here is where we speak of becoming a thing to do it. To smash the narrow pattern of the self is to break free of a mode of being that has one locked up inside oneself and pitted against the outside. It is a great inside that encompasses the outside, that breaks through the small world of "myself" to the outside. Here inside and outside are at root one.

The standpoint of nothingness has been around the East since ancient times. It has nothing to do either with idealism or materialism. Why it is not a materialism I have just explained, but what of the claim often made in Japan that Buddhism is an idealism? This, too, is mistaken. Idealism claims that we have within ourselves a mind and that everything exists within this mind. This claim amounts to nothing more than the inverse of materialism. For while idealism sees everything in the mind, it bases itself on the same duality of mind and matter.

When Buddhism speaks of the mind, however, it is denying mind in just this sense in order to assume a greater standpoint at which the conscious mind of the conscious self is broken down. Of this mind one can say, "becoming a thing, think it; becoming a thing, do it." The Buddhist idea that "things and mind are one" refers to a standpoint for which things and mind no longer exist, and hence where one may speak of things and mind in their proper sense. This standpoint of nothingness belongs to what is primordial in the spirit of the East. It is intuitive as well as active, and therein lies its distinguishing mark.

Seeing the actual form of things, their actual "suchness," is different from the idea of transforming things we find in the West. Western science reduces water to hydrogen and oxygen, and then reconstitutes water out of these elements. Science is free to carry out this kind of transformation by analysis. As science transforms things, it also learns the laws and principles that govern them. Thus the study of nature is wrapped up with the attempt to transform nature. Scientific experiments, especially those that take place in the laboratory, make things not usually found in the world of nature. By removing a variety of contingent elements, they make their facts. For example, the water we actually find in nature contains a mixture of various other things, all of which have to be removed. Although pure water does not exist as such in nature, it is considered one of the pure facts of nature on which one may experiment. Thus the attempt is made to uncover the laws of nature by artificially transforming nature.

Things are different in the East. Rather than transform nature we transform the self. Through one form of action or another, the standpoint of the ordinary ego is converted to the standpoint of no-ego, where one becomes one with things and grasps them in their actuality. This kind of transformation runs counter to the standpoint of the West. For all its differences from other forms of Buddhism, when Shin Buddhism says that reprobates weighed down with sinfulness[5] are granted salvation through the saving power of the original vow, there is a sense in which absolute contradictories are being brought together. Through the saving grace of the Buddha the consummate sinner is made equal to the Buddha. These two originally contradictory realities, the ordinary mortal and the Buddha, become fundamentally one. This union is somewhat different from the act of returning to no-ego discussed earlier, but still shows something more basic than the ego of the ordinary mortal. It is not to be understood by reason. It is beyond logic and the standpoint of reason. For example, when Buddhism speaks of putting Mount Sumeru[6] into a poppyseed, the poppyseed remains a poppyseed and the mountain a mountain. Still, Mount Sumeru is said to fit into the poppyseed. Such an idea goes beyond the limits of logic and reason; indeed, in logical terms, it is idiotic. But when one speaks of putting Mount Sumeru into a poppyseed, the idea of nothingness is at work. This is very much a part of the Buddhist standpoint.

IN NISHIDA'S PHILOSOPHY, as I stated at the outset, the spirit of the East and the spirit of the West are joined together. On the one hand, his is a standpoint of nothingness, of no-ego, that has broken

---

5. Nishitani deliberately uses a Pure Land Buddhist term here, 罪悪深重, though he (or his editors) have supplied the final two characters with an incorrect reading. Instead of *shinchō* the term should be read *jinjū*.

6. According to ancient Indian cosmology, a mountain named "Sumeru" is supposed to exist in the middle of the world.

free of the standpoint of the discriminating self; and on the other, an intuitive, acting standpoint.

Nishida often speaks of "active intuition." Although different from past standpoints of action, it has points of similarity with them. It speaks of seeing subjectively or according to the work of the self. Moreover, the self at work in seeing is not the conscious self but the self in absolute nothingness. At the same time, Nishida's thought is always a logic; his aim is a logic based on the standpoint of nothingness. Thus it may be called a standpoint of active intuition possessed of a philosophical method.

In the West, Christianity takes a standpoint transcending logic: Christ is God. The idea that God took human form and appeared in Christ is the height of contradiction. Ordinary logic has no way to conceive of a God becoming human. That this God was crucified and died is also contradictory in the extreme. Finally, this Christ is resurrected, rises from the dead. Once again we are drawn beyond the pale of the theoretically possible. Thus the foundations of Christian teaching are unthinkable in terms of normal logic. The spirit of the West came about as a union of this spirit of Christianity with the spirit of Greek philosophy and science spoken of earlier. In modern times this synthesis fell apart as science and philosophy were liberated from religion and gradually came to develop their own standpoints, leading eventually to positions like materialism that repudiated religion altogether. In the face of such problems, Christian faith finds itself in a trying situation. It finds great difficulties in closing the gap between religion and philosophy, and particularly the gap between religion and science. The task may not be absolutely impossible, but it is clearly most difficult.

This is not the place to go into detail, except to note that Nishida's philosophy represents an attempt to construct a standpoint in response to this singular most difficult issue for contemporary thought by bringing together the Eastern standpoint of nothingness and the Western standpoint of science and philosophy (or reason and logic). In so doing, his aim was to conceive a dialectical logic based on the standpoint of nothingness or no-ego by delving deeply into the spirit behind the rationalism and logic of the West. By grappling with the dialectical relationship between the one and the many whereby the one and the many unite while remaining contradictory, Nishida gave depth to his own position and thus effected a shift away from a standpoint of nothingness to a standpoint of the logic of dialectic. As noted before, the result was a new unity grounded in the mutual penetration of the spirit of the East and the spirit of the West.

The notion of "pure experience" that Nishida adopts in his first book, *An Inquiry into the Good*, refers to the immediacy of an experience, as when we look at a flower or hear a sound. The idea points to an orientation present in his thought from the beginning. What we usually mean by "experience" when we say that we have experienced something does not really refer to the state of experience as such, because in speaking of our experiences we are usually thinking in terms of a certain entity called an experiencing self. I look at this watch before me and at once suppose some fixed self on this end that is seeing, and some fixed thing on the other end that is being seen. Things like this watch of mine seem to be what they are and nothing more. But the more closely I look at my experience, the less I am able to experience the watch on its own. It has a certain color, a certain roughness of feel, a certain weight, and so forth, all of which combine to make up what is experienced. That there is something else behind these qualities is not a fact of experience but only an idea inserted into the picture for the sake of explaining the experience.

It is the same with the idea of a self as a separate, individual something present within us. To speak of having a mind that sees things, a self within that views what is on the outside, does not refer to experience in its pure form but only to a later explanation of experience. In direct experience there is no self, no thing, nothing separate or individual at all. There is only a bond of many things into a single living whole. This is the way it is with what we call the universe or the world.

There is a single life that vitalizes the universe as a whole. In reality no separate, individual things exist on their own. Nor is there any separate, individual self. The only such self is the one that we have thought up; nothing in reality is so patterned. What exists in reality is at one with the Life of the universe. This view may seem to leave us out of the picture altogether, but it only means that in our looking and listening the activities of looking and listening have emerged somewhere from the depths of the universe. Our looking and listening and all the other things we do issue from a point where all things form a single living bond. This is why these activities are united with all sorts of other things and why we cannot think in terms of things existing on the outside and a mind existing on the inside. This is a later standpoint; the prior standpoint is that of pure experience where subject and object are one and undifferentiated. It is here that all experience takes place.

I remember Nishida once telling me how, on a walk in Kanazawa, a bee or gadfly buzzed near his ear, and that noise suddenly awakened in him an awareness of the standpoint of pure experience. It is the moment of direct hearing, before one has time to discriminate between oneself and any thing. This idea points towards the very standpoint Nishida was later to refer to as "becoming a thing, think it; becoming a thing, do it." It is the standpoint of nothingness or no-ego. Put the other way around, it is a standpoint of active intuition carried out in accord with an egoless self.

In subsequent years, as Nishida's thought continued to develop and expand, this standpoint of nothingness or no-self remained fundamental to it. At the same time he conceived of a great system of logic grounded in this standpoint and tried to find in its foundations a standpoint of reason. Against the rationalist mainstream of Western philosophy, Nishida did not see reason as the highest standpoint. Instead he saw the standpoint of nothingness as the final ground and thus the foundation also for the standpoint of reason. By rethinking the spirit of the West in terms of the spirit of the East, his thought broke the ground for a standpoint not yet attained in the West. In this regard, let me repeat, his thought differs from traditional Western thought, yet neither is it traditional Eastern thought. The standpoint of learning—of reason and logic, of method, of rationalism—that has emerged in the philosophy and science of the West had been lacking in the East. Nishida did not try to force this standpoint of reason, like grafting an imported tree onto a native bamboo, but built up the Eastern spirit creatively from within. Therein lies the greatness of his achievement.

3 Nishida's Diaries

IN 1946 A SPECIAL EDITION of *Philosophical Studies* was prepared in memory of Nishida.[1] As a member of the editorial board, I began to transcribe his diaries for publication. As the work progressed, I came to sense an indescribable atmosphere emanating from the diary. Part of the reason, as I stop to think about it, had to do with the intensity of his Zen meditation related there. Some pages speak of him sitting until after midnight for days on end; others entered during vacations tell of "sitting in the morning, sitting in the afternoon, sitting at night." His zeal led him during the winter vacation to Senshin-an[2] to pass New Year's Day. Allusions to the Chinese Zen master Shih-shuang Ch'u-yüan who stabbed himself with an awl 慈明引錐 [3] are inscribed on the cover of his diary notebooks and several times on the inside; the image seems to have been branded on his mind. Because others have already remarked on these matters, there is no need to repeat them here, except to note that the feelings I got from his diaries were more than the result of an extraordinary spiritual tension, a fierce tension of will that one might even call an irate will.

There is another side to his diaries that struck me in quite another sense. Comments about visiting people are mixed in with his remarks on *zazen* and occur with about the same frequency. In the

1. See above, 39, n. 1.
2. See above, 23.
3. Literally: "Shih-shuang stabs with an awl." The reference is to the story of the Zen master in the Rinzai tradition, Shih-shuang Ch'u-yüan (986–1039), who, unable to sleep one night, pondered the sufferings of people of old and the meaninglessness of his own life, and picked up an awl and stabbed himself in the haunches. The account, in Chinese, appears in Nishida's *Collected Writings* 17:23. The original story can be found in the 雲棲袾宏, a work compiled in the sixteenth century.

entries of his earlier period (that is, during the several years after 1897), we often find phrases like, "In the afternoon, I visited A and B, and at night I called on X and Y." These remarks were marked by ellipsis in the edition prepared for *Philosophical Studies*, although in many cases they represent our only record of certain of Nishida's days. For myself, I was no less impressed by references to his visits than by his remarks on *zazen*. Of course, Nishida was still a young man at the time, and it is hardly surprising that he would call on his friends almost daily, and still less surprising when one recalls that as a teacher he would often have had to see colleagues about some matter or other. Because he began his diary as a record of things he did not want to forget, it is only natural that he would have written down a great many visits and the like. To look at these same things recounted day after day, one is likely to pay them more attention than they actually deserve. But there is more to it than that.

Around this time his diaries contain phrases like "restless heart" and "no peace of heart." In some cases there seem to be reasonable explanations; in others, he records a state of restlessness for no apparent reason. He seems to have simply been incapable of sitting still or relaxing without getting edgy. My own impression from reading the diaries of that period is that he was in the grip of some aimless impulse that rises up out of the shadows, from the dark, inner recesses of life, where body and mind have not yet split off from one another. The symptoms point to a common psychological abnormality that befalls otherwise normal individuals from time to time, a state of mental disturbance in which they cannot sit still without wanting to get up and walk around or visit people. This, to some extent, one senses in Nishida. Not, of course, that he was mentally disturbed at the time. It is no easy matter to draw a line scientifically between the normal and the abnormal. Although Nishida's diaries do not give one the sense of pathological abnormality or mental degeneration, one does remark a certain critical state that had him walking perilously close to the edge—if one can speak in such terms—of pathological abnormality. Had he lacked the strength to resist and to keep his psychological balance, had he not been able to "sublate" his moods into something higher, his state was such that he would have fallen over the edge.

My own belief in the matter is that his intense devotion to "just sitting" provided this strength to resist. His diaries show two sides of Nishida at completely opposite and contradictory poles. On one hand, we see him sitting quietly at a still point; on the other, we see the anxious movement of someone under attack. The ferocious willpower and self-control he brought to his concentrated practice of meditation held the dark forces at bay and helped him keep his mental balance. In my view, at least, Nishida was possessed of a rare depth, strength, and expanse of spirit, a breadth of humanity that enabled him at all times to strike a kind of critical balance between these two extremes that took him far beyond the range of spiritual activity of normal individuals. In our contacts with him in later years we always had the impression of something intense, impulsive, daemonic in him, which I had occasion to see erupt ferociously. Whatever it was, it was reined in, sublated, and transformed by his total personality into a moving force that hardened his will and gave it its tenacity. This *énergie spirituelle* was the source of the fervor of his religious quest at the time as well as of the pure and single-minded pursuit of philosophy that ran throughout his life. It was the soul of his philosophical system. For Nishida religion and philosophy flowed out of that dark impulse and were the way to overcoming it.

Nishida's sitting in meditation shows the infinite quiet seated in the eternal present, while his restless movement shows the infinite dynamism welling up from the depths of life itself. Nishida himself *was* the self-identity of these opposites. His sitting would have taught him how to break away from the standpoint of the conscious self and assume a standpoint of true self-awareness at one with heaven and earth and all things that are. It would also have opened to him his own interiority and shown him the wellspring of an infinite, vital activity. Even the everyday experience of looking at a flower, when seen in its purity, becomes the absolute activity of this wellspring prior to all distinction of subject and object. Insofar as the standpoint of "pure experience" that marks Nishida's early period can be seen as the spontaneous self-unfolding of a universal and shown to contain a dynamism rooted in will, can we not see in it traces of this dark impulse that was elevated through the power of meditation to a creative activity permeating self-awareness? Do not his later ideas of the world as the self-identity of the opposites of space and time, of the creative self-expression of the world, of active intuition as the creative self-awareness of this latter, of the historical body, and so forth, reverberate this balance of opposites as we find it in his diaries? If so, this balance struck in Nishida's own person at the time can be seen to have unfolded into his later logic of place.

4   Rooting Philosophy
in the Japanese Soil

ONE OFTEN HEARS how hard it is to understand Nishida's philosophy. The difficulty lies in the problems it deals with. Nishida always strove to get to the bottom of the intellectual problems of our day and age by delving into them in as deep and holistic a manner as possible. But once he had reached a resolution, a new and deeper problem surfaced to demand a still more radical solution. And so the process repeated itself again and again. This gives us some idea of the difficulty of the issues he was struggling with. To carry on and not give in despite the difficulty eventually obliges us to part with basic modes of thought that have directed philosophy in the past and to cut through biases dominant in our ordinary, everyday thinking. It means opening up horizons new in every respect. That the ideas and logic resulting from this shift should be hard to understand is only natural. Indeed, such obscurity is not unique to Nishida's thought. Other thinkers who have thrown themselves deeply into the questions with which the modern world challenges philosophy, like the later Heidegger and Alfred North Whitehead, are no less difficult to understand.

Without overlooking the difficulties arising in Nishida's philosophy as a result of his attempts to fathom the depths of our times, we see through a study of its development how he passed through the whirlwind of contemporary philosophical currents and moved out far ahead into the future. With time the true worth of Nishida's philosophy will become clear, long after many of the bright lights shining today have dimmed and gone out. A proper assessment of its significance demands the prophetic vision to look back at the present from a vantage point a hundred years into the future.

From before the war until the present, Nishida's philosophy has not escaped its share of criticism of every sort, most of which reminds one of people standing at a great distance from the Himalaya Mountains and each talking about what they see from their own perspective—one from the north, another from the south. On the face of it, they seem to be talking about Nishida's philosophy; the fact is, they are all talking about their own viewpoints. They are simply out of touch with what they are talking about, or at least no more in touch than a group of blind men feeling an elephant. That this state of affairs should have gone on for so long is regrettable. It is high time to start bringing serious research and criticism to bear on his thought.

It is nearly a century since Western philosophy began to be transplanted into Japan. The Japanese philosophical thought that our predecessors have labored to shape deserves the same academic attention in Japan that Western philosophy enjoys at present. So long as there is no change in the current attitude, philosophy will never take root in the soil of Japan. For this reason, I welcome warmly the new edition of Nishida's *Collected Works*.[1]

---

1. Nishida's *Collected Works* were first published in 1947–53. On the occasion of a second edition in 1965, this text was included.

Part 2

Nishida's Thought

5 Nishida's Place in the History of Philosophy

IT IS HARDLY POSSIBLE for me to trace within the confines of a single essay the story of Nishida's philosophy in all its breadth and depth and complexity, however boldly I brush the strokes. In any case, descriptive studies and research of this sort are already available in works like Kōyama Iwao's *Nishida's Philosophy*, Yanagida Kenjūrō's *Nishida's Philosophical System,* and Kōsaka Masaaki's *Nishida Kitarō: His Life and Thought.*[1] Accordingly my aim here is to look at his philosophy from a somewhat different angle.

One of the things Nishida used to tell his students—and this is also repeated, I believe, in a collection of essays published in his memory by former students[2]—was something to this effect:

> In all great thinkers there is a kind of "knack" in what is unique to their way of thinking. To understand philosophical thought one has to acquire that knack oneself. With it you are able not only to understand what they have written but also to construe roughly what they might have said about issues they did not touch on.

Concerned lest his students would think this a much easier task than it actually is, he used to warn them against careless reading habits. Although the remark was directed at getting to the heart of philosophy books, as I think back on it I can appreciate its wider implications. For to understand ideas presented to us in

---

1. Kōyama Iwao, 西田哲学 *[Nishida's Philosophy]* (Tokyo, 1935) and 続西田哲学 *[Nishida's Philosophy: A Sequel]* (Tokyo, 1940); for Kōsaka's book, see above, 22, n. 20; Yanagida Kenjūrō, 西田哲学体系 *[Nishida's Philosophical System]* (Tokyo, 1946).

2. See, for example, Shimomura Toratarō, 西田幾多郎—人と思想 *[Nishida Kitarō: The Man and His Thought]* (Tokyo, 1977), 166.

written form, one has to get at what is behind the ideas, to enter into the creativity that produced them. This true grasp of the creative by creatively grasping the creativity behind creations was part and parcel of Nishida's own philosophy. For him the creative was the most fully real.

Already in his early writings Nishida speaks of the principle of the universe as something creative, something we can ourselves become and work in accord with, even though it cannot become for us an object of consciousness. Or again he speaks of things with form as shadows of something that has no form, or of seeing things by becoming them, and so forth. Such ideas were further elaborated in his last years in his concept of the creative element in the creative world.

Even in philosophical thought, there is something formless and creative behind the forms of thought. Therein lies the true reality of the one whose thought it is. The least we can say is that without this formless creativity thought would never have taken any real form, and therefore the former is more real than the latter. In his *Introduction to Metaphysics*, Bergson notes that one of the marks of a great thinker is a vivid philosophical intuition which, while not itself expressible in conceptual terms, is the creative force behind systematic conceptual thinking. We come to discover this intuition within ourselves, he goes on, by way of sympathy. Nishida says something similar in *An Inquiry into the Good* when he sees a kind of intellectual intuition at work behind all thinking:

> This unifying intuition is essentially the same as the "knack" of a technique. Broadly speaking, behind all great thought like the philosophies of Plato and Spinoza there is a great intuition at work. Since the intuition of intellectual genius differs from ordinary thinking only in degree, there is no difference in quality, and the former is no more than a new, profound intuition of unity.[3]

From this we understand that attentiveness to the presence of the great intuition behind philosophic thought is itself the root

---

3. All references to Nishida's *An Inquiry into the Good* refer to the original Japanese text, which appears in vol. 1 of the *Collected Works of Nishida Kitarō* (hereafter, CW) 西田幾多郎全集(Tokyo, 1980). The passage cited here can be found in CW 1:44.

and stock of Nishida's thought, as it was for Bergson. In other words, the fact that he was able to say this, and to offer it as the way to get to the heart of what one was reading, points to part of the creative soul of his own philosophy — to what he would have called its knack. In so teaching his young disciples, Nishida disclosed at once the character of both his philosophy and himself as a philosopher. In his case, there was no difference between the two.

Let us now turn to the fundamental role that this intuitive element played in Nishida's philosophic thought. As noted above, references to intuition appear already in the beginning of his philosophical pilgrimage, *An Inquiry into the Good*. In the years that followed, of course, his idea of intuition gradually broadened and deepened, always maintaining a consistent basis, which we might call with Dilthey an "isomorphism." I do not mean by this the rigid uniformity of a system of thought but rather the uniformity of something intuitive living and working beneath the transformations of thought — a uniformity of Life. In this sense the unique vitality of Nishida's philosophy is already present in that first book. One often hears it said that "Nishida philosophy" proper begins with the emergence of the idea of "place" (場所 *basho*). In the sense that it provided his thought with a clear and distinctive form, this is of course true. But seen in terms of a more basic and formless philosophical intuition, Nishida's thinking from the start contained an intuition whose uniqueness can hold its own admirably in the company of other leading philosophies. In other words, from its first beginnings Nishida's philosophy contained an intuition that, once more or less understood, enables one to follow his subsequent development and to begin to grasp his complex and penetrating later thought. My concern here is with this empowering intuition.

Such creative intuitions do not come from nowhere. They need to be situated historically in the world of thought. Something creative is shaped by this environment and in turn gives it shape. It is what Nishida has called the transition "from the made to the making." Every historical situation is laden with a task. The more deeply those within that environment are shaped by that task, the more completely and profoundly they awaken to it as their own task, and the more the environment changes as they exert themselves to carry it out. Through this relationship the historical world continues to shape itself. In the world of ideas, too, the unique, self-forming creative power of a given thinker has to be understood not only internally, in terms of a specific philosophical system, but also externally, in terms of the task that is being taken to heart and the intellectual environment from which it has come.

This being so, with what task was the world of thought laden when Nishida's philosophy was taking shape? On the surface, the intellectual excitement after Hegel had come to a standstill in the latter half of the nineteenth century. Philosophy had returned to the academy, but there was none of the academic enthusiasm that had marked the age of Kant and Hegel. Philosophy took on a reflective character that put the stress on its formal side, both in the study of the history of philosophy and in epistemology, methodology, and logic. For the history of philosophy, the most important development of the time was the emergence of psychology as an independent empirical science—a development whose meaning for philosophy has yet to be given proper attention. Of this I shall have more to say later. Suffice it to note here that we are speaking of a period when psychology had broken away from philosophy to become a science and then turned around to dominate philosophy. Epistemology, methodology, and even logic were thought of in psychological terms and psychologists, beginning with Wilhelm Wundt, were engaged in philosophy.

As is well known, the neo-Kantians, having returned to the critical philosophy of Kant, now began to wield their logic-oriented critiques against such psychologism in philosophy. In part their criticism hit the mark, but it also missed the deeper undertow beneath the emergence of the psychologistic approach. Neither those who tried to see philosophy in psychologistic terms nor those who tried to reduce it to questions of logic were fully aware of the critical nature of the problems that had been carried over from the intellectual ferment of the first half of the century. Thinkers like Nietzsche who struggled with these problems were completely ignored. Therefore, if we are to know what the historical task of thought was at that time and what kind of a decision was being called for, we need to turn our attention to the establishment of psychology as an empirical science and the emergence of psychologistic philosophy, and to reflect on what all of this meant for philosophy. The philosophies of Nishida and Bergson began from the idea of pure experience and shared the aim of erecting a new metaphysics in opposition to psychologistic and logistic philosophies that consciously excluded metaphysics. To appreciate their significance we need first to place them in the context of the serious problems of their age.

Only those who live their times profoundly are aware of the issues fermenting out of their particular historical situation, and this awareness presupposes a certain capacity for self-awareness cultivated through long years of tradition. As shaped by present circumstances, this capacity is the matter that is given form by its environment; as something that shapes its own circumstances, it is rather the power that gives form to the matter of the environment. In this sense it is something like Aristotle's "potency." It represents the possibility of a future hewn out of the tradition of the past. Naturally, for this possibility to be actualized, a new form must emerge from the activity of determining the environment while being determined by it. This self-formation is achieved only as a mediation between the future (the task of the historical situation) and the past (received tradition). The deeper the split between the historical situation and the tradition, the more difficult self-formation becomes; at the same time, the more likely it is that a deep level of self-awareness of the historical task will be reached and that the creation of new modes of thought capable of responding to it will be correspondingly profound. This is unthinkable without the element of a capacity for formation cultivated by tradition. In Bergson's case this cultivation goes back to Maine de Biran and Ravaisson, and still further back to Plotinus. In Nishida's case, we can look on one hand to German idealism, and in particular to the philosophy of Hegel, and on the other to the still more latent influence of Zen Buddhism, whose influence was particularly decisive in the intuitive underpinnings of his thought.

In order to deal with creative elements in Nishida's philosophy like the philosophical intuition that lay behind his system of thought, three things are required: first, to lay out the intellectual situation of his time and its inherent historical task; second, to get inside the thought that emerged in response to this task and look for the philosophical intuition that gave that thought its creative power; and third, to see how creatively the received tradition was transformed.

ONE NEED HARDLY mention that in the wake of the collapse of Hegel's absolute idealism the philosophies of realism, positivism, and empiricism appeared. In Germany Feuerbach appeared on the scene but was soon eclipsed by materialism, whether in the historical form of Marxism or in its more scientific forms. In England and France figures like Comte, Mill, and later Spencer had influence worldwide. Their common commitment was to be grounded in the facts and never to deviate from them. Nothing that was not a datum of inner or outer experience, nothing that could not be grasped empirically, was to be allowed. For them the facts alone were true. They did not admit of any reality behind or beyond the facts. Nothing transcendent or transperceptual, no thing-in-itself, nothing "conceptual" or ideal at all belonged to the truly real. They disallowed the idea of any kind of a priori that would precede the facts of experience and rejected the idea of deducing empirical facts from an a priori. The idea of transcendental categories of pure reason as giving structural "formality" to the knowledge of experience, such as Kant had argued, was for them impossible. As for the subsequent attempts to turn things around and see the truth of all things in the *Begriff* or *Idee*, to argue that the real was the rational and the rational the real—this was all pure "construct." In this way the idea of true reality that had dominated the history of Western philosophy from Plato to Hegel was radically rejected.

Western philosophy up to Kant and Hegel had been grounded in Platonism, according to which the Ideas transcending the world of sensible things represent true reality, and God is posited at the foundations of the realm of Ideas. That is to say, Platonism taught a two-world theory that distinguished the sensible world we live in from an intelligible world beyond it and urged the soul to transcend the sensible world by denying it in order to return to the world above. It was this traditional view that was being denied, and only this world, the world of positive fact, was affirmed. Based on this two-world theory, traditional Western philosophy has proved virtually incapable of establishing a standpoint of transcendence while maintaining a foothold in experience and fact. If one plants one's feet on the hard ground of experience and fact, transcendence turns out to be no more than an idealist notion. If, on the contrary, it is the transcendent one seeks, one ends up taking leave of the world of actuality and denying the standpoint of experience and fact. On this point, of course, Aristoteleanism differed from Platonism in that it did not posit such a clear two-world theory, although it did grant an independent transcendence to the standpoint of reason. In the West, empiricist philosophy and rationalist metaphysics continue to stand opposed, the former by aligning itself to antimetaphysics, atheism, and the rejection of religion, the latter mainly by adopting a theism that takes God as a transcendent absolute. A standpoint that was metaphysical and yet empiricist, that maintained ties to God without departing from the actual world of fact, was almost unthinkable in the West. Moreover, post-Hegelian positivism, empiricism, and materialism were antimetaphysical and atheistic (or at least did not acknowledge ties to God). In locating Nishida's philosophy in the history of philosophy, this split between experience and metaphysics is the first important point to note.

Obviously this philosophical tendency took place against the backdrop of the sudden rise of science, particularly the natural sciences. The idea of reducing natural phenomena to simple elements and their compounds, and then positing a necessary lawfulness that regulates movement and change in natural phenomena, was also aimed at the inner and outer life of human beings. This tendency was already present in germ in the Renaissance, and it dominated the Enlightenment. In the nineteenth century it gave birth to two sciences, sociology and psychology, which then emerged as new philosophies equipped with a method to solve the problems of philosophy and therefore ready to take the place of traditional philosophy. The birth of sociology reflects well the situation of modern men and women and their view of the human. Medieval thinkers derived the idea of human beings as equals from the fact that despite their inequalities, they are all one in the eyes of God. Social and class differences were not resolved, only transcended. This maneuver helps explain the attack launched by social egalitarians against the deceitfulness of medieval religion.

The idea of religious equality in the Middle Ages saw in each individual an interior life that embraced the whole person and had its own individuating differences. It required of individuals that they become whole persons in their interior lives. Modern social egalitarianism, in contrast, tended to do away with the interior life of the whole person with these individuating differences. Treating people as equals meant treating them as average individuals. They became simple elements, like the elements of the natural sciences, and society came to be seen as a compound. The egalitarians began to think that behind the vicissitudes of history lay necessary laws that regulated the human elements and their social compounds. The "scientific" knowledge of history was linked to a will to reform reality. This way of thinking was a product of a modernity in which mass movements were on the rise, in which people understood themselves from a collective perspective and the individual as such was conscious of being a member of a group. The clear and distinct, pure rationality of this "scientific" viewpoint was enough to make the average person accede to it. Furthermore, the swift and certain progress of scientific knowledge and the remarkable transformations it was effecting in social structures and lifestyle were enough to make people think that the scientific way of thinking was the only source of truth.

From the beginnings of the modern period, the great philosophers were those in search of a metaphysics to reconcile science and religion. Before Kant the problem was how to bring together the image of the world held by the natural sciences, chiefly mathematics, and the religious worldview that sees all things as related to God. Beginning with Kant, the questions of society and history were added to the problem, and the way was opened to a reconciliation between political and religious views of equality, between the historical idea of "progress" and the religious view of history. These attempts notwithstanding, the scientific standpoint and its accompanying will for social reform rejected the results and took more violent measures. The violence took the form of an attempt to overturn religion from the roots.

When the deceitfulness of religion had come under attack in the Enlightenment, its critics stopped at pointing out the elements of deceit. Here, however, the point is not simply an assault on one or the other aspect of religion, but an exposé of the way in which delusion poisons the very wellsprings of religion and an attempt to explain the process by which this poisoning takes effect. Nevertheless, Comte and Feuerbach, who followed this line, show traces of religious sentiment in their sacralization of humanity. Still, the scientific perspective in philosophy rapidly evolved into a philosophy of materialism; sociology became the "science of society," and the will to social reform was transformed into the praxis of class struggle. The denial of religion moved from the head to the heart. This matter affected not just the established religions or religion in general, but the entire psychic life of the human person; it shook the very foundations of the interior life. It was a question of depriving people of the way to the interior of the self. Such were the implications in following the lead of the scientific standpoint to the denial of religion. Here the problem of science and religion becomes a matter of the gravest concern. (This was also why Simmel, Weber, Tarde, and Durkheim were later to go to such pains to establish sociology as a purely positive empirical science, in contrast to the science of society, which was tied to a political agenda. In so doing, they also set themselves against the Marxist position in trying to include questions of the interior life that arise in considering religion and ethics as part of society.)

The conflict between the standpoints of science and religion spread to the whole of the interior life. The point is important for the consideration of Nishida's philosophy. In *An Inquiry into the Good* Nishida based himself throughout on positive experience and yet at the same time saw religion at the foundation of it all. In this regard his philosophy never wavered. The main questions confronting modern philosophy, and indeed the thought and spirit of modernity in general, come down to the clash between science and religion. It was a matter of human life divided against itself. The significance of Nishida's philosophy is that it took a clear position regarding this basic problem of the modern spirit. To be sure, the various social and historical problems that this position entailed were not taken up in that first book. They would appear in later periods of his philosophy. In general, society and history were not yet being treated as cardinal philosophical problems in Japan. But in taking a position concerning the problem of science and religion, *An Inquiry into the Good* had already touched the roots of modern thought, and furthermore—as we shall show presently—offered an entirely new perspective on the question. This is the second point to be noted in trying to place Nishida's philosophy in modern intellectual history. Its significance will become clearer as we look at other trends in the West.

THE ESTABLISHMENT of psychology and sociology as independent empirical sciences was another important result of the positivist and empiricist spirit of the modern age, that is to say, of the dominance of the scientific perspective. Phenomena of consciousness came to be seen as immediately given facts free of all philosophical categories, a priori, and treated with the same sort of purely positivist attitude that the natural sciences took towards the phenomena of nature. The traditional philosophical approach to problems came to be excluded entirely. For some, like Comte and Marx, traces of the traditional approach remained in the sense that the positivism that analyzed facts was still tied to systematic construction. This was a reflection of their subjective aim (social reform) and their practical ideals. It constituted their philosophical standpoint and showed the concreteness of their thought as a unity of the world of objects and the subjective "ought."

At the same time, a strange self-contradiction surfaced in this approach, especially in its Marxist form. Marxism seeks to ground its theory of knowledge on positive, "scientific" certainty, but when practical aims enter the picture, epistemic certainty hardens into dogma and turns to expressing itself in formulas. In contrast to the scientific spirit of inquiry for which formulas are mere working hypotheses in constant need of reformulation, the Marxist position is withal antiscientific and dogmatic. In the effort to hold on to its philosophic concreteness and at the same time to be scientific, Marxism became unscientific.

At this point another approach to analyzing and describing the workings of consciousness appeared on the scene, one that excluded all aims and ideals and eschewed philosophical constructs. For this psychology even the relationship between the objective world and the subject was open to purely scientific observation and experiment as a conscious process. In its attempt to explain the workings of consciousness, this approach broke ties with traditional modes of philosophical thought in order to be completely scientific. What concerns us here is the way in which a psychology that had cut ties with received philosophical tradition could prompt the emergence of a new and fundamentally different philosophy.

One thinks in this regard of the philosophy of psychologists like Wundt and James, and perhaps also of Fechner and Mach. Wundt spoke of "immediate experience," James advocated a radical empiricism, and Mach argued for a critique of experience. All three were empiricists in the sense that they excluded from experience anything impure and rejected any philosophical construct imposed from without and hence not itself part of pure experience. In this regard their thought differed from older forms of philosophical empiricism. They forged a new philosophical standpoint by breaking all ties between experience and the philosophical. References to "immediate" experience, "radical" empiricism, and the "critique" of experience all point to such a philosophical stance, which always entailed returning experience to pure experience. This trend later gave rise to a number of influential academic centers throughout Europe and has until recently been a particularly dominant element in American philosophy.

There is great significance in the emergence of this standpoint that has escaped the attention of historians of philosophy in general and has been overlooked by historians of ideas. I do not mean that philosophies based upon this approach are particularly important. Whatever contributions they may have made to specialized fields like psychology and physics, Wundt's voluntarist philosophy and Mach's philosophy of rational economics have been overshadowed by the neo-Kantians. Even James's pragmatism no longer fulfills our philosophical needs. The idea of purifying experience in order to have pure experience, and making that the starting point of philosophy, is one thing; the kind of philosophy it leads to is quite another.

No matter how unsatisfactory the results, the underlying historical problem that made inevitable the birth of such philosophies remains momentous. For example, when the neo-Kantians added their criticisms to the philosophy of "psychologism," their critique may have been largely to the point, but this does not mean that they always went as deep as the problem behind the philosophies they were criticizing. For what lay behind these philosophies was the fall from grace of traditional religion and its accompanying metaphysics and two-world theory, as well as the unreliability of both the positivism and materialism that had appeared in the wake of the denial of traditional religion, metaphysics, and earlier empiricist philosophies, all of which contained philosophical artifices in the form of constructs and dogmas. Only our immediate experience was left to rely on. This conclusion amounts to a complete lack of confidence in all forms of traditional philosophy.

This lack of confidence may be considered the outcome of the persistent attempt of science to break down the various standpoints of philosophy from within, but more was involved than mere attention to science could resolve. The issue was more like what Nietzsche had become aware of in his nihilism, something abyssal. Hence it was inevitable that science would be pursued to the point of establishing psychology as an empirical science, but there was nothing inevitable about the philosophy that emerged from this psychology. That is to say, this philosophy proved incapable of solving the problem of the abyss that had opened up. The founders of psychology, when they were carried beyond the founding of their science to philosophy, were not themselves aware of the abyss that had opened up in the aftermath of their science. Nor were the neo-Kantians or phenomenologists who criticized these psychologies; if they had been, they would not have been able to stop at mere logicism. Neither psychologism nor logicism could avoid a basic futility. The situation called rather for metaphysics than for science or criticism. In the meantime, as the forces of science continued to advance, Hegel's metaphysics collapsed, and Christian faith was unable to provide the basis for a new metaphysics. The way to metaphysics was lost, and the clamor of voices calling for a new metaphysics produced no results.

The problem called for a philosophy that would keep its feet firmly planted in immediate and pure experience (in the sense described above) and yet be able to offer new answers to the same fundamental questions that the old metaphysics had addressed. It would not be a "metaphysics" in the old sense of the word, but neither would it be merely a philosophy of scientific psychologism. It would have to satisfy both demands. From the standpoint of traditional philosophy, this amounts to a fundamental contradiction. But the situation was calling for a completely new orientation in philosophy that would be capable of overcoming precisely this contradiction.

First, the tendency of the old metaphysics towards a two-world theory had to be dispensed with. A separate world of Ideas or things-in-themselves existing apart from or behind our experience in this world, and a God conceived of as existing transcendently in that world, could not be admitted.

Second, in spite of this shift away from a two-world theory and the demand to keep in touch with our actual experience, God must be awakened to as the ultimate ground of all things in the world and as the one who grants to human life its natural course. In other words, it was necessary to find a new and different standpoint for religion. In trying to resolve the problem of science and religion in favor of science by accepting atheism and denying religion, positivist and materialist philosophies proved too one-sided to offer a workable solution.

Third, a philosophy based on immediate experience rids itself of the philosophical constructs of traditional empiricism and eliminates from what we usually think of as experience any impurities imported into pure experience from without. But even in its philosophical development, this psychologism maintained the standpoint that established it as a science and hence obscured certain critical problems inherent in that standpoint. This obscurity is most apparent in the way psychologism treats culture, ethics, and particularly religion. Wundt's *Völkerpsychologie* and James's *Varieties of Religious Experience* were epoch-making works that from different perspectives laid the foundations for the psychology of religion. But these thinkers used religious experiences only as source material for psychological study, not as the personal problem of those who have them. While they do not reject religion outright, neither do they inquire into or affirm its subjective side. Compared with Comte and Marx, their approach to science is more consistent but has lost the element of subjective confrontation. It is only natural that a philosophy standing on these foundations should be philosophically futile, failing as it does either to touch the basic problems of human life or to respond to the problems brewing beneath the surface of the times.

A momentous problem cuts into the picture here. On one hand, the metaphysics of idealism as well as the philosophies of positivism, materialism, and empiricism—in a word, all previous standpoints in the history of philosophy—are closed to us. Either they presuppose a worldview that has already become untenable, or, despite their claim to be based on positive fact and experience, they require an experience involving dogmatism and artificial reconstruction. What has brought this state of affairs to consciousness is the spread of science, which has arrived at the point of demanding a fundamental critique of the long history of philosophy until now. On the other hand, the philosophical standpoint of psychologism (which always tries to take experience in its pure and immediate form and to exclude all philosophical constructs in the name of pure science) could not reach the questions traditional philosophies have tried to answer. The basic dilemma here reflects a situation so momentous as to shake the whole history of traditional philosophy and to affect the destiny of philosophy itself.

Where can we look for a way out of this dilemma? We cannot return to a metaphysics affiliated with idealism, nor to positivism or materialism or traditional empiricism. Our only recourse is to return to the standpoint of immediate and pure experience and begin from there. Might not the standpoint of pure experience offer a way to answer anew the fundamental questions about human life inherited from traditional philosophy? Or must the standpoint of pure experience end up in psychologism and its futility? Everything comes down to a question of reexamining the standpoint described as "immediate experience" or "pure experience" or "the critique of experience." It is not a question of returning experience to the here-and-now prior to all our intentions and constructs, thereby taking a firm stance on pure experience. It is rather a question of how to purify experience. In other words, we must ask again whether or not the pure experience we are talking about is truly immediate experience prior to any device. The question carries with it the call for a new metaphysics different from a philosophy grounded only in psychology.

To raise this question in those days was already something out of the ordinary. And it seems to me that there were only two philosophers capable of doing so. One was Bergson, whom we mentioned earlier. The other was Nishida. These two philosophers were able to erect a new system of metaphysics representative of the first half of the twentieth century by taking their start from pure experience in the true sense of the word.

IN THE PREFACE to his *An Inquiry into the Good* Nishida writes:

> For some time now I have had it in mind to try to explain everything by taking pure experience as the one and only reality. At first I read people like Mach, but somehow felt something was missing. In the course of my reading it struck me that it is not that experience takes place because there are individuals, but rather that there are individuals because experience takes place. The idea that experience is more fundamental than individual differences offered a way out of solipsism, while the idea that experience is active also made it possible to harmonize my views with post-Fichtean transcendental philosophy.[4]

In these few words we find the pillars on which the book rests and on whose foundations the considerations that follow will be based.

What does pure experience mean in the true sense of the term? Where does it differ from what psychologists call immediate experience? Why is it that their idea of immediate experience is not truly immediate?

Immediate means subjectively immediate. But from the psychologist's standpoint, the consciousness that is said to be immedi-

_____

4. CW 1:4.

ate and the standpoint of those who observe, reflect, or test that consciousness are always distinct. The observing consciousness and observed consciousness are never the same. Insofar as psychology is a science this distinction is only natural. Indeed psychologists must work on this assumption. The obstructing influence wrought by the act of observation itself on the process being observed should be eliminated as far as possible. But it is precisely here that the limits of what psychology calls immediate experience become apparent. As elsewhere in science, experience entails a separation of subject and object. The process being observed inevitably takes on the quality of something posited as a matter for observation. Even if it is referred to as immediate, its immediacy or directness is that of a mediate, indirect standpoint.

True immediacy, however, must be prior to all mediation and all separation of subject and object. Bergson understood it as "pure duration," while in *An Inquiry into the Good* Nishida took it to mean true "pure experience." Both returned immediate experience to a point prior to the distinction of subject and object. Both assumed a standpoint of experience prior to the reflection of scientific observation or to any processing that experience undergoes as a result of such reflection.

Only by taking experience prior to any work done on it (be it philosophical or scientific) can the ground be laid for a new metaphysics. This does not leave the realm of what we normally call experience, but neither is it the same thing. The standpoint of pure experience implies a kind of taking leave of experience—not to a beyond but to the here-and-now, not to an "over there" but to a "right at hand."

This is where the horizon of a new metaphysics opens up. The transcendence entailed here is not an entry into a world transcending experience, as is the case with traditional metaphysics. It is a transcendence that enters more purely into the realms of ordinary experience. As a transcendence, it breaks through ordinary experience; but the point where that breakthrough takes place is in fact none other than the standpoint of experience in its pure, everyday form. Freedom, goodness, knowledge, religion—everything is questioned from this standpoint. Obviously we are dealing here with something essentially different from traditional metaphysics.

The work of psychologists like Wundt and James forms the foundations for *An Inquiry into the Good,* as it had also for Bergson's *Essai sur les donneés immédiates de la conscience.*[5] Yet Nishida was not arrested by what these thinkers had in mind by pure experience but exerted himself further to see the notion of true pure experience through to the end, as something lived prior to the distinction of subject and object. The same effort lies behind the collection of essays entitled *Thinking and Experience* that followed *An Inquiry into the Good.* There Nishida takes up the standpoints of speculative economics and pragmatism, for example, to contrast the current of pure experience with that of pure logicism.[6] Conversely, he points out that the positions of Mach and James do not represent the standpoint of "true" pure experience. In the passage just cited from the preface to *An Inquiry into the Good,* Nishida remarks how he studied thinkers like Mach with the aim of finding a way to explain everything in terms of pure experience, only to be dissatisfied with what he found.

In *Thinking and Experience* he refers to "true pure experience" — that is, pure experience *sensu stricto* — in these words:

> To begin with, we must make clear what is meant by the standpoint of pure experience in the strict sense of the word. Pure experience is generally taken to be a psychological explanation. But for me psychological explanation contains numerous background hypotheses and rests on the dogmatic assumption that experience is individual and conforms to the categories of space, time, and causality. Since even many of those who profess the cause of pure experience rest their thinking on such foundations, it seems not unreasonable to think of pure experience in entirely psychological terms. But inasmuch as this way of thinking already involves the addition of a certain dogmatic element to experience, it cannot be called true pure experience.[7]

Elsewhere he remarks that ordinary psychologists and empiricists, because they view pure experience from the outside rather

---

5. Published in Paris in 1889. English trans. by F. L. Pogson, *Time and Free Will: An Essay on the Immediate Data of Consciousness* (New York, 1910).

6. "The Epistemological Claims of the Logicists," CW 1:210.

7. CW 1:226.

than from within, do not catch its true form.[8] To view pure experience from within means standing firm in the living, concrete reality of experience itself as it is right now, from moment to moment. To view it from the outside, conversely, means analyzing this dynamic concrete totality into abstract psychological elements and then reconstructing the elements to explain it. So doing universalizes individually lived experience. What psychologists and empiricists mean by experience is something that has already gone through that process. It has already been grounded in certain hypotheses and taken on a certain dogmatism. All their claims to the contrary, they are viewing experience from the outside, not as the occasion of a true unity of subject and object. Again Nishida:

> Psychology studies the self and adopts the same analytic method as the other sciences. What has been grasped by pure intuition it tries to break down into psychological elements like perception, feeling, representation, and so on. For psychology there is no other way, but to turn around and speak universally in such terms is to forfeit the particular traits of everybody. The subtle and indescribable nuances of taste that distinguish oneself from others, for instance, disappear. We are left with only the general pattern of disposition towards a given thing.[9]

This quotation, by the way, belongs to a commentary on Bergson's philosophical methodology, from which we conclude that the philosophies of Nishida and Bergson have in common the return to what we have been calling pure experience in the strict sense of the term. The point is confirmed in passages like the following:

> From the first there were those whose philosophies took their start from reason and those who took their start from experience. Bergson belongs among the latter. But while those who claim to be starting from experience do not usually mean true pure experience but rather something that has been fashioned by the intellect, Bergson strove to eliminate everything dogmatic and to penetrate deeply to

---

8. CW 1:306.
9. CW 1:322–23. The passage appears in "An Essay on Bergson's Philosophical Methodology."

the true form of experience itself. What he got hold of in the process was pure duration.[10]

Of course, there is a big difference between what Bergson and Nishida took this pure experience to be. To put it simply, while Bergson's pure duration is a matter of life, Nishida's pure experience in his first period has to do with will and is more subjective. This fundamental contrast was the source of the great differences that appeared between the two philosophers as their thought developed.

Consider, for example, the following passage from *Thinking and Experience*:

> Each time we enter into a state of pure experience where discursive discrimination has truly ceased and where subject and object are at one, we join the absolute activity that is cosmic consciousness. . . . When I speak of individual experiences pure and simple, I am referring to concrete, lived facts. It is here, on each and every occasion, that I find the deep religious fact of seeing God.[11]

Attention should be drawn to Nishida's use of the term "individual experiences" and "concrete, lived facts." A radical return to individual facts is for him of fundamental importance. His talk of pure experience in which subject and object are at one may seem like an abnormal psychological state or an extremely subjective, conceptual, and idealist standpoint. In actuality, our thinking and feeling, our speaking and doing, do not take place apart from pure experience where subject and object are at one. Those who see this as abnormal or idealistic would do well to take a step back and look at the fact that they are thinking that thought right now. However brief and fleeting the thought, it remains an incontrovertible fact that will never occur again in the universe, before which one can say with Nishida, "The one and only reality there is—try as you will, there is no doubting it."[12] The world of all these facts is the actual world.

In *An Inquiry into the Good* such facts are spoken of as phenomena of consciousness, although of course Nishida does not thereby

---

10. "Bergson's Pure Duration," CW 1:327.
11. CW 1:306.
12. *An Inquiry into the Good*, CW 1:37.

mean to oppose them to material phenomena. As he writes, *"Phenomena of consciousness* may be thought to imply that spirit only exists when cut off from matter. What I really mean is that true reality can neither be called conscious phenomena nor material phenomena."[13] What we usually call mind and matter, or spirit and body, do not belong to pure experience but are only the result of artificial constructs added to it. This way of speaking comes about when people add their own "discriminations" to their experiences. Experience itself is at work before I reflect that "I" am experiencing or that my experience has a certain structure. It arises as an "independent self-sufficing activity." It is a spontaneous and self-unfolding dynamic unity with its own organic system. It is almost like the great forces of nature that make the buds on a tree expand, burst into leaves, and flower.

Insofar as the discrimination affixed to pure experience — so-called reflective thinking — is itself a fact, it represents one aspect of the systematic development of consciousness, of which we shall speak presently. But from what has already been said and from the metaphor of the budding tree, it may seem that individual experiences are to be regarded as determined by a great force ruling the entire universe in necessary causal relationships that link all the events of the cosmos together.

As we noted earlier, this is already to view things from the outside. Seen on its own terms, experience is a spontaneous self-unfolding that takes place from and of itself; it cannot be considered apart from subjective activities like seeing, hearing, and thinking, nor from the unifying work of systematically coordinating these activities. Relationships in the cosmos also need to be seen in terms of this immediately living and developing experience.

Only on this basis can we make sense of Nishida's remark, "Each time we enter into a state of pure experience where discursive discrimination has truly ceased and where subject and object are at one, we join the absolute activity that is cosmic consciousness." But what kind of sense?

13. CW 1:54–55.

WE NOTED earlier that however brief and fleeting our experience may be, it remains an incontrovertible fact. The phenomena of consciousness are forever in transition from one moment to the next, but they function as a spontaneous self-unfolding by constituting a dynamic and systematic unity. This unity also makes it possible for the first time to think about time. Once the lived unity of the contents of consciousness is granted, we are then able to line up the contents in terms of a before and an after, and hence to think in temporal terms. Talk of a unifying development of the contents of consciousness does not of itself entail a temporal frame in which this occurs. Quite the contrary, it is only with the unifying functions of consciousness that we can begin to speak of time. In *An Inquiry into the Good* Nishida writes:

> It is not that the unifying activity of consciousness falls under the dominion of time but rather that time comes into being as a result of this unifying activity. We have to say that there is something immutable and transcending, something outside time, at the root of consciousness.[14]

To turn to this unifying activity of consciousness is to return to pure experience. Pure experience is therefore something that has transcended time, by which we do not mean that it has left this temporal world for another world outside time. The point at which this unifying activity functions is "now," and it is from this now that time comes about even as time is being transcended. We may perhaps borrow Kierkegaard's words and speak of the now as an "atom of eternity" reflected in time. The only difference is in the meaning of "reflected." In Nishida's philosophy we may speak of eternity being manifest in the present in unison with the constitution of time. To borrow from the vocabulary of Nishida's later philosophy, contradictories like time and eternity represent the contradictory self-identity of the present determining the present.

To be more precise, the world is spatial in the sense that it consists of the many that are the self-negation of an all-encompass-

---

14. CW 1:73–74.

ing "one," and temporal in the sense that it is a "one" that is the self-negation of the many. Thus the world is the self-determination of the absolute present as a contradictory self-identity of space and time. Naturally this theory does not surface in *An Inquiry into the Good*, but it is an inevitable consequence of the ideas laid out there. The idea that the unifying activity of consciousness entails something immutable that transcends time is the source of the idea, already referred to, that pure experience unites with "the absolute activity that is cosmic consciousness." The passage from *An Inquiry into the Good* goes on:

> In psychology the origin of such a unifying function reverts to matter in the form of brain. But . . . the fundamental fact is the unifying function, which is an immediate constellation of the contents of consciousness. It is not that this unifying power stems from some other reality, but that reality is established through this activity. All people believe in a fixed immutable principle in the universe according to which everything that is has come into being. This principle *is the unifying power of all things and also the unifying power of the interior of consciousness*. The principle is not something possessed by things and minds; it brings things and minds into being. Reason is independent and self-sustaining, and does not differ according to time or place or person. . . .
>
> The unifying power of the objective world is identical with the unifying force of subjective consciousness. In other words, both the so-called objective world and consciousness are come about through the same principle. This is why people are able to understand the basic principles behind the constitution of the universe by means of the principle within themselves.[15]

Thus the unifying activity through which our conscious experience comes into being is one and the same as the absolute activity that unifies the universe. In each of our experiences the absolute activity that is the unifying force behind the entire universe is reflected. This is why it is not a mere "idealistic" standpoint but one that has direct ties to the basic principle that brings things and minds into being. This law is called independent and self-sustain-

---

15. CW 1:74–76.

ing. That is to say, it is transcendent. This does not mean that it is transcendent in the sense of something that can be an object of consciousness. He says, "Principle as such is creative, something we can become, something we can work in accord with. But it is *not* something we can view as an object of consciousness."[16]

The relationship between this sort of principle—which is transcendent and creative, at once the unifying power of all things and of consciousness, yet itself incapable of being an object of consciousness—and our particular experiences is close to the relationship that Leibniz posited in the monads as living mirrors of the universe. Living and working are themselves a reflection of the universe. Creative activity in this sense is reality, and the universe is the world of this reality. Here we have an intuition similar to Leibniz's intuition of a world of pre-established harmony. Nishida writes expressly: "Reality comes about through mutual relationships; the universe is the sole activity of the only reality there is."[17] Taking his start from the monadology of Leibniz, Nishida later spoke of the world as the self-identity of absolute contradictories, and of us as the creative elements of that creative world as its "self-expression-*in*-self-formation." Such ideas were already present in germ in *An Inquiry into the Good*.

The book opens with a description of pure experience:

> To *experience* means to know facts just as they are. It means to know by casting aside all of one's devices and following the facts. Since even those who use the word "experience" are in fact usually mixing in some of their own ideas, we call it *pure* to refer to the state of experience just as it is, without the slightest addition of opinion or discrimination. It refers, for example, to the moment I see a color or hear a sound, before I have had a chance to think about it as the effect of something external or of myself as sensing it, or even before affixing a judgment about what color or sound it is.[18]

When such pure experience takes place it carries with it a sense of presence wherein the unifying power of the universe and the unifying power of consciousness referred to above are one and

16. CW 1:75.
17. CW 1:72.
18. CW 1:1.

the same. It is an identity we might compare to Schelling's *Identität*, which Nishida calls "a state of immediate experience."[19] What Schelling called "the identity of the real and the ideal" was a standpoint of absolute reason, something conceivable through speculation. It was also, therefore, an idealism. In *An Inquiry into the Good*, however, the identity was grasped in pure experience, in the actual, straightforward facts like hearing a sound. Later Schelling came to espouse a "positive philosophy," which considered the standpoint of rational speculation as merely a "negative philosophy" fixed on *Was-sein* (essential being), and took its stand rather on the *Dass-sein* (factual being) in the experience of reality. In forsaking this standpoint of factual experience for the philosophical mists of myth and revelation, however, he was never to know a standpoint in touch with the ordinary experiences of hearing sounds and seeing colors and fathoming them to their depths. For he did not live to see psychology established as an empirical science.

IT SHOULD BE clear by now that this standpoint of pure experience does not slide into solipsism. Even those psychologists who take up pure experience in psychology omit anything like a substantial "mind" or "soul" from their consideration of conscious processes. From a philosophical perspective, however, such a position can only land them in solipsism. The only standpoint from which to avoid this conclusion is that of a new metaphysics that conforms thoroughly to experience and to the view that the unifying power of consciousness is identical to the unifying power of all things.

This idea shows up in Nishida's reference in *An Inquiry into the Good* to the unifying power at the ground of the systematic development of pure experience as a universal: "The fact of pure experience means that a so-called universal has realized itself."[20] What he means by the universal, he tells us, is what Hegel calls the concept or *Begriff*. When a systematic contradiction develops within a spontaneous and self-unfolding pure experience, a larger systematic unity is needed. The felt need for a greater unity is thinking,

19. CW 1:42.
20. CW 1:26.

at whose ground in fact such a unifying power is already at work. This "power unifying concrete facts" *is* the universality of the concept. "Since our pure experience is a systematic development, the unifying power operating at its ground must be directly the universality of the concept itself."[21]

The concept does not refer here to a mental abstraction. To think in such terms is to fail to conform to pure experience, to set up a kind of "self" within an abstract framework cut off from pure experience and see that self as thinking things. But this is a self that has been thought up. If one stays with experience as such, experience is always a spontaneous self-unfolding with a unity. It is grasped as the differentiating development of something universal. This active universal is the concept. And the infinite unity at the final ground of this development, the highest state of unity free of all clash of contradictories, is called intellectual intuition. This is the standpoint joined to the unifying power of the universe to which we alluded in the previous section.

Now the actual work of uniting that pervades the process towards an ever deeper and vaster unity is our "rightful and true self."[22] This true self is not the self posited through thought. We usually think of the self as an individual and then slip the label marked "the individual" into consciousness. On this point Nishida writes:

> The sphere of consciousness is never confined to the so-called individual, which is no more than one small system within consciousness. We usually take a microsystem with corporeal existence as its nucleus to be the center, but if we try to think of a larger system of consciousness as the axis, this macro-system would be the self and its development the realization of the will of the self. It is something like this with serious devotees of religion or scholarship or art.[23]

To think on an axis of the macrosystem of consciousness is to deepen and widen the connections of the unifying power of pure experience with the unifying power of the universe. Here one

---

21. CW 1:26.
22. CW 1:33.
23. CW 1:39.

passes beyond the frame of "the individual" whose core is corpo-
real existence to a realm where the self becomes the broad and
deep system of experience. The guiding idea of the "universal" behind this way of thinking is derived from Hegel, while that of "intellectual intuition" by and large follows Schelling. In revitalizing
German philosophy from the standpoint of pure experience, Nishida was able to avoid the solipsism to which psychology's standpoint of pure experience was prone.

It is Kierkegaard who returns to the reality of subjective experience by negating Hegel's standpoint of speculative reason. Although the consequences of subjective life are probed deeply and
the underlying psychological analysis is extremely concrete, one
does not find the perspective of "science" in Kierkegaard. It was
only later that psychology came to be established as an empirical
science and that consciousness came to be seen as pure experience.
For Kierkegaard the problem of science and religion is not yet
taken up as the source of an intellectual crisis. That Nishida arrived at a view of religion different from that of Kierkegaard is
related to this fact. "How can we ask after the existence of God in
the facts of our immediate experience?"[24] Both the fact that this
question is posed and the historical circumstances that made it
possible deserve attention. Here is Nishida's response:

> The foundations of the reality that makes up the universe can be
> known in the depths of our own hearts; we are able there to catch
> the face of God. The unbounded freedom of activity of the human
> heart is direct proof of God himself.[25]

Elsewhere he writes:

> Our true self is the very stuff of the universe. To know the true self
> is not only to be joined to the good of humanity in general but also
> to melt into the stuff of the universe and to blend in with the divine
> will. Here religion and morality are indeed exhausted. The law of
> knowing the true self and joining with God is only to be found in
> appropriating the power of the union of subject and object. But to

24. CW 1:98.
25. CW 1:99.

acquire this power is to kill off the false ego completely, to die once and for all to the desires of this world and be born again.[26]

And this, Nishida, goes on, is what Christianity calls rebirth and what Buddhism calls enlightenment.

Confronted by the intellectual quandaries that accompanied the expansion of science, and taking its start from the pure experience that "try as you will, there is no doubting," Nishida's philosophy could not but arrive at such a view of religion. Needless to say, there are all sorts of problems involved. Comparing this view with that of his final essay, "The Logic of Place and a Religious Worldview," one is surprised at the extent of his development. The biggest difference is that in the view of religion we find in his early work, the problems of sin and death were not yet given very serious consideration. Later Kierkegaard was to have a momentous influence on the development of Nishida's religious views. In the end, however, Nishida took a different tack from Kierkegaard, arguing for a relationship of "inverse correlation" between God and human beings that harks back to his own early views on religion.

While admitting the standpoint of science, Nishida's philosophy did not lead to the sort of critique and denial of religion that scientific positivism and materialism did. For example, he refers to the standpoint of pure experience as "seeing something by becoming that thing," or "grasping the absolute state of a thing by trying to become the thing itself."[27] To see something by becoming it is not of course materialism. Matter cannot see things by becoming them. But neither is this possible from a standpoint of mind opposed to matter. To see things by becoming them is a standpoint that kills the ego completely to *become* the principle of the universe. It is a standpoint of pure experience at which one joins to the power that unifies all things. If we call it mind, it is not the mind of a mind-matter opposition but rather a mind that transcends them both, a mind like the mind of which it is said "the mind just as it is, is the Buddha." In Nishida's words, "What Zen Buddhists refer to as 'mind following every shift of location—shifts

---

26. CW 1:167–68.
27. "Bergson's Philosophical Methodology," CW 1:319–20.

of place effective and deep' is the true form of experience in the raw."[28] The mind that changes its perspective as it changes its location is the great free and unobstructed mind able to see things by becoming them. In the terms of Nishida's philosophy, that shifts of place are actually effective and deep means that the mind blends with the absolute activity of the cosmos. Yet these empirical facts are said to be "in the raw." This perspective is altogether different from materialism.

In its attempt to be scientific, materialism led to the rejection of religion and forfeited its capacity to provide answers to the fundamental problems of human life. That existentialism and existential philosophy assumed a standpoint of subjectivity stands to reason. The problem is that in the process they lost touch with the scientific outlook. The standpoint of pure experience that we have just seen in Nishida's philosophy incorporated a position that overcame the one-sidedness into which materialism and existentialism had fallen. His standpoint represents a fundamentally new reformulation of what psychologists had called pure experience, and in developing it he revitalized the metaphysics of thinkers like Hegel by a shift from speculation to facticity. And the intuition constituting the basic formative power of this philosophical standpoint was provided by Zen Buddhism.

Through further confrontation with its own inherent difficulties, the standpoint of pure experience developed into Nishida's later profoundly unique system of thought. For more detail, the reader is referred to the works mentioned at the beginning of this essay. Here I have simply tried to deal with elements in his early thought in which the basic intuition that operated in its later development appears in its simplest form.

---

28. "Bergson's Pure Duration," CW 1:328.

6 *An Inquiry into the Good:*
Pure Experience

NISHIDA'S *An Inquiry into the Good* consists of four sections entitled respectively "Pure Experience," "Reality," "The Good," and "Religion"; but the one idea that pervades the whole is that of pure experience. In the preface to the first edition Nishida called pure experience "the ground of my thought."[1] By *ground* he meant both the starting point from which his ideas developed and the point to which every development, both his individual ideas and his thought as a whole, returns. Not only the fundamental questions of theoretical philosophy—broadly speaking, the questions of thought and reality traditionally dealt with in epistemology and ontology—but also matters of ethics and religion are all seen as concrete developments of pure experience. In that same preface, part 1 of the book is said to clarify the "nature" (that is, the basic form) of the pure experience that grounds his thought, and, together with the three parts that follow, it tries to develop a complete system of pure experience. Hence it is only in the context of the entire book that one can come to see what is meant by the standpoint of pure experience.

That the work is to be read as a whole is evident from the way it is structured. Part 1, "Pure Experience," in which the nature of the pure experience that runs through the entire system is explained, begins with a chapter of the same title. This chapter deals with the basic form of the idea that grounds the entire system, its

_____

1. CW 1:3.

germ as it were. (Indeed the first dozen lines or so of the text speak of what we might call the *materia prima* of pure experience as it appears in such seminal form.) The form of pure experience is developed from an explanation of its seminal form in the first chapter through an elucidation of its systematic development in terms of "thinking" and "will" in the next two chapters. Finally, in a chapter entitled "Intellectual Intuition," it is given its consummate expression as the basic form that it is. In short, the structure of the book reveals a threefold approach to pure experience: as that which brings unity to the system as a whole, as the basic form of the complete unity, and as the germ of that basic form. All three are called pure experience. No matter which part of this whole system one takes, the basic form—pure experience—is dominant and its *materia prima* is present.

In chapter 4 of part 1, "Intellectual Intuition," Nishida says of "infinite unity," for example, that it is "given in the form of so-called intellectual intuition" and remarks further that "true intellectual intuition is the very unifying activity in pure experience itself, the comprehension of life."[2] Again at the end of the chapter he takes up the question of "true religious awakening" by way of conclusion and refers to it as "the appropriation of a vast unity laid across the ground of intellect and will," and as a kind of intellectual intuition, a "deep grasp of life." At the very end of the chapter he adds, "I consider that this fundamental intuition must be at the root of all religions. Religion must lie at the root of learning and morality; through it learning and morality come into being."[3] With these words he closes part 1.

Putting this all together, we see that the intellectual intuition that grounds thinking and will is the same unifying activity in pure experience whose *materia prima* appeared at the outset of the book. The unifying activity is not, of itself, something other than the awareness of unity. Self-awareness is part of it from the start. Nor, as the flow of the rest of the book makes plain, is the unifying activity of itself anything other than unity. True unity is a living unity; it is where the "true self" that Nishida calls "the infinite

2. CW 1:42–43.
3. CW 1:45.

unifier" and "truly the unifying force itself of the reality of the universe" is present.[4] In its ultimate form, this intellectual intuition appears in religious awakening. Hence this essentially religious intellectual intuition is the perfection of the nature (basic form) of pure experience and is an essential part of the *materia prima* of pure experience referred to at the outset. In essence, pure experience is something religious.

Furthermore, in part 4, "Religion," Nishida actually states that "God must be the foundation of the universe and also our foundation; our return to God is a return to that base."[5] This leads him later to write:

> The unity of pure experience is at the ground of our consciousness in all circumstances; there is no way to leap free of it (see part 1). In this sense we may see God as the one great intellectual intuition at the ground of the universe and as a unifier of pure experience encompassing the universe.[6]

Here the pure experience whose nature was considered in part 1, and which was taken up in part 2 in connection with the reality of the universe and in part 3 with a reflection on personality and the good, is spoken of in connection with God who is "the foundation of the universe and also our foundation." To return to the start of the book from this, its final vantage point, already at the ground of the simple pure experiences of "seeing a color, hearing a sound," a road opens up before us that leads directly to God. This is the standpoint of pure experience.

THE MEANING OF PURE EXPERIENCE

AN INQUIRY INTO THE GOOD comprises a complete system of thought that may be described as "a philosophy of pure experience." Seen in the light of the overall development of Nishida's philosophy, the work is simply a first step, a fountainhead. In his preface to the new edition Nishida himself acknowledges that it is but the first in

---

4. CW 1:78–79.
5. CW 1:174.
6. CW 1:186.

a series of four standpoints that emerged over time. But even on its own, *An Inquiry into the Good* is an original *tour de force* that would have assured it a place among other great systems of thought even if Nishida's had not developed further. Nishida's philosophy not only represents Japan's first original formulation of a philosophical system but also merits a place in the history of world philosophy for having opened up an altogether new approach and outlook for philosophical thought and introduced novel possibilities for it. This is apparent already in the standpoint of pure experience that occupies his attention in *An Inquiry into the Good*. In what does the fundamental novelty of this standpoint consist and what is so original about it?

The book opens with the sentence, "To experience means to know facts just as they are" (p. 9). These words express aptly the essence of experience. The term "facts as they are" means that experience is the locus where facts are given most immediately, while "knowing facts as they are" means that experience is the locus where knowing arises most immediately. Or we might say that experience is the fountainhead for both the objectivity of facts as they are and the certainty of knowing what there is to know. The two come together most immediately in experience, at the point where facts are "as they are." If we refer to the unity of the objectivity of facts and the certainty of knowing as "facticity," then "as they are" is the locus of the most immediate facticity.

That I see with my own eyes and feel with my own heart, or at any rate that I am myself present in what is going on, is an essential part of the experience of "knowing facts as they are." I am always on the scene where facts manifest themselves as they are and where the certainty of knowledge arises. Or rather, the scene and my own presence there are the same thing. It is not that the scene of my experience is first set without my being there (in which case, there would be no experience) and that I then enter in. The scene of experience is set by my presence in it. In short, facts, the knowledge of facts, and the actual presence of the self all become immediately one in experience.

As observed above, it is from the locus of pure experience that the standpoint develops at which true knowing (the subject of part 1), true reality (part 2), and true goodness (part 3) appear in their original form and at which they can be examined with appreciation. Moreover, it is also the standpoint that leads to unity with God (part 4).

As we also noted earlier, at the end of part 1 the direct intuition that both transcends reasoning and will and gives them their roots is seen as "a kind of intellectual intuition"—a deep grasp of life—and "the root of all truth and satisfaction." Nishida adds:

> This basic intuition must be at the root of all religion. And religion must be at the root of learning and morality, for it is through religion that they arise. (p. 45)

In part 2, he takes up the question of "reality" in connection with learning (leaving morality for part 3). After drawing attention at the start of part 2 to the agreement between "intellectual convictions" about views of the world and human life on the one hand and "practical demands" in morality and religion on the other—that is, to the fact that "originally, truth is one"—he goes on to take up the questions of "the true countenance of heaven and earth and human life" (p. 46) and "true reality." Here again, it is pure or immediate experience that represents the starting point and foundation:

> Now if one aims at understanding true reality and knowing the true countenance of heaven and earth and human life, one must doubt as much as possible, take leave of all the hypothetical constructions people make, and set out on the basis of direct knowledge which one cannot doubt no matter how hard one tries. . . .
>
> In what then does this direct knowledge consist that one cannot doubt even if one wants to? Simply in the facts of our intuitive experience, that is, in what we know about the phenomena of consciousness. Here the presence of conscious phenomena and our consciousness of them are straightforwardly one and the same, with no interval for subject to be distinguished from object. Between the fact and its knowledge not the slightest hairline chink opens up. Truly one cannot doubt even if one tries to; . . . one can only know the facts as they are. It makes no sense to speak of being in error or not being in error. This kind of intuitive experience forms the foundation on which all of our knowledge must be built up. (pp. 47–49)

The same point is repeated in parts 3 and 4. There is no time or necessity to enter into those formulations here, but if I had to choose a representative passage, it would be the following:

> Not everything we desire or everything we need has to be explainable; they are given facts. We say we eat to live, but the words "to live" are an explanation added afterwards. Hunger does not need any such reason to arise, any more than an infant needs such a reason to start nursing. It only drinks to drink. Not only are our needs and desires direct facts of experience that need not be explained, but they hold the secret to understanding the true meaning of reality. (p. 120)

In short, all experience, including such simple things as seeing a flower, hearing the sound of a frog diving into the water, or eating a meal, consist in "knowing facts as they are." The original form of this experience just as it is, in its pure and immediate form, leads directly to true knowing, true reality, true morality and religion, and the like.

As noted earlier, experience always takes place in the presence of the self. Accordingly, the self-unfolding of experience itself means that the "true self" (p. 78) is realized and examined as it permeates true knowing, true morality and religion, and all such things. These are all ways by which the true self is embodied. The development of pure experience is oriented to our own transformation into a true self and attaining insight into the self's original countenance.

Put the other way around, in order for the Socratic injunction, "Know thyself," to be realized in the concrete, there must be a development towards contact with the true countenance and true reality of heaven and earth and human life that proceeds by way of a philosophical view of the world and human life. And given that "true reality is originally one," this development requires in turn that one pursue the practical question of how to lead one's life by walking the full length of the road of "personality" and thus enter into the world of religion by way of some fundamental intuition that gives one a "grasp on life." All this belongs to intuition understood as the "experience" of "knowing things as they are."

My life cannot for so much as a moment take leave of the place of experience. Try as I might to distance myself, it is to no avail, for my very effort to take leave of experience already belongs to experience; it is an unfolding of experience itself. At each moment experience opens up into an infinite expanse and depth. Its infinite development urges it in that direction, or rather to it and back from it. Even if it is only a question of ordinary, everyday experiences like having a meal, looking at something, or listening to a sound, it is entirely the same. It is said that an old man once reached the Great Enlightenment by looking at a peach blossom; and one Zen master is known to have taught the way to enlightenment by listening to a mountain stream.

In this sense everyday experience suggests passing from the top of one tall mountain to another. And this holds true not only for apparently abnormal experiences but also for those that are ordinary and everyday, so long as a basic intuition and grasp of life are present. For experiences of the self in the here and now, where facts are known as they are, the extraordinary is as normal as the ordinary and everyday. "Working all day and getting nothing done" (p. 45), as the ancient saying goes, are entirely the same. It is only natural that ordinary experiences at times strike us as strange while extraordinary experiences may seem normal.

PROBLEMS WITH UNDERSTANDING THE BOOK

NOW EVEN if we grant that all experience is this way by nature, it is hardly the way we ordinarily think of our own experience. Indeed, we cannot. Let experience take place in its original form before our very eyes, we ourselves can only see it in unoriginal form (in other words, we have not become a "true self"). This discrepancy between what the self experiences and how the self interprets that experience is forever a stumbling block to understanding pure experience and the way of thinking it leads to. That we are in no hurry to change the way we think about our experience just because it has been pointed out to us that our experience is by nature such and such may seem trivial enough in itself, but it is precisely here that the sense of confusion about the book sets in and that all sorts of doubts and suspicions materialize. Accordingly I would like to begin with these questions, which I would divide roughly into two areas.

A first set of difficulties arises from treating the book's standpoint as one of pure theory and reflection. The concept of pure experience represents an entirely new and original perspective, different from any way of thinking in the history of philosophy. As readers, of course, each of us brings our own experiences to the book, as well as our own set of questions arising from those experiences and at least some sort of provisional solution to them. In short, we approach it with our own prejudice.

Obviously prejudice impedes appreciation of novel and original thinking in general, but there is an additional consideration with Nishida's book: from start to finish pure experience is stipulated as "consciousness." Does this not amount to a kind of psychologism or subjectivism? From the standpoint of materialism, it looks to be an extreme form of idealism. But that is not all. Among the variety of idealisms, there is a metaphysics of objective, rational law that maintains objectivity and yet differs completely from the extreme form of objectivity we see in materialism. If, however, the standpoint of pure experience comes to term in what we described above as a basic direct intuition, does not its failure to break free of its moorings in experience ultimately point to a rudimentary limitation?

Already in Plato and Aristotle metaphysics had passed beyond the dimension of "experience" and into that of "reason." The same basic orientation is visible in metaphysics since Descartes, which has set itself up against modern empiricism. Could it be that the standpoint of Nishida's book, which adheres strictly to experience, is better able than these to resolve the complicated theoretical issues involved? Or is it just that its standpoint is too narrow and simplistic? In one form or another, these suspicions are bound to arise. It is no easy matter to replace our preconceived ways of thinking with the idea that the standpoint of pure experience might be able to respond to certain types of problems.

In the second place, even if we are not held captive by our prejudices but try to understand the book's ideas with an open mind, we may still feel that we have not really understood what we thought we were understanding. What we have understood intellectually may not sink in enough to give a true sense of understanding. That such difficulties accompany an approach determined to stay with experience and conform to it, determined to refuse to acknowledge what is usually taken for experience as true experience and to make the return to "pure experience" its starting point, is unavoidable and indeed represents part of what is distinctive about such a standpoint. Through it, abstruse questions lying hidden behind the standpoints of common sense and science and general philosophy are brought to light without being subjected to conscious investigation. This becomes a matter of some significance when we turn our sights intently on the question of the human, that is, when the human looks intently at itself.

Something similar took place when Kierkegaard worked out his standpoint of *Existenz* as one in which the individual (*der Einzelne*) incorporates the dimension of transcendence. In opposition to purely cerebral thinking, he forged a way of thinking according to which understanding is true understanding only when it has been appropriated as one's own (*Aneignung*). This position became the moving force behind his confrontation with Hegel's philosophy and went on to exert a profound influence on contemporary philosophy, religious thought, and literature. This one example should suffice to make apparent the gravity of the question with which we are dealing.

Nor has the gravity of the question been lost on the East, where we find attention drawn to it from ancient times. One thinks, for instance, of the unity of knowledge and action proposed in Confucianism by the Wang Yang-ming school, to which in fact Nishida himself refers (p. 106). Or again, in Zen Buddhism, sayings like "What comes in through the door is not a family treasure" and "A drawing of rice cakes does not fill an empty belly" are too numerous to count. In this sense, the standpoint of pure experience may be said to belong to the heritage of the East.

In short, the desire to appropriate one's ideas, to incorporate one's perspective as part of oneself, belongs to a problematic that touches on the deep foundations of the being we call human; and those who have not satisfied that desire or understood the ideas and perspectives out of which it arises will never really understand, no matter how hard they cudgel their brains into understanding. This fact, inextricably woven into the stuff of human being, finds its most classical formulation in traditions like Zen.

Simply by being a theoretical discipline, of course, philosophy already differs from Zen. Yet it is hardly surprising that the place where philosophical thinking plants its feet and takes its start is in essence the same as it is for Zen. In part this is owing to the nature of philosophy, and it follows as a matter of course that understanding philosophical thought should bring its own sorts of problems. The appropriation of thought embraces difficulties entirely different from those found in intellectual understanding.

These, then, are the two difficulties that impede an appreciation of the ideas that Nishida presents in *An Inquiry into the Good*. First, there are apprehensions having to do with the nature of *experience* in the standpoint of pure experience: whether it leans towards a subjectivism, whether restricting oneself to experience is too narrow and simplistic an approach to cope with complex issues, and whether such a standpoint might not fall short of the wide and comprehensive horizon of the objectivity of "reason" that is found in traditional metaphysics. A second difficulty stems from the fact that it is a standpoint of *pure* experience that requires "appropriation."[7] These two obstacles to understanding are in fact joined at the roots at the basis of the book. We may now turn to a comprehensive consideration of these points by inquiring into the fundamental nature of "pure experience."

THE INDEPENDENT AND SELF-SUFFICIENT
NATURE OF PURE EXPERIENCE

CONCERNING the first question, Nishida notes in his preface to the second edition (1936) that the standpoint of the book "is one of consciousness and may even be considered a kind of psychologism." At the same time, he continues, "During the period in which the book was written, this was not the only thing in the back of my mind," suggesting that he means to give the notion of "conscious-

---

7. Nishitani plays on the Japanese to give 自己化 (literally, "transformation into the self") as a translation for the German word *Aneignung*, which we have rendered here as "appropriation." Nishida himself, as Nishitani notes, prefers the term 自得 (literally, "self-attaining") in the present book (*see* CW 1:63, 168).

ness" a far greater and more widereaching connotation than it normally has. His understanding of the term was literally infinite, going beyond psychology and psychologism, beyond empiricism and pragmatism, and even beyond Kantian transcendentalism and Husserlean phenomenology, to embrace everything. The standpoint of pure experience means that the infinite manifold of beings forms a unity in the here and now, and it is this sense that Nishida attributes to the term *consciousness*. "Consciousness," he says, "is what Hegel calls *das Unendliche*" (p. 57).

If one approaches the book without preconceptions about consciousness, there is little danger of misjudging its standpoint as one of subjectivism. The author himself warns repeatedly against such misunderstanding. For example:

> There is a danger that the term *conscious phenomena* used here may invite misunderstanding. It may be taken to mean that spirit exists on its own, apart from matter. But what I actually mean by true reality can be called neither conscious phenomena nor material phenomena. (p. 54)

Whatever Nishida's intentions, his choice of the term *consciousness* remains a problem. The meaning he gives the word in his book is not the ordinary sense of something that *has been made* conscious — a "phenomenon of consciousness" — but rather a sense of that which *is* conscious. Insofar as this distinction is maintained, it hardly seems adequate simply to adopt the same word *consciousness* to designate the consciousness of being conscious; at best this clouds the discussion. What Nishida himself writes in his preface to the second edition admits as much, and later developments in his thought drive the point home.

As for whether a standpoint based on experience might not be too narrow and simplistic, it should be noted that "experience" here denotes something ongoing and in constant development. Now whatever is in process is always a seedbed of problems. Individuals have their personal problems, executives their business problems, scientists their problems with specialized research, and so on. The world of social interaction, thought, morality, and religion is filled with problems beyond number. If all is experience, then all these problems belong to the development of experience. And this is precisely the claim on which Nishida bases his book.

For Nishida, experience always has its own "structure" and develops systematically. That is, it creates its own structure from within as it unfolds, and this structure in turn always contains a system. The cornerstone of this development is always an infinite unity. Such is the perspective from which Nishida approaches experience and considers problems that arise in the unfolding of experience. This is what he has in mind in positing pure experience as the standpoint for philosophy. What, then, can it mean to claim that from the very start experience is rooted in an infinite unity?

All experience of any kind is always and at each moment possessed of its own unity, and in this "unifying activity" or "unifying power" opens up into a horizon of infinite expanse and depth. At bottom, it always harbors an infinite unity; its development is a constant moving from one infinite unity to another. Behind the scenes of every development of experience there is a unifier at work. Even though it is called infinite, this unity does not mean that experience comes to a standstill. Infinite unity implies infinite opposition and contradiction, and therefore also infinite development. For Nishida:

> In essence this contradiction and unity are one and the same thing viewed from different angles; because there is unity there is contradiction, and because there is contradiction there is unity. . . .
> As one, it is many; and as many, one. (p. 66)

Accordingly, since infinite unity—that is, a unifier at work behind the scenes—is basically only itself and has nothing other than itself, opposition and contradiction must also emerge from within. Here we see a "spontaneous self-unfolding of a single thing," a development that is "self-initiating and untiring" (p. 70). What never ceases to move out of itself is not a dead standstill but an infinite "motion-in-stillness" at whose foundations an "unchanging" unification is always going on (p. 70). It is not without significance that Nishida speaks of *self*-development and *self*-initiating activity. Indeed we might even say that the standpoint of his book is mirrored in that single word *self*-.

The phrase "independent and self-sufficient" appears time and again throughout the book in such terms as "independent and self-sufficient activity," "independent and self-sufficient true reality," and "the independent and self-sufficient system of reality." These are all expressions of pure experience, that is, of what is prior to the distinctions between knowledge and feeling and will, of what is prior to the subject-object dichotomy. Here "self" refers to a unifying power or activity, with no "other" being set up in opposition to "self." If there were an other, the unifying activity would not be infinite. The infinitely unifying activity is powerful enough to survive within any and all opposition or contradiction by passing beyond it and in the process effecting a still more comprehensive unification. This infinitely unifying power is the basic power of life itself, which inevitably requires opposition and contradiction for its development. Without it, no unity would be more than a standstill. Unity and contradiction are "two sides of the same thing." Because there is unity there is contradiction, and because there is contradiction there is unity.

Now the distinction between self and other—or the opposition between subject and object—is the most basic of all antitheses, the source of all discrimination and opposition. The infinite unifying power is able to surpass even this antithesis, emerging from behind it as it were. This is so from the start. (Because it arises from behind discrimination, it is able to surface from within discrimination and to return behind it from the surface. This free movement from surface to background between discrimination and unity belongs to life, while to stop short in either of them means death.)

At any rate, the qualifier "self-" as we find it in talk of self-development and self-initiating activity, and which can only be spoken of in connection with infinite unity, does not refer to a self posited in distinction to an other. Accordingly, the independence alluded to in the phrase "independent and self-sufficient" does not refer to the solitary independence of a relative self opposed to an other, but rather to the independence of what is self-sufficient. Here "self-" indicates something that is at once different from an "other" (and not only an "other person") and at the same time something of which it can be said "self and other are neither one nor two." In other words, it is a unity that is neither simply discriminated from every sort of other nor simply not discriminated from it. It is something of which one can only say it is "independent and self-sufficient," "spontaneously self-unfolding," and "self-initiating and untiring." By nature this kind of unifying activity makes experience possible and is always at work behind the scenes of what we call the experience of the self.

In the East, the standpoint of the self in this sense has been around from time immemorial. We see its clear embodiment in Buddhism, particularly in the Zen tradition. Dōgen, for example, takes "self-joyous *samādhi*" to be the main gate to Buddhist practice and speaks of "dropping off the body-mind, body-mind dropped off." When Hui-hai, author of the well-known work *Essentials for Sudden Enlightenment*,[8] first went to sit in Zen meditation under Ma-tsu,[9] he was turned away with the reprimand, "What are you doing running away from home without a thought to the treasure in your own house? I have nothing here for you. What kind of Buddhism are you looking for?" "What do you mean by treasures in Hui-hai's own house?" asked Hui-hai. Ma-tsu replied, "The one who has just now put that question to me is your treasure house. Everything provided, nothing is wanting. It is there to be used freely. What are you doing turning outside to look for enlightenment?"

The same point was stressed, among others, by Lin-chi: "What is lacking in your present responsive activity! In an instant you enter the Pure [Land]"[10] Or again, in a passage cited in *An Inquiry into the Good*, we hear Nan-yüeh,[11] the teacher of Ma-tsu, say: "Everything is illuminated, you lack nothing. . . . As it was said of old, when you say what something looks like, you are off the mark. Just look into your own house." All of these express the standpoint of the self and help us to see how the experience of one who had thrown himself into Zen lies behind *An Inquiry into the Good*.

---

8. Ta-chu Hui-hai (1089–1163). His book on sudden enlightenment is one of the most important works in all of Chinese Buddhist literature.
9. Ma-tsu Tao-i (709–88) was the founder of the second great line of Chinese Zen. See note 1 of the preface.
10. *Record of Lin-chi* 16:18.
11. Nan-yüeh Huai-yang (677–744).

METAPHYSICS

WHAT THEN is the standpoint of "self-" as infinite unity? Earlier I cited Nishida's apprehensions that the use of the term "conscious phenomena" might occasion misunderstanding as well as his insistence that true reality can neither be called conscious phenomena nor material phenomena. He goes on to say:

> Immediate reality is not something passive. It is an independent, self-sufficient activity. Indeed, it is better to speak of being-in-acting. (p. 54)

Later he explains the basis for this idea:

> As noted before, since both material and spiritual phenomena are identical from the point of view of pure experience, these two kinds of unifying functions must ultimately be of the same sort. The unifying power at the foundation of our thinking and willing and the unifying power at the foundation of the phenomena of the cosmos are directly the same. For example, our laws of logic and mathematics are at once the basic principles by which the phenomena of the universe come into being. (p. 68)

Our experience originates at a point beyond the subject-object dichotomy. This means that at the point where it is immediately constituted—that is, in the immediate form it takes as an experience possessed of its own unity—the unifying power at the basis of our thinking and willing (the world of the subject) is "directly identical" with the unifying power in the phenomena of the cosmos (the world of objects). That even a fact of experience like seeing a flower comes about by virtue of an infinitely unifying force unfolding itself spontaneously from the standpoint of the "self-" means that this unifying power embraces the myriad ever-changing phenomena of the cosmos.

This identity of the unifying forces that underly both the world of the subject and the world of the object calls to mind Schelling's notion of "absolute identity," just as the systematic development Nishida finds there is reminiscent of Hegel's *Begriff.* Nishida mentions both these philosophers explicitly in the course of his book.[12] These comparisons indicate the sort of general concern with metaphysics that shows up there.

The theory of two kinds of unifying power said to be directly identical is a cornerstone to *An Inquiry into the Good*. Given the frequency with which Nishida takes up the question himself, there is no need to embark on further detailed discussion here. There is, however, one matter I would like to take up in connection with the question of metaphysics, and that has to do with what Nishida refers to in his book as "principle." We read, for instance:

> And the unifying power of the objective world is identical with the unifying power of subjective consciousness; the so-called objective world as well as consciousness are both established on the basis of the same principle. For this reason, one is able to comprehend the basic principle on which the universe is established by means of a principle within one's own self. (p. 76)

Clearly Nishida is saying much the same here as what he says in the passages cited earlier. The only difference is that an identical unifying power here means an identical principle from whose perspective everything is to be explained. His phrasing, which speaks of "an identical principle," "the principle within us" (or, in its earlier formulation, "our laws of logic and mathematics"), the "basic principle" on which the universe is established, and our "comprehension" of principles, cumulatively suggests the sort of underlying gridwork consistently found in all sorts of metaphysical systems erected by philosophers, beginning with Plato's theory of Ideas. In that sense at least, Nishida's book may be said to contain metaphysical underpinnings. And yet when we look at the makeup of the system built upon them, we find something fundamentally different from any metaphysics known to the history of Western philosophy. In this sense, it is not really proper to continue speaking of the book's standpoint as metaphysical.

The fundamental difference comes down to this: what is taken to be an identical principle is viewed from what we have called the standpoint of "self-" and is seen as an infinite unifying power present from the start in experience. In other words, the very founda-

---

12. *See* CW 1:25, 42, *et alibi.*

tions of metaphysics in the West are taken over immediately, just as they are, and made into the basis of pure experience. Such a step could not have occurred in the Western tradition of philosophical thought. Given that it requires a thorough recasting of metaphysics, it is hardly surprising that it did not occur to those belonging to the received metaphysical tradition.

Obviously, metaphysics begins from experience, but in its search for principles, it feels the need to pass beyond the pale of experience. Why? In thinking about experience, three preconceptions are generally brought into the picture. First, we think of the conscious acts of knowing, feeling, and willing as separate and distinct. Second, we cling to a differentiation of subject from object. And third, we assume the framework of the "individual" to be absolute, so that experience is always the experience of a given individual.

Experience is usually thought of as a kind of consciousness, which in turn is presumed to arise out of a relationship between the mind and things, or between subject and object, where the subject of experience is assumed to be incapable of overstepping the bounds of existence as an individual. In short, experience is accepted in terms of a differentiation of the "I" and things, of subject and object. The subject in experience is thus taken to be the individual human consciousness possessed of body, sensations, and desires, while the object in experience consists of individual things in the outer world. Through the relationship that these two have to one another, phenomena of consciousness like knowing, feeling, and willing are thought to arise apart from one another.

These three preconceptions are so much a part of common sense and so firmly implanted in our minds that metaphysics did not bother to question them in making experience its starting point. As a result, it had to leave the realm of experience in its search for unifying principles that would overcome the distinction of subject and object in the world of experience, for universal principles free of the confines of individual consciousness. Only in this transempirical realm, it was thought, could the standpoint unique to metaphysics take shape.

Not even in a world of reason beyond the opposition of individual subjects and objects thought to make up the world of expe-

rience was it possible to dispense with the universal distinction between subject and object. The opposition between the realms of
knowledge and of will also remained intact. Thus from the side of
the subject, the universal rationality common to all human minds
(see p. 75), and from the side of the object, suprasensible, law-reg-
ulated principles were seen as correlatives. In terms of knowing,
this correlation was one of pure rational knowing, while in terms
of doing, it was seen as pure rational power (*virtus noumenon*[13]), as
"the good." Finally, at the very bottom of this world of reason God
was posited as the Absolute—an absolute good and absolute truth,
an absolute identity in whom no vestige of distinction between
subject and object remains. The three problematic points in the
starting point of experience are only resolved when we arrive at
God. In short, the whole metaphysical superstructure culminating
in God was set up in such a way as always to lead further and further away from experience and the reality of experience.

Could it be that the metaphysics that represents the main axis
of the Western philosophical tradition has left a basic problem un-
solved? Or perhaps rather that a problem remains at the very
foundation on which metaphysics was erected? The problem is
twofold. On the surface, metaphysics lost touch with experience
and set up a world isolated from our everyday, here-and-now reality. And beneath the surface, in spite of transcending the world
(or rather precisely because of it), metaphysics has been tied covertly to the world of experience. In other words, the three problematic points we found in experience to solve which metaphysics
was brought into being actually lie as unresolved as before. Like
two sides of a coin, the two issues belong to one another.

However much God is seen as an Absolute that cuts through
the subject-object distinction, we still represent God objectively as
an absolute being. Of course theologians agree that it is wrong to
try to represent God, who is beyond the subject and object, in objective terms. Nevertheless, as long as we retain our individual

---

13. In his *Religion Within the Limits of Reason Alone,* Kant distinguishes between freedom of choice *(Willkür)* as *virtus phænomenon,* namely the ground of our actions as natural beings, and *virtus noumenon,* or the ground on which we, as moral beings, assume
maxims to direct our action.

consciousness and subjectivity, the habit of representing God as an object can only continue. We may progress from the subjectivity of individual consciousness to a standpoint of universal reason; but even so, can we really speak of having transcended the subjectivity of the particular individual? What is called universal reason does not seem to have cut all ties to individual minds. It has no direct ties to "low mind" (the mind of sensation and desire at one with the physical body), and yet at the same time it appears to be immanent in the "high mind" (the mind of pure intellect and will that transcends all bodily ties). These two minds, the high and the low, are in fact only two parts of one and the same individual mind, like opposite poles between which the individual mind is tautly stretched. The mind connected to the physical body and the mind that breaks away from that connection are bound into one. Hence when the reason that looks on the surface to be universal, suprasensible, and transindividual is viewed from behind, it is at once seen to be bound up with the individual physical body and its accompanying individual consciousness. No matter how far metaphysics distances itself from the realm of experience in order to enter the lofty realms of the transexperiential, experience follows it each step of the way like a young buck shadowing a doe.

Thus the realm of experience cannot really be surpassed in a metaphysical way by taking leave of the realm of experience. In the end it does not provide us with a place to stand outside the place where experience arises. The idea of transcending the realm of experience has to be understood another way. It must mean a passing beyond what we usually mean by experience — that is, experience laden with the sorts of problems whose resolution drove metaphysics in search of universal reason — that remains forever within the realm of experience and purifies its residence there. The standpoint of pure experience in *An Inquiry into the Good* was set up with this end in mind, and this end in turn is tied up with a way of understanding "principle" altogether different from that of conventional metaphysics.

7 *An Inquiry into the Good:*
Truth and the Self

THAT "there is some fixed, unchanging principle in the universe through which all things come into being" (p. 74) is an idea that runs like a single thread throughout the system of *An Inquiry into the Good*. But this principle is not to be seen only in terms of its connections with things and events in the objective world. According to the passage cited earlier:

> And the unifying power of the objective world is identical with the unifying power of subjective consciousness; the so-called objective world as well as consciousness are both established on the basis of the same principle. (p. 76)

And earlier, in the same vein:

> This principle is at the same time the unifying power of all things and of the interiority of consciousness. It is not that principle is maintained by mind and matter, but that principle brings these into being. Principle is independent and self-sustaining. It does not vary from one time or place or person to another. (pp. 74–75)

Principle is taken here to be an independent and self-sustaining unifying power existing prior to mind and matter, while what we usually refer to as experience grows out of a relationship between matter and mind and differs according to time, space, and persons. To put philosophy on this basis as the empiricists do is to make principle into a subjective concept abstracted from experience through reflective thinking. If, however, we understand principle as something objective and visibly present in the universe, its grasp requires a metaphysical standpoint beyond the realm of experience. But the principle Nishida is talking about functions as a unifier of all things as well as of the interiority of consciousness. In other words, it is the unifying power in pure experience:

> There is an unchanging unifying power at work in the ground of consciousness. . . . The immediate coalescence of the contents of consciousness is a basic fact. Its unifying power does not emerge from some reality other than itself, but reality itself comes into being through its functioning. (p. 74)

Obviously the "consciousness" Nishida has in mind here is consciousness viewed in terms of pure experience.

The idea of an "immediate coalescence of the contents of consciousness" is a good way of expressing the working of principle. At bottom, pure experience is always the spontaneous self-unfolding of a "self-independent and self-sufficient" unifier, but its content is always a coalescence that includes a systematic construct. As mediator and synthesizer of a variety of contents, principle appears in the form of a systematic construct. Viewed in terms of the unifying power of immediate experience as a "being-in-acting," the contents of experience always "immediately coalesce" (p. 74). Here we see the character of principle as something that works.

In the sense that principle represents an "unchanging" unifying power working at the ground of consciousness and is the fixed and unchanging principle of everything in the universe, it is also eternal and unchanging, and in that sense may be referred to as transcendent. It is "independent and self-sufficient," beyond conditions of time, space, and human individuals. In this regard it has something in common with principle as conceived by metaphysics, but in addition it is a principle that functions as the unifying power of immediate experience:

> The unifying work of consciousness is not under the control of time; rather time comes about through this unifying work. At the ground of consciousness there is something unchanging that transcends time. . . .

At the ground of spirit there is always something unchangeable, something that grows larger each day. The passage of time is the continual shift in the unifying center that accompanies this development. And this central point is forever "now". (p. 74)

As a working agent, principle is to be viewed at a point in the ground of immediate experience where time is brought into being, a point that we might call the "eternal now."

This principle should not be restricted to the confines of individual subjective consciousness. Anything so grasped is but

a footprint of principle at work and not principle itself. Principle itself is creative. We can *become* it and work in accord with it, but it is not something we can see as an object of consciousness. (p. 75)

As something eternally unchanging and transcendent and yet creatively at work, this principle does not allow itself to be made an object for viewing. The unifying power itself is the original point that makes it possible for anything to be made into an object for viewing but which remains nonobjectifiable. The only way to see the objectively unseeable is that we ourselves *become* it and *work in accord with* it. Compared with the "seeing" of objects, this is a kind of "blindness" at the ground of such seeing (see p. 40). It is what the ancients called a "seeing of not-seeing." It is the intellectual intuition we spoke of at the outset of the last chapter as a grasp of life.

As something that works, principle cannot be thought of in merely subjective terms; but neither is it merely something objective. Unlike things, it does not "exist in a certain form at a certain place and time." As Nishida says, "If principle . . . were something restricted to one place, it could not perform the work of unification, and would no longer be a true, living principle" (p. 75). Truth is living. And because it is living it cannot be objectified. As such it passes beyond the limits of time, space, things, and persons to serve as the unifying power of all things and also of the interiority of consciousness. The standpoint of immediate experience is not of a sort with standpoints of experience that "differ according to time, space, and persons." It is rather a standpoint of experience of which we may say:

It is not because there are individuals that there is experience, but because there is experience that there are individuals. Seeing experience as more fundamental than individual human differences makes it possible to steer clear of solipsism. (p. 4)

This standpoint, according to Nishida, permits the view that today's consciousness of the self and yesterday's coalesce directly into one and the same system, thus enabling us to speak of an individual lifetime (p. 74). Furthermore, a continuity of consciousness is set up between oneself and others, thus making mutual understanding and communication possible (p. 75; see also p. 55). It includes a "transindividual element" (p. 62) and posits "a universal" at ground.

It is important to note that because the very principle that works as a unifying power cannot be objectified, the only way left us is to become it. The point is stressed again and again because it is such a good expression of the basic standpoint of the book. Speaking of thinking, for instance, Nishida writes:

What pushes thinking ahead is not a voluntary activity on our part; thinking unfolds on its own. Only by letting go of the self completely and becoming utterly one with the object or question that we are thinking about, or perhaps more appropriately losing the self in it, do we see thinking in action. Thinking has its own laws and acts on its own. (p. 20)

To become some object, then, is to become utterly one with it. Take the mathematician pondering a mathematical problem. The activity of thinking must progress entirely according to the principles of mathematics. In terms of immediate experience, this means that by throwing the self into the problem at hand and becoming one with it, a spontaneous, self-unfolding activity of the mathematical principles occurs. This is the true picture of mathematical thinking in action. As Nishida says:

Because the mathematician lets go of the self and sets up a kind of love-relationship with the principles of mathematics, it becomes possible to illumine those principles. (p. 197)

Or again:

That we know a thing means simply that the self coincides with a thing. In seeing a flower, the self becomes that flower. To study a flower and illumine its nature means letting go of subjective conjecture to coincide with the nature of that flower. Even when thinking about principles, principles are never our own subjective fantasies. It is not only that principles are held in common by all, but also that they are in fact the basis on which objective reality comes into being. Steadfast truth is always attained by abolishing the subjective self to become objective. In a word, the deepening of knowledge means that it joins itself to objective nature. (pp. 93–94)

While principles are here given a character no less real than that accorded them by traditional rationalist metaphysics, the standpoint of "thinking about principles" betrays an attitude altogether different from that of rationalist thinking, one of becoming the principle by "abolishing the self." Hence the idea that the nature of principle is to be alive and working. These two aspects combine to highlight the special traits of the standpoint of immediate experience in *An Inquiry into the Good*.

To begin with, the idea of becoming a principle is entirely different from what we generally understand as thinking. In fact, it does not include thinking at all. The same holds true for metaphysics. Similarly, it is usual for philosophers to consider living, nonobjectifiable principles as lying beyond the reach of thinking. And yet it is precisely a standpoint that thinks in terms of "true, viable principle" that is being spoken of. "Thinking" is here thinking the unthinkable and hence is the very negation of thinking in the ordinary sense of the word. We are reminded here of a passage of Yüeh-shan Wei-yen that Dōgen is fond of citing: "How do we think what lies beyond the reach of thinking? We do not think it."[1] This is what Nishida means by intellectual intuition or the "grasp of life."

To abolish the self in things and principles to the extent of becoming them implies, conversely, that we appropriate them. "To identify oneself with" is to appropriate. "Becoming" is appropria-

---

1. Yüeh-shan Wei-yen (745–828). Dōgen cites the passage, for example, in the 坐禅儀 *Zazengi* [Rules for Zazen] and 三十七品菩提分法 *Sanjūshichihon bodai bunpō* [Thirty-seven Conditions for Attaining Wisdom] chapters of the *Shōbōgenzō* 正法眼蔵.

tion.[2] "Working in conformity with" is appropriation. In this sense, to say that principle is living means that it is appropriated. The same holds true of the "grasp of life."

It should be clear that the standpoint of immediate experience is different from both the empiricism and the rationalist metaphysics that have caused a rift in the modern history of Western philosophy. If anything, it draws from the foundations of each what is positive and not to be passed over—from empiricism, the immediate certainty of experience, and from rationalist metaphysics, the real objectivity of principle—and unites them anew. Put the other way around, the standpoint of immediate experience breaks free all at once from the basic difficulties in each of these standpoints and from the principal defects for which each criticizes the other. Without entering any further into this issue, the foregoing should give some idea of the essential novelty and originality of Nishida's book.

The passages cited earlier in this section conclude with the following statement that brings the same characteristic features into relief:

> But this is not only so for knowledge; it is the same for the will. What is purely subjective can do nothing at all. Will can be actualized only by following objective nature. To make water move is to follow the nature of water; to control people is to follow their nature; to control oneself is to follow one's own nature. Our will becomes effective only to the extent that it becomes objective. The reason Śākyamuni and Christ still have the power to move people after thousands of years is that theirs was a highly objective spirit. Egoless persons, those who have abolished the self, are the greatest. (p. 94)

Plain as these words are, they express the standpoint of an original philosophy. Without an understanding of the ideas of will, nature, and spirit developed in the book (which we shall not embark on here), there is no way to appreciate what Nishida means when he writes that "will can be actualized only by following objective nature" or that Christ and Śākyamuni possessed "a highly objective spirit." The standpoint of *An Inquiry into the Good*

---

2. See note 7 of chapter 6; CW 1:75.

anticipates the position of "becoming a thing, think it; becoming a thing, do it" that Nishida was to assume in later years—apparently simple words tied to an extraordinary process of speculation.

THE TRUE SELF

IN THE PASSAGE just cited, Nishida refers to "egoless persons, those who have abolished the self." Throughout *An Inquiry into the Good* phrases like "abolishing the self," "doing away with the self," "forgetting the self," and "oblivious of oneself and things" appear again and again. Obviously the self that is to be abolished is the subjective self that we normally represent objectively as "oneself," the abstract self that is represented as floating in the air and removed from the real world. This abstraction of the self is what distances us from reality and hence also from the true self. For the basis of true reality is what the book calls "the unifying power of consciousness." In more concrete terms, it is a unifying power in the double sense of a power that unifies all things in the universe and unifies the interiority of consciousness; it is the unifying power within immediate experience, within which the self is also to be found. As a true self, it is completely nonobjectifiable.

The subjective self that we usually think of in terms of everyday experience lurks like a phantom in the shadows of empiricist philosophy and metaphysics. It is only when this self loses its hold that the true self becomes present. To say that the subjective self floats in the air, removed from the real world, implies that "subjectivity and objectivity do not exist in separation from one another but are related like two sides of one and the same reality"—the subject as the unifier, the object as the unified—where "we ourselves are always the unifiers of reality." Nishida continues: "It may look as if the self can be viewed objectively, but this is not the true self; the true self is the observer of the present, its unifier" (p. 78). Hence the true self is the self that sees the objectified self from behind, or rather, from a point directly in front of it. The subjective self assumes a form in which the seeing self becomes oblivious of itself in the self that is seen. The fundamental problem that embraces all others, as we shall see later, is this: how to shake the true self out of this narcosis and come to know it. The true self is thus the spontaneous, self-unfolding unifier in the interiority of consciousness. Or in the terms of the text, it is at once "the unifier of reality" and "the very power that unifies the reality of the universe" (p. 79).

Nishida thus sees the unifying self latent in nature — "Nature, too, possesses a kind of self" (p. 87) — and even claims that "an appearance of a unifying self" is to be found in individual plants and animals (pp. 84–85). In a later passage, he adds:

> Only with this kind of unifying self, and then with a purpose and significance to nature, does nature come alive. This unifying power that is the life of nature is not a mere abstract concept fabricated in our minds, but a direct fact that reaches us in perception. When we see a favorite flower or cherished pet we at once grasp something in its entirety. What we grasp is its self, its noumenon. (p. 86)

The unifying power — the life — of nature is thus intuited as the noumenon, the thing-in-itself, the self within a single plant or animal. The unifying self behind the whole of nature, the very power that unifies nature, appears as the self, the noumenon, of each and every living being. Our true self is a self able to perceive itself in the unifying self behind the whole of nature, in the self with which nature is provided. It is a self capable of grasping the life or unifying power of nature immediately and intuitively. It sees itself as the unifying power of the universe visible in every tree and flower.

Earlier we spoke of "becoming things and principles" as an act of appropriation. The true self is the unifying power at work in this appropriation of things and principles to the self. Accordingly, Nishida can write:

> We can only conclude that the subject in the proper sense is the noumenon of reality. The noumenon that truly animates things is the unifying power that is the fundamental activity that brings reality about, and therefore must be a subject in the true and proper sense. (pp. 81–82)

It is evident that this true self as "the very unifying power of the universe of reality" is altogether different from the ordinary subjective self. Indeed it becomes manifest only when it has broken away from the confines of such a self.

Nishida stresses ideals and sentiments, arguing that "as our ideals and sentiments deepen and spread out, we are ever more capable of understanding the true significance of nature" (p. 87). Only from a standpoint where knowledge, sentiment, and will are one can we be assimilated with—become—the unifying power that is the life of nature and thus attain an intuitive grasp of the purpose and significance of nature. Knowledge alone is not enough. The introduction of ideals means that the original unifying power is not only the alpha but also the omega. It is infinite in the sense that it is beyond determination. The true self is the "infinite unifier" (p. 78) and as such is at work in the very midst of immediate experience, which is never apart from it. Its unbounded creative advance gushes forth as if from an inexhaustible wellspring, and as the spontaneous self-unfolding of an independent and self-sufficient unifying power, it is forever flowing back to its source. The infinite unifying power is a reality in the here-and-now and at the same time an ideal (approximating Hegel's notion of *Idealität*). The discovery of a unifying self at the deep ground of living nature thus amounts to an "ideal" perspective. But of this we shall have more to say later.

Despite the claim that the true self sees itself in nature, within nature this unifying self remains something potential. It is the same with the claim that we see ourselves in individual living things. It is only in the mind or spirit that the unifying self becomes visibly real and appears as something truly able to see itself:

All reality comes about through unity, and it is in the spirit that this unity appears as a clear and distinct fact. Only in spirit does reality become complete—an independent and self-sufficient reality. (pp. 91–92)

Only in arriving at the spirit does the true self make its appearance. (p. 85)

This self of ours that is the unifier of the spirit is originally the unifying activity of reality. . . . As for where this unifying power or self comes from, it is the manifestation of the unifying power of reality, an eternally unchanging force. This is why we always feel the self as a creative, free, and infinite activity. (pp. 92–93)

This standpoint of spirit is one where unity has become aware of itself. Nishida explains its appearance by identifying infinite unity with infinite conflict, an idea we have seen to be fundamental to *An Inquiry into the Good*. In advancing from conflicting contradictories within one unity to a still greater unity, "our spirit becomes conscious of itself as the unifying activity of reality" (p. 90). At the same time, "the movement that opposes spirit as its object is conceived of as nature" (p. 181). Thus the distinction between spirit and nature comes down to a difference of perspectives towards one and the same reality, not to two distinct unifying forces:

> There is no opposition of subject and object in the fact of immediate experience, no distinction between spirit and matter, but only a single reality of mind-in-things and things-in-mind. (pp. 180–81)

And again elsewhere:

> A deep understanding of nature implies a recognition of spiritual unity at its ground, that a complete and true spirit must be at one with nature, that there is only one reality in the universe. (p. 96)

The recognition of a spiritual unity at the ground of nature means that the true self, the power that effects unity in the universe of reality, perceives itself in the power that brings unity to the life of nature, in the self of nature itself, in the self of a single flower or animal. To say that true spirit is at one with nature means that to study a flower is to become one with the essence of a flower, that steadfast truth is always had by abolishing the subjective self and becoming one with objective nature, that only by following objective nature is the will actualized. It is a dynamic of abolishing the self to become nature and its principles:

> Just as the objective world can be said to be a reflection of the self, the self reflects the objective world. Without a world for the self to see, there is no self. Heaven and earth have the same roots [as the self] — all things are one body [with the self]. (p. 156)

The last phrase, minus the bracketed additions, which are my own, is a saying of Seng-chao, frequently cited in Zen. I will not go into it further here, except to note that it represents a perspective in which one senses the influence of Zen.[3] We should also note that Nishida follows up on the allusion by quoting passages presenting the gist of Brahman, Saint Paul, and Confucius. In any case, the two movements Nishida discusses here represent the two aspects that make up the self-awareness of the true self.

THE TRUE SELF AS PERSONAL

THE VIEWPOINT just treated forms the foundation for part 3 of *An Inquiry into the Good*, entitled simply "The Good." Here Nishida speaks of the true meaning of the claim that the infinite unifying power at work in immediate experience is "personal."

The notion of the person is not generally considered to have any connection to the idea that "heaven and earth have the same roots—all things are one body." On one hand, such a position seems to bury the idea of personality; on the other, a standpoint of human personality is felt to be removed from the things that make up the cosmos. This only serves to draw greater attention to Nishida's attempt to bring the two movements together. From the start, the ordinary way of viewing personality in terms of the subjective self is rejected. For Nishida, "the true person appears where the [subject] self has been forgotten" (p. 151). Personality is the unifying power of consciousness in the sense of immediate experience:

> True unity of consciousness is a pure, uncomplicated activity that appears naturally without our knowing it [unknowingly]; it is the original state of independent, self-sufficient consciousness without any distinction of intelligence, emotion, and will, without any isolation of subject from object. At such times our true personality expresses this totality. . . . Our personality is at once the dynamic of the unifying power of the universe. (pp. 151–52)

This perspective on personality leads Nishida to conclude that

> the realization of personality is for us the absolute good. . . . While the desires of this personality are the unifying power of conscious-

---

3. Seng-chao (384–414) was the brilliant disciple of Kumārajīva.

ness, they are also the manifestation of an infinite unifying power at the ground of reality; to realize our personality is to become one with this power. (p. 152)

As for these "desires of personality," Nishida adds that "they can only reach self-awareness in a state of immediate experience in which we have not yet begun to think and discriminate" (pp. 153–54). Only an action arising from an inner necessity of the self can be called a truly good action. Hence the kind of good deed that realizes the desires of personality and reaches self-awareness only in immediate experience implies a sense of seeing the true self:

> To follow the inner desires of the self in all sincerity, that is, to realize the self's true personality, does not imply setting up a subject in opposition to an object so that things without obey the self within. On the contrary, in utterly obliterating the subjective fantasy of the self and becoming completely one with things, the true desires of the self are satisfied and the true self becomes visible. (p. 155)

In other words, self-awareness of the true self comes about when the subject-object opposition is overthrown. As noted earlier, this self-awareness comes about in seeing the self reflected in the objective world and the objective world reflected in the self. The passage continues:

> In one sense, each one's objective world is a reflection of that one's personality. Or, better, apart from the independent, self-sufficient system of reality itself that appears before each individual, there is no true self for each individual.

It is at such times that fundamental elements of the standpoint of immediate experience appear. This also suggests why this philosophy, while having affinities with the tradition of Western philosophical history, can be said to possess distinct characteristics belonging to the spiritual tradition of the East (and to Buddhism in particular). Nishida makes the point forthrightly:

> As is the case with the basic Buddhist idea, self and cosmos share a common foundation. Nay, they are directly one and the same. This accounts for our sense of the significance of the whole of infinite reality in the self's interiority — as infinite truth in knowledge, as in-

finite beauty in feeling, as infinite good in will. To say that we know reality does not mean that we know things outside the self but that we know the self itself. (p. 164)

At its ground level, the claim that self and cosmos are basically one — that the self has the same roots as heaven and earth and is one with all things — points to knowledge of an infinite reality whose significance lies in infinite truth, good, and beauty. This "ground level" refers to the point at which the true self is the "infinite unifier" and a "unifying power itself of the reality of the universe." This infinitely unifying power is the alpha and omega of all things. As an infinite, it is transcendent; as a matter of immediate experience, it belongs to the reality of the here and now. This is the point at which the one reality, independent and self-sufficient, represents a motion-in-stillness and a stillness-in-motion. It is here that reality reveals the significance of ideals in Nishida's sense of infinite truth, good, and beauty. The following passage contrasting spirit and nature may also be read in this vein:

At those times when the unity of reality is at work within, we feel as if we are in control of reality as ideals of the self, as if the self is engaged in free action. And since this unifying activity of reality is infinite, we feel the self to be something infinite that embraces the cosmos itself. (p. 93)

At its ground level the one reality, independent and self-sufficient (that is, reality as a whole "self" with no "other" standing opposed to it), unfolds itself spontaneously. Here the infinitely unifying activity of the universe of reality in its self-unfolding and self-unification constitutes the true self. And when this unifying activity at the level of "spirit" becomes manifest in the self itself and as the self itself, the true self becomes the true self of self-awareness. For "the true self appears only when it reaches spirit." Here the self-unfolding and self-unity of the reality becomes clearly manifest in the interiority of the mind, in a mental state that obtains "when the unity of reality is at work within." This is what Nishida means when he speaks of the self acting freely as if in control of reality and of the sense of being an infinite self that encompasses the cosmos.

In brief, the idea that self and cosmos have a common ground, that to know reality is to know the self, is one of the fundamental ideas of Buddhism and in fact is profoundly consonant with Dōgen's famous words: "To practice and confirm all things by conveying one's self to them, is illusion; for all things [dharmas] to advance forward and practice and confirm the self, is enlightenment."[4]

This is the heart of the standpoint of "immediate experience" that Nishida advances. It shows up in his book at every turn. For instance, in his chapter on God (3 of part 4), he writes, "The most basic explanation necessarily returns to the self. The secret key to explaining the universe lies in this self" (p. 180). Again, at the end of part 3, "The Good," we read:

> In closing this chapter, I have one more thing to say. In explaining the good academically, various explanations are possible, but in actual practice there is only one true good and it can be expressed succinctly: to know the true self. The true self is the noumenon of the universe, and in knowing, the true self not only joins as one with humanity in general but fuses with the noumenon of the cosmos and merges with the divine will. Both religion and morality find full expression here. The way to know the true self and join with God consists only in acquiring for oneself the power of the union of subject and object. Acquiring this power means killing off our false ego and dying to the desires of this world in order to be reborn (as Mohammed says, the Kingdom of Heaven stands in the shadow of the sword). This is the only way to reach the point of a true union of subject and object. This is the ultimate meaning of religion, morality, and art. In Christianity it is called being born again and in Buddhism, enlightened insight. The story is told that when Pope Benedict XI asked Giotto to show him a work demonstrating his talents as a painter, Giotto simply drew a circle and handed it to the Pope. In morality we must attain to Giotto's circle. (pp. 167–68)

Interestingly, Islam, Christianity, and Buddhism are taken together here. But the fact that the secret key to everything—to joining as one with the good of humanity in general, fusing with the

---

4. *Shōbōgenzō,* "Genjōkōan," trans. N. Waddell and A. Masao, *The Eastern Buddhist* 5/2 (1972): 133.

noumenon of the cosmos, and merging with the divine will—is found in the self-awareness of the true self, and that this self-awareness is symbolized by a circle, shows clear ties to Zen.

THE DESIRES OF THE TRUE SELF

IN THE FOREGOING I have singled out for discussion a few points that might seem problematic from the first two parts of *An Inquiry into the Good*. In part 3, "The Good," Nishida develops his theory of ethics. In connection with this section, I would like next to ask how the basic standpoint of the whole book appears there; in other words, to ask what was the motive behind connecting the realm of ethics with the realm of reality on one hand and with that of religion on the other to form a unified whole. In a sense, we already have our answer in the passage from the end of part 3 just cited: "in knowing the true self one not only joins as one with humanity in general but fuses with the noumenon of the cosmos and merges with the divine will." But let us look at the matter a little more closely.

For Nishida, "the good is the realization of ideals and the satisfaction of desire." In answer to the question, "Whence do these desires and ideals arise, and what then is the nature of this thing we call the good?" he answers:

> The will is the deepest unifying activity of consciousness; it is the self itself at work. In short, the original desires or ideals that are the cause of the will arise from the nature of the self itself. We might call them the power of the self. (p. 145)

The "nature of the self itself" here refers to the quality of its natural essence. Nishida continues:

> Just as each thing gives full play to its natural gifts—the bamboo those of the bamboo, the pine tree those of the pine tree—so the good of the human being consists in giving expression to the innate nature of its humanity. (p. 145)

As these words make plain, he is approaching the good from a fundamental standpoint of immediate experience, as the deepest unifying activity of consciousness, as the working of the self itself. This is corroborated in the passage that follows the one above:

> Since our consciousness in thought, imagination, and will as well as in what are called perception, emotion, and impulse all have an internal unifier working at their ground, every phenomenon of consciousness is a development and completion of this unifier. And this deepest unifying power that unifies the whole is our "self" and it is the will that presents this power best. Since in this view the development and completion of the will represent at once the development and completion of the self, we may speak of the good as the development and completion of the self, as *self-realization.* In other words, the harmonious development that our spirit attains to in developing its various abilities is the highest good. (p. 145)

In this way, the pursuit of the problem of the good, the "deepest unifying activity of consciousness," leads to talk of "desires," "ideals," and "spirit." What can this mean? Following up this question may provide us with a clue to one of the fundamental aspects of the standpoint of immediate experience.

Nishida repeats again and again the point that immediate experience is a unity of consciousness in which subject and object are united. Moreover, this unity of consciousness appears as an ineluctable desire arising from our own interiority. It is a fact of the immediate experience in which subject and object are unified. He writes, for example:

> Our every wish and desire[5] is a given fact that is not to be explained. . . . The first time an infant nurses at the breast, . . . it drinks only in order to drink. Not only are our wishes and desires such inexplicable facts of immediate experience, but they are the key through which we understand the true meaning of reality. The complete explanation of reality does not merely tell us *how* it exists but also *why.* (p. 120)

---

5. Nishida draws a contrast between 欲望 and 要求, in which the latter is more basic and closer to human nature. To avoid the misleading connotations of the standard English equivalents for these Japanese words ("desire" and "demand"), we have rendered the contrast through the terms *wish* and *desire.*

These lines conclude his chapter entitled "Values." At the outset of that chapter he distinguishes between theoretical inquiry, which asks after causes or reasons—the "why"—and practical inquiry, which asks after ends—the "wherefore." What he means to say in his conclusion is that a full-fledged grasp of reality comes about only when we advance from the realm of theory to that of practice and are able to unify the two without incongruity. It is for this reason that he stresses the importance of the aspects of emotion, telos, and ideal for the elucidation of true reality, and in particular why wishes and desires represent the secret key to "understanding reality."

This viewpoint was presented at the beginning of part 2, "Reality." There Nishida stressed the claim that the intellectual conviction in a philosophical view of the world and of human life and the practical demands of morality and religion have to be maintained together, that "truth is one," that the truth of knowledge is directly the truth of practice, and vice versa. In the same context he spoke of the requisite unification of knowledge and sentiment, of philosophy and religion. All of these represent the goal at which immediate experience aims and at the same time are always implied in the unifying power that forms its foundations. They are the alpha and omega of immediate experience, the root and trunk that hold it together. To set out from this point is for us a matter of ineluctable inner desire. As "inexplicable given facts," they are a manifestation of the independent, self-sufficient activity of the one and only reality, of an absolutely "self-" activity.

In an instinctive, impulsive, unconscious act like an infant's first nursing at the breast, as in things prior to the separation of subject and object, we may be able to see a cosmic "pre-established harmony" or, in a sense to be explained later, the love of God. This aspect of an undichotomized subject-object is also a basic part of immediate experience. But as experience, immediate experience is always a unity of disparates. As a unifying activity, it is prior to the subject-object separation, and yet its contents are a structured unity and this unity is a mode of subject-object union. The undichotomized subject-object is simply the presence of the unifying function in this systematic unity.

In this concrete unity the impulsive and unconscious appear elevated to the level of the will. Unity is always volitional. That is to say, it rises to consciousness as will in the interiority of the subject. Viewed from the standpoint of immediate experience where subject and object are one, the will is more than a psychological phenomenon. "The will," Nishida writes, "is the deepest unifying power of our consciousness and also the most profound manifestation of the unifying power of reality" (p. 110).

Again in this last sentence we find encapsulated the position that Nishida reiterates throughout *An Inquiry into the Good*. The claim that the will is the deepest unifying power of consciousness expresses the basic idea taken up from the very beginning of the book and — it hardly needs repeating — points to the voluntaristic quality of Nishida's standpoint at this time. As we saw earlier, this idea is the basis on which he sets out to clarify the question of the good (see pp. 106–7). Concerning the idea that the will is the most profound manifestation of the unifying power of reality, he writes, for example: "What we call nature is a manifestation of the will; we are able to grasp the true significance of the dark mysteries of nature through the will of the self" (p. 110). To carry this idea a step further, we might see "the unifying self latent behind nature" referred to above present even in a single plant or animal as "that thing's self, its noumenon." This amounts to "viewing the function of the will of the self objectively" and hence to saying that "as our ideals and sentiments grow deeper and wider, we are more and more able to understand the true significance of nature" (pp. 86–87). Here we find again the transition from "nature" to "spirit" we saw in part 2. But let us pause here a moment, for the "desire" that surfaces in the infant's nursing at the breast appears here at the stage of "spirit" interwoven with elements of the "ideal."

We began from the position that "the good is the realization of ideals and the satisfaction of desire." Regarding where such desires and ideals arise and what the nature (or essential quality) of the good is, we have seen Nishida claim that desires and ideals, in their original form as "causes" of the will, emerge from the "nature" of the self itself, from its "power." The will is thus the deepest unifying work of consciousness; it is the very activity of the self itself. In other words, desires or ideals represent the power through which the will comes into being as the activity of the self; they are the power of the self itself, the cause of the will. The will is "the best manifestation of the unifying power of reality" and therefore the deepest unifying function of consciousness. Moreover, this power itself arises from the (innate) nature of the self itself. This is how we know that Nishida considers desires or ideals to be a manifestation of the innate nature of the self.

In Nishida's ideas of activity, power, and nature we may see a reflection of three corresponding ideas basic to Aristotle's philosophy: *energeia* (or *entelecheia*), *dynamis,* and *physis.* In fact, Nishida comments in the context from which we have been quoting: "What Aristotle called *entelechy* is the good" (p. 145). However, Nishida's characteristically voluntaristic standpoint of immediate experience differs from Aristotle's in seeing "the self itself" in the unifying activity and power that encompass the human good and the reality of the universe. The will is the unifying function of the "independent and self-sufficient activity" that forms the ground of conscious phenomena and also of the universe of reality. And the "potential" or "potential oneness" within this activity is the noumenon of the self itself and the power that arises from it. This power is the "desire" of the self itself. Nishida writes:

> The voice of the deepest inner desire of the self holds great authority; there is nothing more awesome in human life than this. (p. 145)

The satisfaction of this desire is said to "arise in the realization of ideal desires" (p. 144). This being so, what can this term "ideal" mean?

In this book Nishida always speaks of the three notions of ideal, spirit, and the infinite in relation to one another because all three belong to the deepest dimension of immediate experience. As early as part 1, in a chapter entitled "Intellectual Intuition," speaking of intellectual intuition as "the manifestation of a great unity in the development of a system of consciousness," Nishida remarks:

> If our consciousness were merely of a sensory nature, it would probably amount to no more than a state of ordinary perceptual intu-

ition; but a spirit that is ideal requires an infinite unity, and this unity is given in the form of what is called intellectual intuition. (p. 42)

Moreover, learning, art, morality, and religion are manifestations of this unity. But what is this "infinite unity"? In the same passage Nishida remarks of the direct insight into the "true form of reality" through intellectual intuition:

> Seen from a strict standpoint of pure experience, experience is not constricted by such modalities as time, space, and individuals; on the contrary, these discriminations come about through an intuition that transcends them. (p. 42)

He then alludes to Schelling's standpoint of "absolute identity" as similar to his own in that it is a standpoint of intellectual intuition and of the union of subject and object. But unlike Schelling's, of course, Nishida's is always a standpoint of experience. This distinction also shows up in his claim that intellectual intuition is of a kind with ordinary perception and that no clear-cut line of demarcation can be drawn between them. The following is a good expression of the distinguishing characteristic of Nishida's standpoint in *An Inquiry into the Good*:

> Even ordinary perception . . . is never simple but always structured and contains an element of the ideal. . . . This element of the ideal . . . is not simply something that structures perception itself but is constitutive of perception itself; through it perception is transformed. There is no limit to how rich and profound the element of the ideal latent in the ground of intuition can become. (p. 41)

The reason that ordinary perception can become ever more rich and profound is that, as pure experience, it transcends modalities of time, space, and individuals and is born—or rather comes to its nature—at a point free of the subject-object distinction. Another reason is that it opens directly, in a spontaneous and self-unfolding way, to an infinite unity within learning, art, morality, and religion. Nishida even adds that "the naive intuitions of an infant are all of this sort" (p. 42). (One might think here of the example given earlier of an infant nursing at its mother's breast.) Here, too, the reason is that, as the stirrings of the innate human nature of the self, intuition leads directly to "the great unity in the process of development in the system of consciousness." As a manifestation of this infinite unity, true intellectual intuition is called "the unifying activity itself in pure experience" and "the grasp of life" (p. 43).

Earlier the will was said to be the most profound unifying function of consciousness. Here intellectual intuition is described as the unifying function itself and even as a standpoint beyond will. Of the relation between the two, Nishida writes:

> Just as intellectual intuition is at the ground of thought, it is also at the ground of the will. Since our willing something is an intuition of a subject-object unity, will comes about through this intuition. The progress of the will is aimed at the completion of the development of this intuitive unity. This intuition is working at the ground of the process from start to finish, and the point of its completion is the realization of the will. This intuition explains why we think of the self as active in the will. There is no other self than this. The true self bespeaks this unifying intuition. (pp. 44–45)

Pure experience is said to be a state in which subject and object are one. But this oneness is always a unity of a discriminated rupture. Thought arises at the point of discriminated rupture, while will arises where unity is at work; and at the ground of both is intellectual intuition as "a fusion of intellect and will" and "a mutual oblivion of ego and things" (p. 43). The will contains an element of progress that is based on intellectual intuition every step of the way.

Attention is drawn here to the idea that the will is a unifying activity and that intellectual intuition is "the unifying activity itself." While ever restoring to unity the ever-occurring rupture, pure experience effects a systematic development in the form of a constructive unity. This unifying activity is the will, but the activity of unity is thought to come about in such a way as to return at each occasion to the activity itself. What is more, the unifying activity is always a manifestation of the unifying activity itself. In other words, will comes out of the unifying activity itself and returns to that activity. To advance is to return to the start. This is more or less what Nishida has in mind in saying that intellectual intuition is at the ground of will, and that, as an intuition of a subject-object unity, will arises through intuition.

From another angle, the same can be said of thinking. Nishida posits intellectual intuition at the ground of thought by arguing that "on the one hand, the fundamental intuition in thought is the ground of explanation, and yet on the other hand, is the dynamism of thought and no mere static form of thought" (p. 44). By the "ground of explanation" he means that thought returns to a basic intuition, and by "dynamism of thought" that thought begins from a basic intuition. All systematic development takes a form wherein *egressus est regressus, regressus est egressus.* Nishida himself borrows Leibniz's terminology, "Evolution is involution" (p. 92).

Intellectual intuition is the ground at which thought and will become one, "intuition that transcends intellect and will and yet grounds them both" (p. 45). It is the alpha and omega of the independent and self-sufficient development of pure experience that is a motion-in-stillness. And it is here, too, that the true self is to be found. This is what he means in saying that there is no other self and that the true self bespeaks a unifying intuition. The will at all times comes to completion by departing from and returning to this intuitive unity. This is why he speaks of the point of completion of intellectual intuition as consisting in the realization of the will, in the satisfaction of the self's desires. At the same time, he insists that an ideal spirit requires an infinite unity and that this unity is given in the form of intellectual intuition. The true self, freed from the restrictions of space, time, and individuals, seeks infinite unity, and the desires and ideals arising from the innate nature of the self are satisfied in an intellectual intuition that is the completion and realization of the will. This means that the potential that constituted the basic unifying power in pure experience—the potential one that is the true self itself—realizes itself or is its own actualization. But what is this ideal spirit? In what sense do ideals and spirit fit into the picture?

SPIRIT AND IDEALS

IN HIS CHAPTER on "Spirit" in part 2, Nishida notes that the spirit that is usually set up against nature is actually an abstraction of the unifying activity from a single reality in which subject and object are one. To separate objective nature and subjective spirit from each other as independent realities is simply an abstract viewpoint floating free of the facts of immediate experience. But such ideas do not arise without cause. The one and only reality in which subject and object are united contains within itself a permanent rupture, so that opposites are able to emerge by breaking through the bottom of its pre-established structural unity. One systematic unity collides with another, and the desire for a new unity to overcome the contradiction is born. If the unifying activity is then abstracted by cutting away the element of unity and bringing it to consciousness on its own, this abstraction comes to be conceived of as spirit. This is what happens in knowledge when a rupture occurs in the content of thought and the desire for a new unity arises, or when there is a conflict of motives within the will.

In short, because "on the one hand reality is infinite conflict and on the other is infinite unity" (p. 90), a desire for new unity is continually being born. This desire is the setting in motion of the "unifying activity itself" referred to earlier as a basic intuition; it is a manifestation of the self's innate nature (what Aristotle calls *physis*) and the self's own power. Here the unifying function reaches consciousness as spirit. This is why Nishida argues that will comes about through intuition because to will something amounts to an intuition of a subject-object unity.

Thus the birth of a desire for a new unity means that a greater and deeper unity is emerging as a new possibility from behind an already realized unity like a shadow that was not there before. It is the same with thinking as with will. This is why he said that the basic intuition becomes the basis for a new explanation and at the same time represents the dynamism of thought. Where this "power" takes effect, new possibilities are also stirring like new life fermenting in the heat. This power or possibility (what Aristotle calls *dynamis*) is pregnant with infinitude. Behind it lies the indeterminate, beyond the reach of all the determinations that belong to what has been actualized. If this possibility is seen as the unifying activity itself that is basic intuition, then this latter includes an "infinite unity." Each occurrence of the unifying function begins and ends there. Just as intellectual intuition is at the ground of thought and will, so it is from intellectual intuition that thought and will begin and there that they return. Seen from the ongoing development of thinking and willing, this ground is a kind of bottomless bottom. Thought and will seek an infinite unity which is at once the "ideal" of their infinite destination and always latent in the here and now. In achieving a provisional completion in the actual world—that is, in provisionally realizing its goal—this ideal is called over from the infinite destination into the present[6] and "given in the form of intellectual intuition." For reality by nature includes both sides of infinitude: infinite conflict and infinite unity, and yet ultimately it is a unity. (This ultimate unity will appear later in Nishida's discussion of religion as absolute unity or occasionally as nothingness. This is the locus of the true self, the place where it is and relates to God.)

In its original sense, spirit represents the presence of a unifying activity in the one independent and self-sufficient reality. This unifying activity implies an infinite possibility and is open to infinitude. Put the other way around, because it is upheld by the completely undetermined power of the unifying activity itself, spirit cannot be separated from ideals. The unifying activity of spirit is infinitely open to a greater and deeper unity and seeks infinite unity. Conversely, through the unifying activity, spirit may be said to conceal an infinite unity at its base. This is the element of the ideal in spirit. (As noted earlier, this concept is not far removed from Hegel's notion of *Idealität*.) This is what Nishida means by his claim that "an ideal spirit requires an infinite unity" (p. 41). In the chapter in part 3 on spirit he writes:

> We do well to consider the fact that wherever spirit is, there conflict is, as an indication that ideals go hand in hand with spirit. Ideals signify contradiction and conflict with actuality. (And because this means that our spirit appears out of conflict, spirit is never without agony. In this sense there is some truth to the pessimists' claim that the world is a world of suffering.) (pp. 90–91)

---

6. Nishitani appears to be playing with Japanese to create here the effect of Heidegger's play on the word *Zukunft* as a "coming-to" the present.

Spirit is accompanied by ideals because it represents a dimension open to infinitude, and ideals contradict actuality because a power seeking infinite unity lies at the ground of that which limits actuality and also of that which breaks through those limiting determinations. This is where the above-mentioned suffering comes in. It is also where our sense of the self as a "creative and free infinite activity" comes into the picture. As to why the self should be so felt, Nishida comments briefly:

> This self of ours, the unifier of spirit, is originally the unifying activity of reality. . . . At those times when the unity of reality is at work within, we feel as if we are in control of reality as ideals of the self, as if the self is engaged in free action. And since this unifying activity of reality is infinite, we feel the self to be something infinite that embraces the cosmos itself. (p. 93)[7]

In the foregoing we have frequently touched on the idea that the unifying power of reality is the unifying power of consciousness and at the same time of the universe. When this unifying power is directly at work within, the ideal spirit is given the infinite unity it seeks, and this unity in turn generates the sense that the self embraces the universe, controls reality as its own ideals, and can act freely.

Representing the unifying function in the independent and self-sufficient activity of the one and only reality, the idea of the spirit leads to talk of ideality, infinitude, and freedom. This is once again apparent in Nishida's chapter on "Freedom of the Will" in part 3, where he seeks to refute the case of the fatalists who deny free will. The argument runs like this: In what we call the world of nature, only those phenomena occur that cannot but occur according to the laws of nature; no other possibility at all is allowed. But conscious phenomena do not simply occur the way natural phenomena do. They involve a self-knowledge of what is occurring. Nishida continues:

> And this knowledge or consciousness means precisely an inclusion of other possibilities. The consciousness of picking something up,

---

7. See above, 124.

for example, entails inversely the possibility that we might not have picked it up. To be still more specific, there is always something of a universal nature in consciousness. In other words, consciousness possesses an element of the ideal. Without it, it would not be consciousness. And the fact that this is the nature of consciousness means that aside from such events as actually occur it can entertain other possibilities. It is the special quality of consciousness to be actual and yet include ideals, to be ideal and yet not depart from actuality. (pp. 115–16)

Regarding the inclusion of self-knowledge in conscious phenomena, Nishida notes earlier in the book:

The actual phenomenon of consciousness is identical with our consciousness of that phenomenon; the two cannot be distinguished as subject and object. Between the fact and the awareness there is not so much as a hair's breadth. (p. 48)

Now the element of the ideal is connected to the essence of consciousness as this kind of immediate experience in which subject and object are one. Without this ideal element, to repeat, it is not consciousness. But now what can such ideality, reduced to its most elemental, rudimentary point, refer to?

The element of the ideal is said to be something of a universal essence. "Universal" means, for instance, "color" as distinct from red, blue, and so on. In general, it is the standpoint of knowing that includes universals. Or in other words, knowing is the point at which something universal has been posited as a locus. Insofar as even perception includes knowing in some sense or other, it contains the universal. That is, it entails what we might call the disclosure of a locus able to embrace the sensation of red and the sensation of blue. We may perceive only the presence of the color red, but other colors like blue and green, while not actual, are present as possibilities. In short, perception means perceiving red as the "color" red.

In the previous section I cited Nishida to the effect that even ordinary perception is always a structuring activity and contains an element of the ideal (p. 41). Insofar as universals have the power to distinguish between particular colors and relate them to one another, and insofar as they represent a locus in which all colors are thereby unified into a system, the perception that includes these universals as a power-in-locus can also be referred to as a structuring activity. To say that perception includes such universals and is a structuring activity means that it entails knowing. In this sense, the work of knowing is also present in perception. Moreover, this knowing is also one with a self-knowing. Self-knowing belongs to the perception of a color.

This is what Nishida means by claiming that the actual phenomenon of consciousness is identical with our consciousness of that phenomenon. This is also why he can speak of "something of a universal nature" and of an "element of the ideal." In this latter, the qualification "ideal" refers simply to a dimension lying behind the actual, a dimension that seeks a greater and deeper unity capable of embracing actuality and other possibilities. If "being conscious" and "knowing" are essential to consciousness, and if therefore consciousness includes something universal, then Nishida's claim that there is no consciousness without an element of the ideal makes sense. This also makes intelligible his argument that it is of the essence of consciousness to be actual and yet include ideals, to be ideal and yet to remain in actuality.

The foregoing has had to do with the phenomena of consciousness in general, but the same can be said of its highest stage, the realm of spirit. Earlier we cited Nishida's statement that "there is no limit to how rich and profound the element of the ideal latent in the ground of intuition can become" (p. 41). The perception of the artist, for example, has direct ties to the realm of spirit. It actualizes an infinite unity in the form of intellectual intuition and leads to an appropriation of a deep grasp of life. All such *approfondissement* is a deepening of the self-knowing contained in consciousness; it implies new breadth and depth to the progress of the element of the ideal towards infinite unity. Put the other way around, the unifying function of consciousness (that is, of immediate experience or reality) always arises from an infinitely deep ground to act as a unifying activity. The activity of unifying activity is none other than will, so that as self-knowing deepens it goes hand in hand with the development of will towards the realization of the ideal. Knowing serves to posit a locus that allows the many to stand side by side in their mutual conflict and opposition. Willing is the activity of uniting the many into one.

Knowledge and will are thus two sides of the same development, a development that we may characterize as an infinite *approfondissement* of "the universal" in the nature of a power-in-locus:

> Seen in terms of the ideal at the ground of consciousness, this actuality is simply one example of the ideal. It is simply one process of the self-realization of the ideal. (p. 116)

The words actually come from a discussion of the problem of freedom. In that context "actuality" implies the whole of what we call the world of nature, completely ruled by the iron laws of nature without any other possibilities, while the "ideal" points to a standpoint of freedom beyond the world of nature and its necessary laws — in a word, to the realm of spirit. As the ideality in consciousness, the universal is directly connected to this larger picture. Alluding to Pascal's "thinking reed," Nishida cites the passage from the *Pensées:* "But even if the universe were to crush him, man would still be nobler than his slayer, because he knows that he is dying and the advantage the universe has over him" (p. 117).[8] The self-knowing within consciousness in general has a direct connection with these ultimate questions of human existence. The distinguishing mark of the standpoint of immediate experience that Nishida works out in *An Inquiry into the Good* consists in seeing even the most elemental things of consciousness as leading directly to something ultimate. The following passage on the problem of ideals is a good illustration:

> The element of the ideal, of unifying activity, at the ground of consciousness . . . is not a product of nature; rather nature comes into being as a function of this unity. Indeed here is the infinite power that is the basis of reality, a power beyond quantitative determination. It lies entirely outside the necessary laws of nature. Our will is free because it is a manifestation of this power and is not subject to the control of the laws of nature. (p. 117)

---

8. The original appears in the *Pensées*, no. 200. The translation is by A. J. Krailsheimer (Harmondsworth, 1966), 95.

Here we see spelled out the meaning of the assertion that from the standpoint of the ideal at the ground of consciousness, actuality is simply one example of the ideal.

Freedom arises only at the stage of spirit. As noted earlier, spirit represents the point at which the unity of reality reaches self-awareness. Spirit is what results when the unifying activity is no longer latent, when it becomes a fact of actuality. This is what distinguishes spirit from nature:

> All reality comes about through unity, but it is in spirit that unity appears as a clear and distinct fact. Only in spirit does reality become complete — an independent and self-sufficient reality. (pp. 91–92)[9]

This is the source of the connection of spirit with infinitude and ideality that we have been discussing. Reality is originally an independent and self-sufficient activity, an infinite unifying power, but if it is manifest in spirit in this original form, it follows as a matter of course that spirit should arise in connection with infinitude. The infinite power at the foundations of reality is at work in the ground of consciousness as that unifying activity itself, but spirit emerges from this working as one aspect of the unifying activity of conscious unity. For this reason spirit undergoes an infinite development in the search for infinite unity, and this development is none other than will. At the same time, spirit always posits a locus in the here-and-now directed towards infinite unity. This is self-knowing or self-awareness. As noted earlier, development is a kind of unfolding-in-internalizing. Moreover, insofar as the unifying activity of consciousness includes the infinitude of spirit, it carries the sense of an ideality. Ultimately, this is so because the unifying activity of consciousness represents the working of the infinite unifying power of reality.

The spirit in which will and self-knowing are one is our self itself. At bottom this self, the true self, is simply the unifying activity of reality itself. "This self of ours that is the unifier of the spirit is originally the unifying activity of reality" (p. 92).[10]

---

9. See above, 120.
10. See above, 120.

Freedom of will must be seen in this light. Whatever development consciousness undergoes, insofar as it is a spontaneous self-unfolding from within, it may be seen as will. Ultimately this is based on seeing the infinite power of reality as the prime mover behind all developments of consciousness. But in the spirit, where reality is manifest in its original form, the will must also display its original meaning as a manifestation of the infinite power of reality. In other words, the will must show itself, as the unifier of the spirit, to be the unifying power of a primordial reality and in this sense must issue from the self. This is what Nishida means when he writes that "we feel most free when we work from the inner essence of the self, . . . in other words, when the causal motivation issues from the deepest inner essence of the self" (p. 115).

When our self has displayed its original form as the unifying activity of reality, it is self as "person." In this case, the ideals of will consist in satisfying the desires of the personality as a whole, and this is what we call "the good":

> Since the good is something that satisfies the inner desires of the self, and since the greatest desire of the self is the desire of the basic unifying activity of consciousness, namely, the desire of the person, the greatest good for us is the satisfaction of that desire, the realization of personality. This demand of the person is both the unifying power of consciousness and the manifestation of an infinite unifying power at the ground of reality. To actualize our person is to join ourselves to this power. (p. 152)

As we have seen, then, the unifying activity of consciousness is the infinite power of reality in which an element of the ideal is present at the ground of consciousness. And our will is said to be free because it makes this infinite power in reality manifest, and the desire for the self-realization of the person is said to manifest this same power. This was the basis for talk of "ideals at the ground of consciousness" and "an ideality or unifying activity at the ground of consciousness" whose deepest form of expression was "the great desire of the self," namely "the basic unifying activity of consciousness or personality." Here we find the real meaning of the initial claim that "the good is the realization of ideals and the satisfaction of desire."

The cornerstone of all of these claims is the standpoint that finds the true self at the point where the unifying activity of consciousness and of the universe are identified, a standpoint that pivots on immediate experience. To reintroduce a passage cited earlier:

> True unity of consciousness is a pure, uncomplicated activity that appears naturally without our knowing it; it is the original state of independent, self-sufficient consciousness without any distinction of intelligence, emotion, and will, without any isolation of subject from object. At such times our true personality expresses this totality. (p. 151)

And this total true human personality, we recall, is for Nishida "at once the dynamic of the unifying power of the universe."

A few pages later he adds that

> the desires of our total personality can only reach self-awareness in a state of immediate experience prior to the exercise of reflection and judgment. In this case personality appears from out of the inner recesses of the spirit, giving voice to a kind of internal desire that gradually comes to take over one's whole mind. (pp. 153–54)

In this context "giving voice to a kind of internal desire" refers to "the unifying activity of consciousness and the manifestation of an infinite unifying activity at the ground of reality" (p. 152). And this is what Nishida understands as self-awareness in a state of immediate experience. The actualization of personality is the self-awareness of true self, for "the true self of each individual is not something outside of the independent and self-sufficient system of reality itself that appears to each one of us" (p. 155).

Such a viewpoint requires that we let go of the merely subjective self that treats subject and object as separate things as well as of the subjective self that this subjective self considers to be the self:

> The point at which the subjective fantasy of the self is completely obliterated so that one can unite with things is rather the point at which one is able to satisfy the self's true desire and to see the true self. . . . To fulfill the greatest desire of the self and to realize the self is to actualize the objective ideal of the self, namely its unity with

the objective. Seen in this light, good conduct is always love. All love is the feeling of a unity of self and other. It is the feeling of a oneness of subject and object. Love is not only a matter of person-to-person but is also present in the encounter of a painter with nature. (pp. 155–56)

Since we have already touched on this point earlier, I shall not go into it further here, but there is one point in the above quotation that merits comment.

The highest desire of the self, the desire of the person, opens up into love where self and other are at one, and this love does not stop at human beings but is broadened to include all things. Given that the desires of personality issue from "the deepest inner essence" of the self and manifest the infinite unifying power at the ground of reality, this is only natural. In any event, it should be noted that personality is considered here against the background of the cosmos. From a standpoint that sees the actualization of the person as the union of self and other, one moves from family to nation to humanity as a whole:

The good is the realization of ideals and the satisfaction of desire. Seen from within it is the satisfaction of sincere desires, the unity of consciousness that culminates in the mutual oblivion of self and other, the loss of subject and object in one another. Seen as an outer fact, it culminates in a unified progression from the development of small individuality to humanity in general. (p. 163)

Thus even where the realization of personality is broadened to include all of humanity, when seen from within it remains a unity of consciousness of which Nishida can say "subject and object are lost in one another, ego and things are oblivious of one another, heaven and earth act as one single reality" (p. 156). Love is also seen as a standpoint that shows these two aspects. Looked at in terms of the ground of immediate experience, this follows as a matter of course. For self and universe have an common ground. (As mentioned in passing above, this is one of the fundamental ideas of Buddhism.[11])

---

11. See above, 125.

It is in this light that we should read the oft-cited passage at the close of part 3 of *An Inquiry into the Good*:

> There is only one true good and it can be expressed succinctly: to know the true self. The true self is the noumenon of the universe, and in knowing the true self one not only joins at one with humanity in general but fuses with the noumenon of the cosmos and merges with the divine will. (p. 167)

Good and love are seen in terms of the realization of the person, which in turn is treated in terms of the infinite unifying power of reality. In this way Nishida's argument proceeds naturally from the problem of the good to the problem of religion. By locating the true self in an identification of the unifying activity of consciousness with the unifying activity of reality, Nishida is able to connect the problem of reality with the problem of the good and that problem in turn with the problem of religion. This idea of the true self is the cornerstone of his idea of immediate experience. Here we get a glimpse of the consistency that marks the realms of reality, the good, and religion from a standpoint of immediate experience and the way they are comprehended as a process of deepening. All I have tried to do is touch on this matter by focusing on the ideas of desire, ideals, and spirit.

8 *An Inquiry into the Good:* God

THE TRUE SELF is not only related to a universal reconciliation with other persons and a fusion with the noumenon of the cosmos; it also has a profound affinity with God. Besides entailing a problem of reality (part 2) and a problem of the good (part 3), the true self also entails a problem of religion (part 4). The standpoint of immediate experience is bound to God from its very ground. We must therefore touch on this point in concluding our treatment of *An Inquiry into the Good*.

The final three chapters of part 2 deal respectively with nature, spirit, and God. God is there described as "the foundation of infinite activity" and "the ground of reality." Consider the following, for example:

> A deep understanding of nature cannot but acknowledge a spiritual unity at its ground. Further, to be true and complete, spirit must be at one with nature; that is to say, there is only one reality in the universe. And this one reality . . . is an independent and self-sufficient infinite activity. And it is to the foundation of this infinite activity that we affix the name of God. God is certainly not something transcending this reality from the outside. The foundation of reality is directly God; God is what unites spirit and nature as one by doing away with the distinction between subjectivity and objectivity. (p. 96)

The one reality, as an independent and self-sufficient infinite activity, is an infinite unity that never admits of objectification; but

God is actually none other than the nonobjectifiable ground of this reality.

Now the true self was also said to be that infinite unity. The true self means *becoming* objective nature by losing the small self; and in our becoming nature, nature is appropriated or transformed into the self within an infinite unity. The true self is also a union of spirit and nature, of subject and object. This is "the great self" (p. 101) that seeks the unity of self and others. How does this great self relate to God? Clearly God is conceived of as something inseparable from the true self. God does not transcend the true self and stand outside it. God must be "proved immediately in the self's immediate experience" (p. 98). The standpoint of immediate experience includes at once the way that leads to God. Let us listen to what Nishida himself has to say in this regard:

> This being so, how are we able to seek the existence of God in the facts of our immediate experience? Within the very breast of creatures as small as we are, bound to the limits of space and time, . . . the unifying power of infinite reality is there. Because we possess this power, we are able to seek out the truth of the universe through study, to express the true meaning of reality in art, to know in our innermost heart the foundations of reality that structure the universe — in short, to comprehend the face of God. The infinitely free activity of the human mind is direct proof of God as such. As Jacob Boehme says, we see God with *umgewandtes Auge*. (pp. 98–99)

What is this "inverted eye" in our innermost heart?

In knowing our true self we merge with the good of humanity in general where self and other are joined as one; we fuse with the noumenon of the cosmos and become one with the substance of the universe and merge with the will of God. The way to know the true self and join ourselves to God lies in appropriating the power to unite subject and object as one. This state of appropriation is called being born again in Christianity and enlightened insight in Buddhism. The inverted eye refers to this rebirth and enlightenment, to knowing the true self and uniting with God:

> Those who wish to know the true God must equip themselves with the eye to do so by disciplining themselves accordingly. For such

persons the power of God in the entire universe . . . is felt as a fact of immediate experience. This is what it means to see God. (p. 100)

To know the true self is to become one with God. Enlightenment is a vision of the divine, seeing God with inverted eye. The infinitely free activity of the human mind is direct proof of God. In other words, when the unifying power of the universe of reality is experienced immediately as the infinite activity of the human mind and appropriated as such, the power of God throughout the universe becomes a fact of immediate experience. We know God as the foundation of reality and comprehend the face of God. As the infinite activity that unifies the universe, God is a "complete nothingness," and yet at the same time "there exists an incontrovertible principle" according to which "because he is able to be nothing, there is no place where he is not at work" (p. 100).

In dealing with religion in part 4, Nishida adopts the same view as in parts 2 and 3, namely that the principal axis around which everything revolves is the way that leads to the true self by breaking through the subjective self. Part 4 opens with the words:

> Religious desire is a desire for the self, the desire for the life of the self. . . . Authentic religion seeks the conversion of the self and the renewal of life. . . . As long as an iota of belief in the self remains, we cannot speak of authentic religiosity. (p. 169)

This conversion of self is here again said to consist in "letting go of subjective unity completely and becoming one with objective unity" (p. 171). In so doing, one attains "absolute unity" and a "state of subject-object union." Of itself, consciousness includes an infinite differential development, but this "cannot possibly withdraw from the unity of subject and object" which is "the alpha and omega of consciousness" (p. 172). In this sense the state of oneness of subject and object is "not only the fundamental desire of consciousness but actually its original state" (p. 171). This telos of the development of consciousness is at the same time a state forever present beneath the surface of consciousness. The "apex of conscious unity" lies in what was referred to earlier as a "motion-in-stillness, stillness-in-motion."

Religious desire is simply this desire for ultimate unity of consciousness, for a final state of subject-object unity. And as such, it is "the desire to be one with the universe" (p. 172). This desire represents a movement (or rather a motion-in-stillness, stillness-in-motion) from one ultimate conscious unity to another. As such, religious desire also desires that "our self perceive its relativity and finitude at the same time as it joins as one with the power of absolute infinitude, hoping thereby to gain true eternal life" (p. 169), that is "to live by God alone." To live at one with God and the universe therefore represents "the deepest and greatest desire of the human heart and mind." Unlike any other desire, "religion alone is the solution of the self itself" (p. 172). Only when it reaches oneness with the universe and God — only when it arrives at religion — does the self itself find a solution.

The term *the self itself* does not refer to the small, subjective self that is encompassed by an individual life. It is rather a self in search of a greater unity, a unifying power directly at work within immediate experience, such that we must say that it is not that there is experience because there are individuals, but rather that there are individuals because there is experience. Desires that issue from this self are already present in "the birth of a common spirit" in morality, and religious desire is the "epitome" (p. 171) of all the desires of this greater self. The absolute unity referred to earlier is just such an ultimate unity, "a cosmic unity of consciousness that joins together the consciousness of all people" (p. 180).

It should be clear from the foregoing that the position Nishida takes in *An Inquiry into the Good* is one in which joining as one with the good of humanity, fusing with the noumenon of the universe, and merging with the divine will coincide with knowing the true self. This standpoint of immediate experience in independent and self-sufficient development reaches its greatest and deepest level in religion.

In this book Nishida accepts provisionally the general definition of religion as "a relationship between God and the human person" (p. 173). But if we look at things from the perspective of the foregoing, we naturally come to a view rather different from the normal view of the divine, the human, and the relationship between the two. God is seen as "the foundation of the universe"

(p. 173), but not in a sense that makes God transcendent to the world, controlling it from the outside. For Nishida God is rather "directly the ground of this reality" (p. 178), and the universe is "not something created by God but an expression or manifestation of the divine." So, too, with the relation between God and humanity. For Nishida our spirit "has the same ground as God" (p. 176) and represents "the partial consciousness of God," so that he can speak of "a divine-human identity of essence" and a "divine-human identity of substance" (pp. 174, 177):

> God must be the foundation of the universe as well as our foundation. When we return to God we return to the foundation. Further, God must be the telos of all things, and that means also the telos of humans. (p. 173)

And a few pages later he adds:

> Our God must be the internal unifying force through which heaven and earth are set in place, through which all things are nurtured; there is nothing other that can be called God. (p. 176)

This God "contains the deepest truth of human life" (p. 176). These words form the keystone of the view of religion of *An Inquiry into the Good*, giving expression as they do to the standpoint of immediate experience from which we cannot depart for so much as a moment. Such a view of religion may seem to smack of a tendency to what we might call Eastern meditation, but there is more to Nishida's view than that. He writes, for instance:

> The true meaning of religion consists . . . in our lived experience of a grand cosmic spirit breaking through the consciousness of self at the ground of consciousness. Faith is not something given from without through legend or logic, but something that must be cultivated from within. As Boehme says, we arrive at God through the most inward birth (*die innerste Geburt*). We see God directly in this inner rebirth; in our belief we discover the dynamism of the self's true life and feel infinite power. (p. 177)

The point here is to get a grip on "the significance of the divine-human union. As his own words make plain, Nishida rejects the idea that "one gets a sense of the true significance of religion by rubbing out the spirit of initiative and living a passive life weak in ambitions and free of distress" (p. 170).

GENERAL CHARACTERISTICS OF THE IDEA OF RELIGION

I SHOULD NOW like to touch briefly on the general characteristics of this positive and novel approach to religion that Nishida develops in *An Inquiry into the Good*. The opening passage of part 4 is interwoven with biblical quotations, and allusions to Christianity are scattered throughout the book. Nonetheless, one is struck by the fact that he does not hesitate to raise objections against what are ordinarily taken to be matters of fundamental Christian doctrine. For example, Christianity conceives of God, the creator of the world, as transcending the world from without. For Nishida, this concept goes against reason and is not the deepest form of religion (p. 175). In the same connection, he observes that "things like simple reliance on divine assistance and fear of divine retribution are not true Christianity" (p. 169). He is also opposed to the idea of divine revelation[1] on the grounds that "the only divine will we can know are the laws and principles of nature; there is no other divine revelation" (pp. 175–76).

This last point touches on one of the distinguishing features of Nishida's view of religion in this book, deriving as it does from the book's attempt to find the converging point of philosophy and religion. As remarked earlier, "nature" along with "spirit" is made one of the essential elements in the notion of "reality," and the idea of "principle" in nature is given a place of foundational importance. Now all of this follows quite as a matter of course if it is a convergence of religious desire and intellectual certainty of a philosophical sort that is being sought. Hence for a view of religion that sees God as the foundation and unifier of the universe and the universe as an expression of God, it follows that there is no revelation apart from the laws and principles of nature.

---

1. Nishitani draws attention to the fact that Nishida uses 天啓 to render the term "divine revelation," rather than the more common theological word 啓示.

Special attention should be given to the fact that such a view of religion encompasses within itself the standpoint of the natural sciences. After stating that the universe is an expression of God, Nishida comments in this regard:

> There is nothing, from the movement of the sun, the moon, and the stars without to the workings of the human heart within, that is not the expression of God. At the ground of each of these things we can worship the light of the divine spirit. . . .
>
> Just as Newton and Kepler were struck with awe by the sight of the ordered movement of the heavens, the more we study natural phenomena, the more we come to acknowledge a single unifying power in control behind the scene. The advance of learning is nothing other than just such an ongoing unity of knowledge. (pp. 178–79)

Nishida alludes again to Newton and Kepler by name a few pages later (p. 182).

What is it that makes it possible for this view of religion to incorporate the advance of learning and hence the standpoint of the natural sciences as a positive dimension of itself? Particularly striking here is the frequency with which the names of mystics like Augustine, Eckhart, and Boehme (not to mention Dionysius and Cusanus) come up in the chapters of part 4. What is more, they are generally introduced in the context of the *approfondissement* of the basic position of pure experience to religious experience. In other words, once the standpoint of immediate experience has entered the realm of religion, it is related to the experiences of the mystics. In this regard Nishida explicitly singles out the examples of mystical experience recorded in William James's *Varieties of Religious Experience* (p. 189). This affinity with the mystical is another of the distinguishing marks of *An Inquiry into the Good*.

Mysticism is usually set up as the exact opposite of science. How then can mysticism form the foundation for a religion capable of incorporating scientific research in a positive sense? How are these two traits of Nishida's view of religion reconciled with one another? Furthermore, why is it not ordinary Christian doctrine (orthodoxy) or theology or faith but rather an unorthodox mysticism that Nishida absorbs into the standpoint of science and philosophy in his book? The first reason that comes to mind is that mysticism does, after all, set its feet squarely on the ground of experience and, like all experience, can be related to rational knowing (the grasp of principles in things). The difference, however, is that experience in general belongs to a dimension prior to (or lower than) reason, whereas mysticism is experience belonging to a transrational dimension.

This feature of mystical experience is of great importance for religion. For when experience in general shifts to the rational knowing of academic learning, it must distance itself from the immediacy of experience and hence lose its living quality. Mystical experience, in contrast, keeps its experiential standpoint, even when it is displaying its own inner principles and rationality. Transrational mystical experience includes in itself the rational principles that allow it to be an object of academic study without forfeiting its unifying power or unifying function. This enables mysticism to grasp rational laws not as abstractions but as living principles. Contrary to the usual opinion, mystical experience is not purely and simply unscientific. Hence it is not without good reason that the standpoint of immediate experience advanced in *An Inquiry into the Good* becomes affiliated with mystical experience when it enters into the realm of religion in search of its end.

To carry the point further, the position Nishida assumes in this book is that immediate experience is always coincident with the standpoint of an absolute self; that its development is always the independent, self-sufficient, and spontaneous self-unfolding of a conscious unity prior to the distinction of subject and object (what *An Inquiry into the Good* calls the one and only reality); and that fusion with universe and with God does not take place apart from the self's knowing the true self, actualizing the true self, and truly becoming itself. In short, it is a position at one with the standpoint of mysticism.

It is in this light that we need to read the passage cited at the end of the preceding section (p. 177; p. 149 above). There we see a clear confrontation with ordinary Christian doctrine, theology, and faith, which divides faith into two sorts: what is given from without and what is cultivated from within. The former relies on legend (mainly mythical) and theory (such as theological dogma).

As noted earlier, however, this kind of faith not only clashes with reason but also fails to represent what is deepest in religion. The reason for Nishida's aversion for clashes with reason stems from a commitment to take seriously in religion the intellectual certainty of a philosophical *Weltanschauung* and view of the human; and the reason for his claim that Christianity has not reached the deepest level is that it has not arrived at the point where the self knows the true self.

In other words, the clash with reason stems from a reliance on what is given from without, whereas the deepest faith consists in an inner spiritual rebirth of the self and in the "vision of the divine" and "discovery of the true life of the self" that this rebirth makes possible. The idea of a "faith cultivated from within" refers to a dying to one's self to be reborn in God. It is the point at which the self becomes truly alive in being born again. Nishida cites Boehme in this context, and at the start of part 4 cites the famous lines of Saint Paul, "I live now not with my own life but with the life of Christ who lives in me" (Gal. 2:20, p. 169). The passage has been a favorite of Western mystics through the centuries.

Furthermore, this faith through mystical experience is related to a lived experience of the grand universal spirit at work when the subjective self at the ground of consciousness is broken through. The meaning of the term *lived experience*[2] overlaps with that of the term *experiment* in the sciences. In the book Nishida speaks of "uniting with nature" by letting go of subjective opinions and of "becoming" things and their principles. Just as in medieval Western mysticism, knowing God qua God is sometimes referred to as a *cognitio experimentalis,* so here *experience* combines religious and modern scientific connotations. Here, too, we see his standpoint of religion being made to include the realm of science. Thus the defining trait of his view of religion is that it sees the universe as an expression of God, that it recognizes divine revelation in the rational laws of nature and affirms Newton and Kepler along with

---

2. Modern English has come to restrict the word *experiment* to its scientific denotations, thus disabling the connotative connections with *experience* that Nishitani and Nishida have in mind. Accordingly the term has been rendered rather more literally here, and in an earlier appearance on p. 149 above.

the mystics. All of this results from seeing immediate experience as revolving about knowledge of the true self.

To know the true self is to join as one with the good of mankind, to be fused into the noumenon of the cosmos, and to merge with the divine will. Here "religion and morality are present to the full" (p. 167). Here, too, we are able to understand Nishida's talk of the divine and the human sharing "one body" and "one nature." This identity of body and nature does not refer to a superficial identity conceived in merely abstract, intellectual terms. The idea of God and humans sharing one body harkens back to what Saint Paul and Boehme have to say about dying to self and living in Christ, or about breaking through the self to the birth of a new human in the self.

If the idea of God and humans sharing one body seems odd, one might stop to reflect on the notion of the Holy Spirit in the Bible. In the Christian view, the Holy Spirit is one of the three persons of the divine essence, although it seems generally to remain in the shadows behind the other two persons of the Trinity (the Father and the Son). Still, the Holy Spirit signifies divine "life" and "love" and is regarded as the divine power that binds God and humans religiously. It has therefore been given great importance in the mystical tradition that deals with the union of the divine and the human. Seen in this light, the idea of God and humans sharing one body becomes easier to understand.

THE MEANING OF PERSONALITY IN GOD

FROM WHAT has been said, there must be a great integration of God, universe, and the self to which immediate experience ultimately returns. This point of transindividual unity, of universal conscious unity, of absolute unity, is religion. In religion we come to know our true self by joining as one with the consciousness of all people, by fusing ourselves with the cosmos, by merging with God.

Now God, we recall, is seen as the ground of the universe in which all things, from the movement of the sun, the moon, and the stars without to the workings of the human heart within, are expressions of God. To refer back to a passage cited partially above:

the more we study natural phenomena, the more we come to realize a single unifying power in control behind the scene. . . . On further reflection, we see also that nature and spirit are not things
completely unrelated. . . . There must be some further single unifying force at their ground. . . . This unity is God. (p. 179)

These are not assertions Nishida makes from a standpoint of
speculative metaphysics but facts of immediate experience. The
"single unifying force" at the ground of nature and spirit is this
immediate experience itself. The claim that "there is only one
unifying power at the ground of the myriad phenomena of the
universe" (p. 77) is made from a standpoint for which "the phenomenon of consciousness represents the one and only reality." In
other words, the self is the infinite unifier and the power that
unifies the universe of reality. It is in this sense that Nishida was
able to speak of nature as possessed of "a kind of self" such that
even when we look at a single animal or plant, our intuition gives
us "a direct grasp of the unifier in its entirety" (p. 86) and hence
an insight into "the self of the thing." This grasp of the "unifying
force that is the life of nature" and which permeates the self of a
blade of grass and the self of nature as a whole is immediate experience as intellectual intuition. At such times we already find ourselves occupying the standpoint of the unifying power of the spirit:

> Thus this unifying self present behind nature . . . is not something
> unknowable and without relationship to consciousness, but is in
> fact the unifying activity of consciousness itself. . . . Our subjective
> unity and the objective unifying power of nature are basically iden-
> tical. Viewed objectively, this represents a unity of the intellect,
> emotion, and will in the self. (p. 87)

Seen as a rupture or clash that takes place in the interiority of
the system of a single spontaneous and self-unfolding reality, nature and spirit represent the dimension of subject-object opposition. Here spirit is seen as the unifying element and nature as the
object of the unifying. But in the facts of immediate experience,
subject and object are always a unity which can only be called "a
single reality of mind-in-things, things-in-mind" (p. 181). Immediate experience has as its basis an absolute unity that forms the

ground of this one reality prior to the distinction of nature from spirit. And this absolute unity is nothing other than God:

> The God who is the ground of reality . . . must be the ground of the facts of this immediate experience, in other words, the ground of our conscious phenomena. (p. 181)

This is why God is said to be the unifier of the universe and the universe is the expression of God.

When Nishida later comes to ask, "What kind of being is this God that unifies the universe and gives reality its ground?" he follows the theory of reality in part 2 that he developed into a theory of personality in part 3—defining God as "spirit" in terms of "a single great person who is the ground of the universe" (p. 182). He sees spiritual phenomena as cognitive, emotional, and voluntary activities each governed by its own laws, and God—the unifying force behind these spiritual phenomena—as a great personality:

> From the phenomena of nature to the historical development of humanity, there is nothing that does not take the form of a single great thought and great will; the universe is a personal manifestation of God. . . . Reality must directly be the thought as well as the will of God. (p. 182)

Of course, even though God is spoken of as a person, this does not imply a transcendent personality outside the world. What Nishida means here is that all things come about through the unity of God—"the unifying activity of God is at once the unifying activity of all things"—and that this fills us with a sense of an "infinite love" that makes us think of God as personal. Even so, "there is no love of God apart from the unfolding of the things of nature." Indeed it is because the unifying activity of God is the unifying activity of all things that pure experience is a unity "from which we cannot leap free" (p. 185). In this sense God may also be seen as "the unifier of pure experience that encompasses the universe."

Nishida sees God, therefore, as "the one great intellectual intuition at the ground of the universe" (p. 186), and argues that "all ideas of universal unity that govern our spirit are the self-identical consciousness of God" (p. 183). This "self-awareness of God," as he also calls it, is the point at which we reach a self-awareness in which we know our true self by uniting with the self-awareness of God. It is the point at which the unifying activity of pure experience that embraces the universe joins with the unifying activity of God nonobjectively (that is, as an activity). At the conclusion of part 1 he speaks of intellectual intuition as an "apprehension of the profound unity lying at the ground of intellect and will" (p. 40), adding that "the true self is this unifying intuition" and that this in turn constitutes "true religious awakening" (p. 45).

Intellectual intuition here appears as a standpoint in which pure experience comes to term in its mode of unifying activity as the unifying activity of God, which is described as the one great intellectual intuition at the foundation of the universe. Here, too, we see the true intellectual intuition as a "deep grasp of life." This point represents at once the origin and the climax of pure experience.

FREEDOM AND LOVE IN GOD

NISHIDA ALSO speaks of the love of God and the freedom of God, both of which are issues related to the personality of God as the "great person who is the ground of the universe."

Concerning divine freedom he remarks that "God is free in the sense that he is the foundation of all beings, that nothing exists apart from him, that the manifold of things that are all issue from the inner essence of God." In this sense, God is "absolutely free" (p. 184). At the same time, the "freedom of will that is one of the constitutive elements of the individual person is a self-determining universal" (p. 187).

In considering the relationship between the freedom of God as a great person at the ground of the universe and the freedom of individual persons, we may revert to what was just said regarding intellectual intuition. Given that intellectual intuition is "the unifying activity itself in pure experience" and a "grasp of life," that pure experience is not confined to the modalities of time, space, and individuals, that there are individuals because there is first experience, and that transindividual conscious unity itself is the true self whose unifying intuition unites subject and object as one (embraces the universe), it follows that true intellectual intuition and true freedom are not different things. What we have here is a knowing-in-doing and a doing-in-knowing. In its original sense, freedom is synonymous with the "systematic development" of pure experience (p. 35) and the unifying activity within this systematic development is nothing other than the true self. This is why knowing the truth of the universe, "obeying the greater self," and "realizing the greater self" (pp. 32–33) all amount to the same thing. Our "person" is not something other than the basic unifying power of pure experience; it is "already the unifying power of the universe in action" (p. 152). This is where we find true freedom at work. Freedom here consists in a unifying activity in which self is not set off from something other that is transindividual. In other words, freedom is something prior to the determining form of the "individual" (that which sets one individual off from another); indeed, it is the fountainhead from which such determinations and discriminations spring in the first place.

This helps us understand how Nishida can refer to the free will of individual persons as the "self-determination of a universal." The essence of free will in individuals consists in the unifying power of a "cosmic consciousness" in the "transpersonal" sense of something that joins subject and object as one and unifies the reality of the universe. Individual freedom is the self-determination of just such a "universal." In this respect, the unifying power of cosmic consciousness is at once the unifying power at work in the consciousness of our pure experience. This is the context in which the relation between the absolute freedom of God and our own freedom has to be considered for Nishida.

As the unity of the universe, God is "the one living spirit" (p. 183). At the same time,

> the existence of such a divine spirit is not merely a matter of philosophical debate but is an actual fact of spiritual experience. At the bottom of the consciousness of each and every one of us this spirit is at work. (p. 188)

After noting that God is the one great intellectual intuition at the ground of the universe and the unifier of pure experience that encompasses the entire universe, Nishida goes on:

The unity of consciousness cannot be an object of knowledge; it transcends all the categories of knowledge and refuses our every effort to give it form, and yet at the same time through it all things come into being. Thus what we call the divine spirit is inscrutable in the extreme and yet at the same time is intimately bound up with our spirit. At the ground of this unity of consciousness we are able to come into direct contact with the face of God. As Boehme says, heaven is everywhere — wherever you stand, wherever you go, all is heaven. And again: one reaches God through the depths of the inner life. (pp. 186–87)[3]

These lines give us a glimpse of the approach to freedom in *An Inquiry into the Good.* The conscious unity that resists all definition and yet on whose basis all things come about is the unity of pure experience that embraces the universe and the unity of cosmic consciousness where our true freedom lies. At the bottom of this unity of consciousness we come into direct contact with the divine visage, which has deep ties with our own spirit. True freedom as a living unity of pure experience merges nonobjectively — in a single unifying activity — with the absolute freedom in the person of God. In other words, where "God is the unifier of the pure experience embracing the universe," God's absolute freedom and our own true freedom are bound intimately together.

It is the same with our intellectual intuition, which always takes the form of a unity with God, "the one great intellectual intuition at the ground of the universe." This union is a kind of starting point for the activity in which "the universal determines itself" and a point at which, wherever we stop and wherever we go, we are always in heaven. There is where our individual freedom arises.

Where such intimacy and unity are found, there freedom, intellectual intuition, and love are one. "In God there is knowing-in-doing and doing-in-knowing. Reality must directly be the thought as well as the will of God" (p. 182). It is here that "knowledge and love are one and the same spiritual activity" (p. 197).

And again:

---

3. The passage that Nishida is apparently referring to appears in Boehme's "Sixth Treatise," secs. 37–38.

One can only know absolute and infinite Buddha—or God—by loving him. To love him *is* to know him. The teachings of the Vedas of India, the Neo-Platonists, and the Holy Gate of Buddhism,[4] speak of knowing, while Christianity and Pure Land Buddhism speak of love and reliance. While each of these approaches has its distinctive characteristics, in essence they are identical. (pp. 199–200)

The standpoint of pure experience of *An Inquiry into the Good* ends in an elucidation of this essence of religion.

---

4. For Shin Buddhists, the Holy Gate 聖道門 refers to the way of salvation through self-power, in contrast to the Pure Land Gate 浄土門, which seeks salvation through Other-power.

9 The Philosophies of Nishida and Tanabe

PERHAPS the simplest way to approach the question of the difference between the philosophies of Nishida and Tanabe is by way of the criticisms that Tanabe leveled against Nishida's philosophy on numerous occasions and from a variety of perspectives. But while these criticisms are surely a handy tool, the matter is not so simple. For one thing, Tanabe's criticisms contain evident misunderstandings. But even leaving these aside, some question remains, to put it bluntly, whether Tanabe was aiming his critique at what Nishida's philosophy was really trying to say. Indeed it is my impression that a close examination of the points of Nishida's philosophy that Tanabe criticized reveals that Nishida's views often are surprisingly similar to Tanabe's own. In particular, their philosophies share a distinctive and common basis that sets them apart from traditional Western philosophy: absolute nothingness.

Clearly the idea of absolute nothingness originated in the intellectual history of the East, but the fact that it has also been posited as a foundation for philosophical thought represents a new step virtually without counterpart in Western philosophy. In being transplanted to the East, Western philosophy takes an unprecedented change of direction. Moreover, absolute nothingness itself is not a mere idea or mental construct. It is something realized, awakened to in the quest for the truth of life, something encountered at the ground of our Existenz. Accordingly, a philosophy based on absolute nothingness entails a change in the nature of philosophy itself. The very nature of philosophical thought qua thought changes. On this basic point, then, the philosophies of Nishida and Tanabe seem to stand on common ground. For all the differences of terminology and logical system that separated them, when one looks closely at the core of what each was trying to say, the gap that may at first have looked like a vast chasm gradually narrows and in many instances even seems to have been bridged by identical views. Again, this apparent convergence may be a function of a common underlying foundation.

Nevertheless, it cannot be without good reason that Tanabe has subjected Nishida's philosophy to repeated criticisms and vigorously argued for basic differences between their respective philosophies. Regardless of whether his criticisms always take into full account the true intention of Nishida's philosophy and whether he has in each case properly understood Nishida, there must be some sort of philosophical explanation behind his criticisms as a whole, and this is our main concern. To be sure, the thought of both men made great strides and underwent considerable transformations after Tanabe first published his article "Looking to Professor Nishida's Teaching,"[1] which criticized the standpoint of Nishida's book *The Self-Conscious System of the Universal*. Still, the range of criticisms Tanabe has leveled against Nishida's philosophy in the meantime remain substantially consistent in their intention.

The key objection Tanabe raised in his initial article concerns the "place [*basho*] of absolute nothingness" that Nishida posited as the foundation of his self-conscious system of the universal. For Nishida, the place of absolute nothingness is taken as the locus out of which self-awareness emerges. If self-awareness is said to consist in the self's determination of itself *in itself*, then self-awareness becomes transparent in the act of the self's annulment of itself and culminates in a self-awareness of absolute nothingness. It is as *located in* this place of absolute nothingness that the self moves and has its being.

Nishida's position further implies that all things that move and have being annul themselves and come to be seen as shadows reflected within the self. Behind it all, a kind of seeing takes place with no agent doing the seeing. The realization of this absolute

---

1. The article was published in *Philosophical Studies* (see above, 39, n. 1) in 1930. The Japanese title, 西田先生の教を仰ぐ, contains a double entendre so that the "looking to" carries both a sense of respect and a sense of questioning.

nothingness is a religious experience and also the foundation for a philosophy that rests on a position of seeing-without-seeing. Philosophy becomes a standpoint wherein acting is seeing.

Tanabe contends that to begin from a religious experience, the self-awareness of absolute nothingness, and then set up the locus of absolute nothingness as the fundamental principle of a philosophical system, is to assume an unrestricted totality as a simple given from which all sorts of universals emerge as lower realms of determination. Such philosophy cannot avoid the charge of emanationism. Moreover, to identify acting with seeing is to land oneself in a position of "contemplative resignation" where "raw actuality and conduct"[2] are all turned into shadow-being.

For Tanabe, the root problem behind Nishida's notion of the place of absolute nothingness lay in the conflation of the standpoints of religion and philosophy. Accordingly, Tanabe's critique focused on the important but difficult question of the relationship between religion and philosophy as they bear on the issue of absolute nothingness. In the aforementioned article he notes that whereas the self-awareness of absolute nothingness is inherently transhistorical as a religious experience, as a philosophical principle it is a differential element that appears relative to the working of historical reality at each step of the way. Through it historical and relative philosophical self-reflection becomes a dialectical process involving self-negation. In his view,

> The transhistorical that is presumed to be the foundation of the historical is actually one differential involved in the direction that things are taking in history. It is simply the Idea[3] forever being sought in the latter.[4]

For Nishida, in contrast, transhistorical is viewed as "an integral whole rather than simply as an infinitesimal orientation. . . . It is posited as the *principium* of a system by means of which it orders

---

2. The phrase is Nishida's.

3. Nishitani uses the German word *Idee* here to draw attention to its Platonic use. The same effect is had by capitalizing the English word in these cases.

4. *Collected Works of Tanabe Hajime* (hereafter, CWT) 田辺元全集 (Tokyo, 1963–64), 4:311.

164 / NISHIDA'S THOUGHT

and systematizes what is historical and relative."[5] For Tanabe, this amounts to turning philosophy into religion and hence abrogating its unique standpoint. Therein lies the basic point of Tanabe's criticism.

This "basic suspicion" gave rise in turn to further doubts, among them a question about the irrationality inherent in history. In Tanabe's view, actual historical beings cannot express fully the religious meaning of an interior life based on seeing in terms of absolute nothingness. The irrationalities of history become intelligible only through a principle of self-negation that is both located within self-awareness and opposed to it. Historical beings can be seen only in action or at work. To see them in this light is to see them in terms of absolute nothingness and yet to see them as welling up from a source beyond the reach of work or action. Beneath the things of history flows a wellspring deep out of sight of self-awareness. This is the principle of negation, the same dark depths from which work arises. Moreover, since seeing is possible only through acting, seeing in terms of absolute nothingness must of necessity be mediated by seeing things at work in terms of being, which means that seeing remains an Idea sought by means of reflection on that mediation. Conversely, seeing in terms of absolute nothingness is merely an infinitesimal orientation achieved at a standpoint that sees things by making them into being. For "there is never any way to achieve self-awareness except in accord with noetically conditioned contents."[6]

Tanabe handily sums up in the following passage:

> The boundless, unfathomable something that underlies irrational historical reality represents a source of activity permanently hidden from view. Seeing is possible only through the mediation of a principle of negation opposed to the self. Religious self-awareness, therefore, conforms to this irrational historical reality and is mediated by the determinations of the historical *noema* but arises when this historically determined standpoint is freely overturned. Further than that it does not go. For this reason religious self-awareness

---

5. Note the use of mathematical terms, *differential* and *infinitesimal*, which appear frequently in Tanabe's writings.
6. CWT 4:317.

must not be set up as the ultimate principle of philosophy in the form of an integral whole that would include history.[7]

This first critique of Nishida contains the principal themes of Tanabe's later thought: a stress on the irrationality of historical entities and on a principle of negation thought to ground this irrationality, a decision to make acting rather than seeing the basis of his standpoint, and an attempt to regard absolute nothingness as a differential principle that comes about merely by conforming to irrational reality and then freely overturning that standpoint.

Behind these ideas, as well as behind his critique of Nishida's philosophy, lies an approach to the notion of absolute nothingness completely different from that found in Nishida. Clearly not everything in the basic standpoint of Tanabe's essay, in his grasp of Nishida's thought, and in the criticisms he levels against it is warranted. In the preface to a later work, *Hegel's Philosophy and Absolute Dialectic*, Tanabe himself admitted that his appreciation of Nishida's philosophy at the time was inadequate.[8] In particular, traces of a Kantian approach colored his view that the self-realization of absolute nothingness is an Idea to be sought. This attempt to interpret the standpoint of action in Kantian fashion was one that Tanabe later abandoned as he drew closer to Nishida's standpoint and came to think of absolute nothingness more in terms of the subjective self-awareness of the self. Still, the distinctive elements mentioned above remained intact, so that every philosophical rapprochement with Nishida's philosophy in Tanabe's later years went hand in hand with an intensification of the confrontation.

Together with the question of an irrationality inherent in history, the problem of evil occasioned a second set of questions for Tanabe. A principle of negation permanently opposed to the seeing agent was taken to be basic to the working agent and even made into a force aimed at negating the worker in its activity. The principle of negation turns out to be will seeking to negate itself, value-opposing will that wills evil, will clinging to the standpoint

---

7. CWT 4:318.

8. The collection of essays was published as a book in 1931 and is included in vol. 3 of Tanabe's *Collected Works*. The passage to which Nishitani is referring appears on pages 79–80.

of "seeing things in terms of being." But how can the self-awareness of absolute nothingness become the place (*basho*) of this kind
of negative will? In his own words, "Is not a principle of value-opposing as self-negation incapable of entering into the system of
awareness of a universal whose ultimate principle is the self-
awareness of absolute nothingness?"[9]

Tanabe raises a third problematic, concerning Nishida's criticisms of phenomenology and Kantian philosophy. Tanabe insists
that Kant's concept of "consciousness in general" is only possible
as something historically conditioned. For Nishida, he contends,
the acting universal becomes consciousness in general insofar as it
reflects a self-awareness of absolute nothingness that sees the content of the self in terms of nothingness. Moreover, the acting self,
as long as it is seen as such, is not yet truly the self that sees by
"making into nothingness." For Tanabe this sort of contradiction
in the acting self points to the depths of irrationality inherent in
history and interposed between the self and the self-awareness of
absolute nothingness. Fundamentally, it points to the presence of
a principle of negation prohibiting the self-awareness of absolute
nothingness from encompassing all things within itself. Thus consciousness in general arises in the reflection of the self-awareness
of absolute nothingness on the acting universal—as Nishida claims
it does—only insofar as a principle of negation at work behind the
acting universal is included within absolute nothingness and insofar as history is made rational. Thus consciousness in general must
be constituted on the basis of historical conditions.

By the same token, when we think in terms of an intelligible
universal contemplating Ideas with consciousness in general in its
conceptual aspect, the transhistorical nature of Ideas only makes
sense as that which continually and differentially rationalizes each
moment of history in accord with history. The intelligible universal cannot escape historical conditioning. But in regarding the
self- awareness of absolute nothingness as an ultimate and all-en-
compassing universal, Nishida's philosophy took the Ideas that reflect this universal as transhistorical in the sense that they simply

---

9. CWT 4:320.

have nothing to do with history, and thus his philosophy overlooks the historical conditioning of Ideas.

The differences between Tanabe's position and Nishida's become most noticeable in this matter of the historical conditioning of consciousness in general and Ideas. Tanabe's standpoint shows the influence of the Marxist thought popular when he was writing. In addition, the attempt to posit a principle of negation at the roots of irrationality of history in order to ground action and to explain its inherent contradictions, and then to offer this principle of negation as a principle of darkness, suggests certain affinities with Schelling's theory of freedom. Tanabe's objections to Nishida's philosophy, as well as the stimulus to begin constructing a system of his own different from that of Nishida, originated in this principle of negation. Curiously, it almost seems as if the principle of negation that thoroughly opposes and rejects the tendency of the self-awareness of absolute nothingness to embrace all things mirrors the image of Tanabe himself desperately struggling to escape the embrace of Nishida's philosophy. In any case, this principle of negation was the starting point that moved him to maintain the centrality of a standpoint of an acting self that "sees by making into being" and to pursue philosophy in accordance with actual historical entities. The same holds true of Tanabe's attempts to understand absolute nothingness as arising differentially with actual events in history and as consisting in the free overturning of the relative standpoint of these actions. His determination to establish the principle of negation is the basis for all these developments.

In erecting his principle of negation, Tanabe was inevitably drawn more and more into a Hegelian framework and through his struggles with Hegel's dialectics was led to a posture of "absolute dialectics." In the process, his initial motivations deepened.

THIS IS NOT the place to go into the story of Tanabe's engagement with Hegel's philosophy during this period.[10] Instead, let us turn

---

10. Readers interested in this question are referred to Kōsaka Masaaki's *The Philosophies of Nishida and Tanabe*, reprinted in vol. 8 of his *Collected Writings* (see above, 22, n. 20) and to the following chapter of the present collection.

at once to a discussion of Tanabe's thought after the unique standpoint he developed in the pages of *Philosophy as Metanoetics*.

In this work absolute nothingness is defined as absolute mediation, and the power of absolute mediation is seen as absolute Other-power. The mediating work of absolute Other-power and the manifestation of absolute nothingness is nothing other than the death-and-resurrection we see in the repentance of relative beings.

That Tanabe's philosophy reverted to a standpoint of absolute Other-power may be seen as a result of something latent in his thought from the start. As we saw in the essay discussed in the previous section, Tanabe maintains a firm footing in our action or praxis as relative beings and considers absolute nothingness to manifest its transcendence only differentially, that is, by effecting a conversion of relative beings through absolute negation and thus offering them an orientation to their action. In that essay it is clear that the integral standpoint that embraces all things through the self-awareness of absolute nothingness does not get beyond the level of an Idea to be sought.

This position recalls his standpoint in an earlier work, *Kant's Teleology*,[11] a standpoint of "self-aware finality" that seeks to advance the view of the power of reflective judgment developed in Kant's third critique. While it would be going too far to claim that Tanabe treats absolute nothingness objectively in this book, nonetheless it retained the sense of something reflected, of something that has reached self-awareness through reflection. For him, the subject remains a relative self who reflects, and where absolute nothingness is brought into awareness as something that backs up the subject like the lining in a jacket. As such, this standpoint differs from one where the self itself is said to be turned inside out. It contrasts with a standpoint where the subject transcendently submerges itself into absolute nothingness to become an "absolute nothingness" sort of subject.

In *Hegel's Philosophy and the Absolute Dialectic* Tanabe moves beyond this early standpoint of reflection to a dialectic, one of whose

---

11. CWT 7:61–65.

elements is absolute nothingness viewed in terms of an absolute-ness similar to that operative in Hegel's absolute knowledge. Absolute dialectics is converted from the speculative standpoint of Hegel to a standpoint of praxis; and Hegel's absolute knowledge is replaced with absolute nothingness while Kant's theory of ethics and Marxism are sublated. Nevertheless, it cannot be said that Tanabe's position is "mediated" by absolute nothingness inasmuch as the self as a relative being is consistently maintained as the subject of moral practice.

As a result, Tanabe was left with two alternative strategies to see his approach through to the end: either the self itself would have to be turned inside out into a self of praxis by directly assuming a standpoint of the subject based on absolute nothingness; or the self would have to be turned in on itself as a relative being so that it could no longer emerge in praxis and action, this despair in turn effecting a conversion that would bear witness to the absolute nothingness that made it possible. The former alternative would mean the thoroughgoing pursuit of an approach of "self-power"; the latter, an orientation towards absolute Other-power.

As remarked earlier, a dialectical conversion through praxis of the relative self and absolute nothingness remains forever a conversion that occurs within the standpoint of practice, which could thus pass through contradiction unscathed. The contradictions are not in fact absolute. Even if the subject of praxis is said to die through absolute negation and come to life again, the ground of the subject is converted to absolute nothingness through a negation of radical evil and through that conversion is preserved. Life through death in the true sense has not yet occurred. There is a sense in which the continuity of the standpoint of praxis and the self-identity of the subject have yet to be left behind. This is not true absolute negation.

True absolute negation implies an impasse at which all praxis is closed off, a Great Death in which the self-identity of the subject breaks down. If one maintains the position that the self can never escape the mode of being of a relative being, and hence that absolute nothingness appears only in accord with such relative being, reaching that impasse is inevitable. The more one advances, the closer one is led to a limit situation in which the self-identity of the subject and the praxis that it grounds (the so-called praxis of self-power) become impossibilities. Meanwhile, absolute nothingness can only emerge in the form of an absolute Other that stands opposed to the self. Absolute nothingness can only take on the qualities of absolute Other-power. If absolute nothingness and the self are then both to be mediated dialectically, this mediation can only take place in a dialectic of paradox. The self whose self-identity has broken down is restored to its self-identity in this Great Death, resurrected as a "self that is not a self" by absolute nothingness as absolute Other-power.

In *Philosophy as Metanoetics* Tanabe tells us that he was confronted with this impasse by the experience of the war, but that he broke through it by voluntarily abandoning himself in "repentance." From there the way was opened for a standpoint of action-faith-witness[12] in which "death-and-resurrection" are bestowed on one by absolute Other-power as absolute nothingness (that is, by a Great Nay-in-Great Compassion).

In this way Tanabe's thought reached the conclusion to which it was clearly predestined by the distinctive motives that guided it from the outset and that provided a basis for his differences from Nishida. The distinguishing features of Tanabe's philosophy referred to above—the resolve to take as its starting coordinates praxis or action and the self of relative being who is the subject of action; the stress on original evil and the irrationality of history (in other words, the radical nature of the principle of negation) as the basis for this resolve; and finally, in consequence of this same resolve, the view that absolute nothingness manifests itself differentially—all these features, if carried through to their conclusion, disclose a tendency towards the action-faith-witness of absolute Other-power.

The idea that absolute Other-power appears with the dialectical nature of the power of an absolute mediation, and that absolute nothingness is taken to exist only in the work of absolute mediation, also belonged to the direction of his thought from early on. Consistent with Tanabe's claim that absolute nothingness is real-

---

12. As explained in that book, action-faith-witness refers to 行信証 , elements that figure in the title and content of Shinran's major work, the *Kyōgyōshinshō*.

ized only differentially in accord with the praxis of the self as relative being, its transcendence is not simply objectified as an *an sich* posited on the "other side," not even when this absolute nothingness has shown its true transcendence as absolute Other-power. If it were, it would cease to be absolute nothingness. It has rather to be conceived as the power that brings the self of self-power to its death-and-resurrection, as something that operates only through the mediation of self-power. It must be something working to bring the praxis of the self-powered self to despair and to restore it to life as the praxis of a "self that is not a self." While this absolute Other-power serves in a mediating capacity, its work as such is mediated through self-power. And the work of Other-power thus mediated through relative self-power carries the relative praxis that has been mediated through absolute Other-power over into a mutual mediation among other relative beings. Conversely, it is only through the mediation of this reciprocal mediation among relatives that the absolute is mediated to each relative being.

The love of God is mediated so as to render God's love of us and our love of God one. This love of God is then mediated by love of neighbor, and conversely the love of neighbor comes about through the mediation of the love of God. Only in the neighbor can one love God. By the same token, love of neighbor is only possible if the self has been broken down through God's love for us.

Absolute mediation means that the activity of mediation circulates in this way throughout the entire network of relationships between absolute and relative, relative and relative, so that nothing is left unmediated. If *ōsō* (going-to) can be taken to represent the mediation of the relative to the absolute, and *gensō* (returning-to)[13] the mediation of relatives among each other, then *gensō* is possible only through *ōsō* and *ōsō* is possible only through *gensō*. The totality of such dynamic connections is made possible by the activity of absolute nothingness, which enables conversion to take place wherever these relationships obtain. This is why Tanabe insists that absolute nothingness does not set itself apart from absolute

---

13. *Ōsō* and *gensō* are terms from Shin Buddhism referring to the pursuit of salvation and the compassionate pursuit of the bodhisattva to save all beings, which Tanabe adopts into his philosophy of absolute mediation.

mediation. In carrying through the view that absolute nothingness appears as absolute negation in the practice of the self as relative being, we must revert to this standpoint of absolute mediation.

NOW HOW does all of this compare with Nishida's philosophy? While Tanabe's philosophy pivots on action or praxis, beginning with the opening section of *An Inquiry into the Good*, Nishida's philosophy revolves around the axis of self-awareness. Self-awareness does not here refer to something merely subjective and inward; it has nothing to do with what we usually call self-consciousness. The notion of self-consciousness is the result of an attempt to reflect on self-awareness by first positing the framework of a conscious self. True self-awareness arises outside the framework of this supposed self, at the very point that this self breaks down.

In *An Inquiry into the Good* self-awareness is treated as pure experience, of which it is said not that there is experience because there is a self, but rather that there is a self because there is experience. In his later years, Nishida came to think of self-awareness as nothing other than the point at which our self becomes the self-expression of the world, as the creative element of a creative world. It is the point at which the world as the self-identity of absolute contradictories determines the world itself, where the world becomes self-expressive and creative. The self shapes the world through its work, but the world is such that the very self that works to give it shape is itself formed out of the world. The world is a world of infinite creative individuals, a world of one-in-many and many-in-one.

In the advance of the "one" to self-negation, countless independently coexisting individuals emerge; in this sense the world is "spatial." In the advance of the "many" to self-negation, the life of the individual dissolves moment to moment into the world as a single totality; in this sense the world is "temporal." But the moment at which these many are negated into the whole represents the point at which the single totality is reflected in each of the individuals that make it up. At this moment the world determines itself and reflects itself in the positing — that is to say, in the work — of its multitude of individuals. (Hence, after the manner of a contradictory self-identity, spatial becomes temporal and temporal becomes spatial.)

In each such moment the absolute present determines the present itself. In this kind of present, what will appear in the course of the everlasting future is already included and reflected. And for the absolute present to determine the present itself means that absolute nothingness is determining itself, which is the basis for the world's self-determination. Thus when Nishida says that the self at work is the creative element of the world, the world's reflecting itself to itself, the work of the self takes on the sense of the self-determination of the absolute present and the self-determination of absolute nothingness.

In the work we do to shape the world, the world that has shaped us into shapers of the world is reflected to its profoundest depths. Our work penetrates to the foundations of the world and arises from those foundations. The beginning of the world appears at the point of our work. This is the only way that our work can be a truly creative element in a creative world. To be such a truly creative element of the creative world is to project a reflection; reflecting is creating. In other words, working is seeing and seeing is working. Or again, we may speak with Nishida of acting intuition, of the self as historical body, or of the self as the point at which the world expresses itself.

That an individual becomes creative means that it becomes an entirely independent individual—an individual in the true sense of the word. This in turn implies that the individual is a creative point in a creative world, a point at which the world expresses itself and awakens to itself. To say that in acting intuition an individual is always and everywhere an absolutely independent individual means that the world is creative in that individual.

Put more concretely, the contradictory emergence of one absolutely independent individual alongside others is the world's way of expressing itself as a totality of many individuals. Hence the fact that each of the multitude of individuals remains an individual means that the whole remains a whole, and vice-versa. This is the absolute contradiction of the multitude of individuality and the whole, of the one and the many, and yet it is in this very contradiction that the world is world and individuals are individuals.

The world that is a single totality of many individuals is a world that is a self-identity of absolute contradictories. The individual, as the embodied self-awareness of that world, emerges as a self-identity of absolute contradictories. Where the world determines itself, there also our self comes to self-awareness; where our self comes to self-awareness, where we see in work and work in seeing, there the world determines itself. The world expresses and reflects the world itself, and therein occurs the self-determination of the absolute present, the self-determination of absolute nothingness.

It is already apparent that Tanabe's standpoint, which focuses on action and praxis, and Nishida's standpoint, whose central feature is self-awareness, are extremely close and yet very far apart.

For Tanabe, the self as a relative being working through self-power reaches an impasse that is broken through in repentance. The self of the relative being is thereby negated and its fundamental emptiness[14] brought to light. As such it is also mediated by the Other-power of absolute nothingness (that is, is resurrected and saved). Conversely, absolute Other-power is only self-negating absolute Other-power by being mediated by the self-power of relative beings. In more concrete terms, the reciprocity wherein one relative being and another become negative mediations for one another comes about through the negative mediation of absolute Other-power; meanwhile, absolute Other-power, too, is what it is only in the mediating act of bringing about that reciprocity through its own self-negation.

For Nishida, however, the single totality comes about after the manner of a self-negation of a multiplicity of individuals, while the multiplicity of individuals conversely arises through the self-negation of the single totality. In our self-awareness we represent the point where the world as a self-identity of absolute contradictories comes to self-awareness. Our self-awareness comes about permeated, as it were, by the self-determination of absolute nothingness that forms the bedrock on which the world determines itself. The term *permeated* signifies that while individuals and the whole are indeed separated from each other as absolute contradic-

---

14. Here Nishitani uses the term *kūmusei*, which is not found in the work of Tanabe he is citing.

tories, the fact that an individual is always an individual means that the whole is always the whole, and vice versa. In other words, our self-awareness is permeated by the self-determination of absolute nothingness in a self-identity of absolute contradictories. In this sense we may speak of a "self-determination of the individual *in* the self-determination of the world, a self-determination of the world *in* the self-determination of the individual."

Now these two standpoints are by and large the same in that they represent a standpoint of a "self that is not a self" turning on the axis of absolute nothingness. In Nishida's philosophy the idea that the self is a creative element, the self-expressive point of a creative world, is such a standpoint. This is also the meaning of the claim that absolute nothingness relates to the self as transcendence-in-immanence and immanence-in-transcendence. And in Tanabe's philosophy, even when it is said that the self is brought to death-and-resurrection through the mediating power of absolute nothingness, absolute nothingness also seems to require this quality of transcendence-in-immanence and immanence-in-transcendence.

Again, in Nishida's philosophy each individual stands absolutely independent of every other and has its own particular world so that each is the perspectival center of the world. At the same time, as the point at which the world expresses itself, these individuals represent multiplicity in an identical world, and to that extent are self-identical in an absolutely contradictory way. Conversely, individuals can be called absolutely independent of each other only when they die the same death and live the same life from the same source of the world.

In Tanabe's philosophy, too, reciprocity between one relative being and another is based on the mediation of absolute nothingness. Of course, it is from this standpoint that Tanabe hands down his critique of Nishida's concept of the self-identity of absolute contradictories. We shall touch on this matter later, but the main point for Tanabe is this: when one relative being and another, as autonomous beings, are mediated by absolute Other-power after the manner of an absolute negation-in-affirmation and thereby enter into a relationship of reciprocity, or when they become fellow travelers in the complete mode of being of *ōsō-in-gensō*, they must maintain their relative autonomy and yet enter into an identical life and death — that is, they must elect the same path of death-and-resurrection. What is more, this death-and-resurrection must contain the sense of self-awareness if one is to speak of "witness."

A distinction has been drawn between two standpoints, the one turning on an axis of action or praxis, the other on an axis of self-awareness. For the one, the "action" of the self that is not a self is not to be separated from its "witness." For the other, self-awareness means that in terms of the "historical body," working is seeing. In short, the two positions look to be virtually the same in that they share the basic standpoint of a self that is not a self, a standpoint that turns on the axis of the transcendence-in-immanence and immanence-in-transcendence of absolute nothingness.

As stated at the outset, when we compare these standpoints to the various directions that philosophy has taken, the similarities between the two are all the more striking. Still, even a cursory reading of their respective works convinces one that there are indeed fundamental differences between the philosophies of Nishida and Tanabe. The question is where we are to locate them.

THE PHILOSOPHIES of Nishida and Tanabe share the standpoint of a self that is not a self whose axial center is an absolute nothingness that relates to the self after the manner of a transcendence-in-immanence and immanence-in-transcendence. A closer look, however, discloses a major divergence in their understanding of the meaning of the "self that is not a self."

To begin with, in the context of Tanabe's idea of metanoetics, the "self" of "self that is not a self" is seen as a self engaged in repentance. Things like seeing, hearing, thinking, and self-awareness always refer to individual acts, to common, ordinary things that individuals do. Repentance does not. The sinfulness that requires repentance and the "ought" that urges to repentance are common and ordinary, but only in the particular individual is repentance actually carried out. Self-awareness, in contrast, is given to everyone, although usually it is given to a self confined to the framework of discriminating consciousness. When this framework is broken through, then, self-awareness shows its original countenance. Furthermore, what is thereby disclosed is not different from the self-awareness that was there from the start. It is not that the self becomes something else, but only that it has become aware of a different mode of being. Ontically, so to speak, it remains the same even though its ontological ground has shifted.

Given the tendency to take *ontological* as referring to a logic of the grammatical subject and *ground* as referring to a substratum, there is some danger that these terms may lead us astray from Nishida's philosophy, which is based on a *basho*-logic of the grammatical predicate. But the point is simply this: the point at which the world determines itself is the point at which the self becomes the self-awareness of the world. In this context talk of a self that is *not a self* is meant to point to an ontological surpassing of the ordinarily given self. But since there is no ontic change, it remains a *self* that is not a self. Furthermore, inasmuch as self-awareness is a fact given to all, its ontologically detached mode of being is also a natural orientation given to everyone. Of course, whether one chooses to take that course is a matter of free choice. We must speak here of a necessity of freedom and a freedom of necessity.

In any event, to any individual who takes hold of the fact of self-awareness and probes deeply into it, breaking through the discriminating self, the original countenance of self-awareness is unveiled as an originally given fact. This breakthrough of the self is like a disclosure of *Existenz*. In this case any path will do; indeed, the question of whether some particular path (for example, the path of repentance) is required does not even arise. (In Nishida's case, this would probably depend on Zen and the like.) Such things do not belong to philosophy. For philosophy it is enough to exhibit self-awareness and the truth of everything connected to it at the point where the conscious self is broken through, and to have a grasp of the logic behind this disclosure.

Metanoetics presents a completely different case. Repentance cannot be given to everyone. Even if a breakthrough of the self caught in the impasse of self-power is effected, what appears in the breakthrough is not something originally given by nature, but always something being given at that moment as a grace. Hence the self is not allowed to transfer to the place where the self *was* broken through; it may only take a stance at the place where it *is being* broken through, that is, in the action of breaking through. Hence even though mention is made of a self that is not a self, the self has not undergone change in any ontological sense. We cannot speak of the self having gone outside itself, of an "outside" that remains outside and yet becomes an "inside," a self. The only thing permitted the self is that it return within itself, to an inside without an outside. It bears its recognition of the powerlessness and sinfulness of the self bravely to the end, there to encounter the workings of something radically other to the self. No ontological change is involved; the self is the same ignorant mortal it always was. All we can say is that light had been shed on its *avidyā* (darkness of ignorance), that it has become all the more aware of its *avidyā* and at the same time been saved in that *avidyā*. The absolute negation brought about by the encounter with absolute Other-power sets the self absolutely apart from absolute Other-power.

On the one hand, the self is made to realize itself here as an ignorant sinner (*bonpu*) without possibility of redemption. The meaning of absolute negation rests, as it were, merely in the self of the ignorant sinner in whom there is no light. On the other hand, the meaning of absolute negation consists in compassion, in the original vow of Amida Buddha. This is what Tanabe speaks of as "Great Nay-in-Great Compassion" in which there is no darkness. In addition, the activity that absolutely divides light and darkness in this way is at the same time the working of an absolute mediation. It is an activity that saves ignorant sinners just as they are in their ignorance and sin. This is why Tanabe says that the "self that is not a self" always refers to the ignorant sinner.

Hence the conversion implied in the term *no-self* is not to be understood in an ontological sense but only in the sense of a value judgment, that is, as a conversion in which the powerlessness and sinfulness of the self, just as they are, form the core of the Buddha's work of salvation. Such conversion is oriented to prevent the self from being other than it is either ontically or ontologically, to reject any attempt of the self to become different (that is, to transform itself through self-power). Paradoxically, the attempt to reject the ontological enlightenment of the self by holding fast to a common, ordinary, ontic self is the only ontological self-enlightenment possible. The self's original countenance as an ignorant sinner is none other than this: it is an unredeemably ignorant mortal.

In sum, in Nishida's philosophy the self of discriminating consciousness is a delusion, and it is in breaking through that self that the true fact of self-awareness appears. It is precisely in philosophy that we find the tradition of thinking of the self in terms of a subject-object dichotomy, forgetting that the self is in the world and that our very consciousness and thought are facts that belong in the world. An inverted notion of the self as something standing outside the world has crept of its own accord into the way we think of the self. We need to turn back and recover the sense that knowing the self is a fact in the world and in that light to probe more deeply into self-awareness. Only then will we see that there can be no self-awareness apart from the world's creative expression of itself. In this sense the "self that is not a self" can be called the original self. In brief, the self of discriminating consciousness is an empty delusion and the self that breaks through it is true fact.

Things are different in Tanabe's philosophy, where it is precisely this inverted, deluded self, the self of *avidyā* and passion, that must be the original face. The stubborn, ineluctable fact remains: delusion is delusion. Nothing we know about it can change that. Indeed efforts to break free of it, or even the self-awareness of having left it and come to know the truth (what Tanabe calls the standpoint of the "saints and sages"), are said to be untruth and delusion. The emptiness of the self is illumined by the light of absolute Other-power, and the self is redeemed in this very emptiness. The "self that is not a self" is nothing other, then, than this emptiness of the self in which the double meaning of death-and-resurrection is fused into one.

There is, of course, another side to the idea of the self that is not a self in Tanabe's thought, and that is the sense in which the self that has gone through death-and-resurrection empties itself for the sake of others in the form of good deeds.[15] As we remarked earlier, this element of *gensō* is inseparable from that of *ōsō* in

---

15. The term is a Buddhist one and plays a great role in the spirituality of Pure Land Buddhism.

which the self dies and is resurrected through the working of absolute Other-power. They are two sides of the same coin. There are problems here to which we shall return later in this essay.

The differences just noted oblige us to take a step further and conclude that Nishida and Tanabe have fundamentally different conceptions of philosophic inquiry. Nishida's philosophy follows traditional lines as they have come down from antiquity. His approach labors to resolve a variety of epistemological and metaphysical issues that arise from the ordinary standpoint of the self, and in the process to break through the ordinary position of the conscious self and then consider various problems from the vantage point of that breakthrough.

As mentioned earlier, however, for Nishida, traditional philosophy had not broken away from the standpoint of the conscious ego with its opposition of subject and object, but continued to use the terms of an object-logic (that is, a logic of the grammatical subject), while his own thinking begins from a standpoint of radical realism that surpasses the tradition entirely to establish itself on a logic of place (that is, a logic of the grammatical predicate). His is a standpoint in which one breaks through the conscious ego and thinks about facts by becoming the facts one is thinking about. It does not merely philosophize, as has been done in the past, but *becomes* philosophizing. It practices philosophy from the standpoint of which Nishida says, "Becoming a thing, think it; becoming a thing, do it."

The standpoint of Tanabe's philosophy is diametrically opposed to Nishida's. Paradoxically, it denies the standpoint of traditional philosophizing, not to mention the standpoint of practicing philosophy by becoming it, as belonging to "the saints and sages." His is a standpoint of "absolute critique" which begins from the impasse that philosophy seen as a way of wisdom ends up in, and leads to a metanoesis of the ignorant mortal that ruptures the standpoint of reason that has served as the basis for all philosophy up to now. From there he turns back to criticize the standpoint of philosophizing reason (including the reason that criticizes reason itself). All traditional standpoints are criticized that do not lead, as they should, to the death-and-resurrection of the ignorant mortal. Two opposite poles are brought together here: one puts oneself at the lowest rung as a mere ignorant mortal, and one is brought to live by absolutely transcendent Other-power. In this light, all ordinary philosophy appears as a form of blind adherence to self-power. Hence his standpoint of a "philosophy that is not a philosophy," entirely different from the philosophy of the "sages."

In the foregoing, I have mentioned a few basic points on which the philosophies of Nishida and Tanabe seem to differ. In what remains I should like to take up a couple of questions related to their thought that this comparison has brought to the surface.

ONE MATTER should be touched on briefly first. Among the criticisms Tanabe has leveled against Nishida's philosophy not a few appear, on the surface, to be clearly based on misunderstanding. This includes critiques of even some of Nishida's most fundamental ideas. For example, Tanabe interprets the notion of acting intuition as an action performed for the sake of intuition, as an intuition of nothingness, or as an intuition embracing the whole of self-identity. And then he says that we must not assume such a standpoint of contemplation to regard absolute nothingness as an object of observation. Even the cursory account given above should suggest that acting intuition is nothing of the sort. Nishida's acting intuition is not like the intellectual intuition of Plotinus but surpasses it as a self-determination of the absolute present, a self-determination of absolute nothingness (inseparable from the self-determination of the individual), and also as nothing other than all our ordinary thinking and acting. In this sense it is even referred to as "eschatological ordinariness."

Even everyday things like eating and dressing originally include an element of no-mind. In no-mind the world reflects the world itself. Each and every work we perform in the present pierces through to the beginning of all time in the absolute present, to the wellsprings of the world, and is wrought from there. To think of no-mind as something removed from us is to mistake the conscious self for the true self and then try to understand no-mind by reflecting on it. It is rather we who are removed from no-mind and not the other way around. But even if we distance ourselves from no-mind it does not leave us. It is closer to us than we are to ourselves (that is, to our conscious selves); it is originally what we ourselves are (and obviously not just the unconscious). As Nansen,[16] for whom "ordinary mind is the truth," says:

> If you turn to the Way and try to follow it, it turns its back on you.
> The Way does not belong to knowing, neither does it belong to not-knowing.

In other words, the very attempt to know things by reflecting on them obstructs our knowing them, but it is not therefore mere ignorance that is being recommended. It means that a simple act like sweeping the floor is itself a way of seeing. It matters not who is doing it. It is always a question of "following things mindlessly." If it were not, hardly any sweeping would get done. But in normal circumstances it is only "we" who are at a distance from what is going on. We are always our original, no-mind self, but in most cases do not become the original self that we are. The point is that to work is at once to see and to see is to work, which is what Nishida meant by acting intuition. It is not a matter of acting for the sake of intuition, or of intuiting nothingness.

Tanabe also criticizes the "self-identity of absolute contradictories" because it supposes that talk of self-identity rests on the possibility of its being intuited. From this it follows, for instance, that "absolute contradictories" can be reduced to a self-identity, thus dissolving the contradiction; that even the state of dialectical contradiction is in fact turned into a logic of abstract identity; and that everything is reduced to a contemplative form of mysticism in which the absolute and the relative are unified through identification. To judge from some of Tanabe's other criticisms leveled from a variety of angles, it seems that he interpreted the self-identity of absolute contradictories as the content of a contemplative intuition. With an idea of identity as a sort of substratal ground, Tanabe seems also to have understood the notion of *basho* as a kind of substratum, in the process twisting Nishida's logic of the grammatical

---

16. Nan-ch'üan P'u-yüan (748–834), a disciple of Ma-tsu who founded his own school. He appears in the famous story in case 7 of the *Mumonkan*, "Nansen Kills a Cat."

predicate into a logic of the grammatical subject. The stress that Nishida put on the groundlessness of the creativity of the infinitely creative world as a self-identity of absolute contradictories, as a one-in-many and a many-in-one, is missing. Precisely because it is creative without an underlying ground, the self-identity of absolute contradictories represents not a logic of identity but its very opposite.

Acting intuition is thus the virtual dialectical opposite of the standpoint of knowing intuition found in Plotinus. For instance, when we say that there is an absolute discontinuity between earlier ideas in consciousness and later ones even though they are ideas of one and the same self, this means that the unifying self that is posited here as a substratum is no more than an *idea* of a conscious self. Even when we consider absolute nothingness the ground of the self, to the extent that we are thinking in terms of a substratum it is merely an extension of the conscious self. Clearly this is a logic of identity, but when earlier and later thoughts occur as self-determinations of the absolute present in such a way that "with no place to dwell, this mind is born," that a continuity arises between these discontinuities in the form of a self-awareness of an identical self, this self is not a substratum and its self-identity of absolute contradictories is not the identity of which the logic of identity speaks. For it is a self-identity whose identity turns away as soon as we try to reflect on it. When this mind is born without any place to dwell, groundlessly, there is no intuited identity.

The self-identity of contradictories that comes to awareness in acting intuition is altogether different. In broader terms, it is the same with the world as a self-identity of absolute contradictories. Self-awareness is said to be the self's knowing the self in the self. This is already part of the standpoint of the "self that is not a self." This is why it is said that self-awareness means that the self becomes the point at which the world comes to self-expression. This relationship is one I consider impossible from a standpoint of the logic of identity.

In this connection, Tanabe's criticisms of Nishida's ideas of "expression" and "formation" also seem to contain misunderstandings. But I will not enter further into these matters here.

ALTHOUGH Tanabe's criticisms seem to entail misunderstandings, does not their appearance point to unresolved problems in Nishida's thought?

Nishida's philosophy begins from a standpoint of acting intuition based on the collapse of the standpoint of the conscious (or reflective) ego that informs our ordinary notions of the "self." It is a standpoint of radical realism according to which we think a thing by becoming it and do a thing by becoming it. The reflective self represents a standpoint of the opposition of subject and object. The scars of such a standpoint survive in one form or another in traditional philosophies. This is the case, for example, in Kantianism, where objects are the constructs of transcendental consciousness, but also in materialism. For the idea of a conscious self thinking about material things continues to work in the shadows of a standpoint where matter replaces consciousness as the elemental principle. Or again, a standpoint that thinks in terms of an absolute entity like God or the One transcending the relativity of subject and object, insofar as it sets the absolute "over there" and continues to see it objectively or in terms of a substratum, remains in the shadow of this seeing self.

It had not occurred to philosophy in the past to transcend the opposition of subject and object by taking the opposite approach. But Nishida's philosophy probed deeply into the insight that any standpoint based on objective logic (that is, a logic of the grammatical subject) can never shake free of the shackles of the reflective self even when it has advanced beyond the reflective self, and from there set up a logic of place (that is, a logic of the grammatical predicate). In so doing he inaugurated a new phase in philosophy that completely surpassed the standpoint of the conscious self that had previously held sway, overtly or covertly.

Looked at the other way around, did this insight not at the same time create a problem for Nishida's philosophy? For the standpoint of the conscious self, however inverted and removed from the truth it may be, is still one that the ordinary person falls into quite easily—not that people deliberately opt for this standpoint, but that they slide into it unwittingly and hence have a hard time extricating themselves from it. That even those philosophies that have disowned this standpoint have not been able entirely to escape its confines bears witness to just how difficult that task is. Bergson notes how deeply ingrained in us is the tendency to spatialize time and represent it as a straight line. The same is true of our natural tendency to think of things in terms of the conscious self. One of the great facts of life is that we usually position ourselves on a standpoint of "discrimination," far from the true facts of things. The same holds true of our penchant for delusion.

Nishida, however, seems not to take sufficient account of this fact philosophically or to find for it an appropriate place in his overall system. This fact does figure in Hegel's thought where, as is well known, discriminating understanding is surpassed by the loftier standpoint of speculative reason and yet allocated the role of a negative moment in the overall dialectic of his philosophy. This is an outstanding feature of his thought and one that is lacking in many other systems. I do not find its equivalent in Nishida's philosophy either. To be sure, he speaks of the world as containing radical evil and introduces the profound notion of a "logic of inverse correlation" as a religious world view. But the problem of the conscious self is not the same as the problem of evil.

In doing away with the standpoint that thinks of things in terms of a conscious self in order to assume a position of thinking a thing by becoming it and doing something by becoming it, Nishida's philosophy emerges into the world of truly factual fact, but in the process he seems to have lost sight of the fact that ordinary people do not think of things by becoming them, and hence he does not provide an answer to the questions of precisely how this kind of inversion takes place and what its essential features are. From the standpoint of one who has exerted unparalleled efforts to close in on the true form of facts, things like the conscious self and its inversion seem to need breaking down completely but are not faced philosophically. A standpoint that requires one not to stop at philosophizing but to *become* one's philosophizing seems to leave no other choice.

In this regard another problem arises. Nishida does little philosophizing about philosophizing itself. If the standpoint of the conscious self were seen not only as something to be broken through but as a problem in itself, the meaning of the philosophy that makes this breakthrough would become equally problematic.

For religion it is enough simply to break through the conscious self. Religious people do not concern themselves with what religion is (those who do are the philosophers of religion). For philosophy, philosophizing itself can become a matter to philosophize about. But for all its concern with problems of religion, morality, science, and so forth, what significance practicing philosophy has for these problems and what place it holds among them did not seem to be questions that Nishida put systematically. This lacuna appears to be connected to the fact that Nishida did not treat the standpoint of the conscious self as a problem in its own right but philosophized from a position where the conscious self had already been broken through, where one engaged in philosophy by identifying with philosophizing. I have the impression that this approach of Nishida's hindered him from philosophizing about philosophy itself. This is particularly apparent in the fact that in taking up the religious worldview philosophically by way of his logic of place, he made no mention of the momentous question of the relationship between religion and philosophy.

As noted earlier, Tanabe's 1930 article "Looking to Professor Nishida's Teachings" did address this question. Its keynote was that the standpoint of the self-awareness of absolute nothingness is a religious standpoint and that to make it a philosophical one is to conflate philosophy with religion, thus endangering philosophy, which must never depart from reflection.

Later Tanabe himself spoke of the self-awareness of absolute nothingness, always insisting that this self-awareness be understood not as the intuition of an integral whole but as a differential manifestation. In seeing philosophy as metanoetics, absolute nothingness becomes absolute Other-power, and the general standpoint of philosophy is abandoned as the standpoint of those who displace the absolute by self-power and do not awaken to the ignorance of the self. This finally leads Tanabe to his "philosophy that is not a philosophy" with its standpoint of death-and-resurrection based on absolute Other-power. In it he saw the death and rebirth of philosophy itself and aimed his absolute critique at philosophy in general for not having gone through this process.

Clearly Tanabe's focus here is on unearthing the standpoint of the ordinary conscious self and becoming aware of it as our "mortal ignorance." At the same time, the standpoint of philosophizing has been brought to the point of reflecting on itself in the radical form of the demand to be resurrected by first dying. The dialectical opposition to the standpoint of becoming one's philosophizing is patent. Tanabe's philosophy makes a strength of what is in fact the Achilles' heel of Nishida's philosophy.

To repeat: I see no way around the conclusion that the criticisms Tanabe directed at Nishida's notions of the "self-identity of absolute contradictories" and "acting intuition" are, if taken literally, based on misunderstandings. The closer we look, however, the more it appears that his criticisms hit on problems inherent in Nishida's philosophy. Still, in spite of the problematic areas that Tanabe pointed out, Nishida's philosophy also contains the disclosure of a great truth that refuses to be undermined by these criticisms. This may become clearer if we air some doubts concerning the standpoint of Tanabe's philosophy.

THE CLAIM that in Tanabe's philosophy the standpoint of a "philosophy that is not a philosophy" works through metanoia or repentance to establish for itself a logic of absolute critique, raises some questions. Here I should like to take up the one that I consider the most basic: the matter of the relationship between metanoia and philosophy as absolute critique.

Metanoia cannot be separated from the standpoint of the ordinary person who is brought to repentance. The foundation of metanoetics appears to consist in this: the rupture between the self that has been led to an awareness of its own ignorance and absolute Other-power at once turns into a mediation, so that the self that has been led to resurrection through death performs acts of requital for other relative beings and seeks the way of repentance with them. The standpoint of the "philosophy that is not a philosophy" also appears to be based on the faith-action-witness of the "self that is not a self," which has been led to resurrection through death in absolute obedience to absolute Other-power. Absolute critique, then, would appear to represent a standpoint of reason that is not a reason, a kind of transrational rationality once the standpoint of reason and other standpoints like it on which general self-power philosophies stand have fallen to pieces in the self and voluntarily let go to be resurrected through the working of absolute nothingness as absolute Other-power. Strictly speaking, this death-and-resurrection of reason is a death-and-resurrection of reason in the self, and in this sense absolute critique must be an absolute critique of the self by the "self that is not a self."

In philosophy there is no avoiding criticism of the ideas of others. Tanabe himself undertook critiques of Kant and other thinkers who had influenced him greatly. Such criticism of others contradicts the view that repentance or metanoia is to be directed exclusively against itself. The contradiction is removed only by exposing all such critique as really self-criticism, that is, a critique against a standpoint one had adopted oneself under the influence of others. The critique is then carried out in the self where, as it were, "self and other are not two." Yet even this reading of Tanabe's criticisms leaves some questions unanswered.

At bottom, absolute critique must be a standpoint of absolute infallibility. As the action-faith-witness of absolute nothingness (or absolute Other-power), absolute critique must at least include a claim of absolute infallibility. Since the standpoint (that is not a standpoint) of the self "that is not a self" is mediated by absolute Other-power in the form of a death-and-resurrection, this action-faith-witness precludes the possibility of error. It is a standpoint of decisive faith, nonretrogressive action, and self-evident witness.[17] This claim derives from the religiosity that is the foundation of absolute critique, whose absolute infallibility lies in the mediating power of absolute Other-power to which the self as ignorant mortal is awakened in salvation. But insofar as absolute critique is metanoia and self-criticism, it requires their incessant repetition. This is why Tanabe insists that the conversion of absolute nothingness is forever differential. The standpoint of the self that is not a self displays a constant tension despite the decisiveness of faith — or perhaps we should rather say because of it. Between the self that

---

17. These terms are drawn from Shinran, in obvious deference to the framework within which Tanabe composed his *Philosophy as Metanoetics*.

is *not a self* and the *self* that is not a self there obtains an active unity of absolute contradictories that is nothing other than self-critique.

Now when this standpoint of the "self that is not a self" ventures outside the realm of religion to set itself up as a "philosophy that is not a philosophy," problems naturally arise. On the one hand absolute critique may be seen as a self-critique, but on the other, it cannot, as philosophy, avoid criticizing others. The standpoint of absolute critique is itself a criticism of standpoints other than its own. The critique may be directed at a point where self and other are no longer two, but this does not eliminate its meaning as a confrontation with the other. As a philosophical position, it cannot but entail elements hard to reconcile with metanoia. As self-critique, absolute critique consists in the active unifying of a tension or contradiction within the self that is not a self. As a critique of others, it cannot avoid tension with them. Even a philosophy based on the self that is not a self must take a position as a self in relation to others if it is to criticize them. In so doing it carries something of the same meaning as, for example, Tanabe's philosophical confrontation with Kant, where the self can only set aside the tension of self-criticism that it carries within itself to embrace the tension with the other. Does this not entail something not covered by (or retreating from) the standpoint of metanoia?

Tanabe sets up an opposition between his philosophical standpoint of the ignorant mortal and the philosophy of the "saints and sages." The latter, he says, is too far beyond his reach for him to do more than admire it from a distance. Here we see a pure expression of metanoetics. Elsewhere, however, he remarks that the philosophy of the sage belongs to an *an-sich* and *ōsō* mode of being and thus fails to measure up to the philosophy of metanoetics, a judgment whose logical justification he pursues at great length. As a critique leveled from a philosophical position, this is all very much in order. But he goes on to a standpoint of dialectical wisdom that theoretically refutes the logic of the sage as well, which is something qualitatively different from the standpoint of the ignorant fool engaged in metanoia.

It is of course possible to interpret this knowledge as a grace bestowed on the ignorant mortal together with death-and-resurrection. But even though this knowledge is a faith-witness of absolute Other-power, its influence does not necessarily carry over to the various philosophical theories that Tanabe constructs on the basis of this knowledge. These are rather his own theories, set up by way of the self-power of "Other-power-*in*-self-power." He is driven to this theoretical position by the aforementioned critique of the other.

Following the course of self-criticism, both absolute critique and the transcendence of the rational insight of the sage revert to the action-faith-witness of the penitent ignorant mortal. The transcendence of rational insight occurs through religious action-faith. But this means that the transcendence of rational insight that takes place through a dialectic, as we saw in the critique of other philosophies—in other words, the standpoint of a philosophy that is not a philosophy—has no direct connection with the transcendence of rational insight that takes place through the action-faith of the ignorant mortal. To engage in dialectics seems to me qualitatively different from engaging in the action-faith of metanoia. When all is said and done, I am left with the impression that the connection between the metanoetics and philosophy is not sufficiently clear.

Doubts of this nature do not apply to theology and religious doctrine. Christian theology, for example, can take a position of action-faith and yet engage in the dialectics of apologetics. Unlike philosophy, it has its foundations in sacred scriptures. The same applies to Shinran's *Kyōgyōshinshō*, which relies entirely on doctrine. Criticisms against others (like the *kyōsōhanshaku*) are the work of the self that is not a self in the sense that they are absolutely dependent on the sūtras. Because it is not a philosophical standpoint, this apologetic approach[18] to the criticism of others does not chafe against the absolute infallibility inherent in the action-faith-witness, nor is it incoherent with the self-criticism of metanoia.

(Repentance is not presented here as a form of dialectics or apologetics. That Shinran wove a strong thread of repentance into his *Kyōgyōshinshō* and yet did not make this the foundation of an apologetics may be due to his sense of a qualitative rift between the two.)

---

18. The same word is used for *apologetics* and *dialectics*.

In contrast, philosophy represents free inquiry without reliance on sacred texts. In order to take this position, absolute Other-power, too, had to be absolute nothingness. The claim that such free philosophy rests on the standpoint of the self that is not a self means that two normally opposite approaches are possible.

In the one approach, the action-faith-witness of the self that is *not a self*, together with its absolute infallibility and absolutely unobstructed freedom, are taken to represent the philosophical standpoint of *the self*. This amounts to making the philosophy of the self even more absolute than philosophies of self-power do. This approach is diametrically opposed to metanoia.

The other approach is that of a metanoia towards *the self* that believes and yet has no faith, acts and yet regresses, awakens and yet strays into delusion. It is a self-criticism of the delusion of self-power. With this approach, however, there is no way to come to philosophy as an absolute critique that includes a critique of others. The standpoint of philosophy as metanoetics is supposed to sublate these two polar opposites through negation. Still further difficulties remain regarding just how this union of the standpoints of metanoia and philosophy is supposed to take place.

In the foregoing I have discussed what I take to be a fundamental problem in the philosophies of Nishida and Tanabe, or at least my own failure to understand. It is my fondest hope that others will take up the further study of these two great systems of philosophical thought produced in our country.

10 Questioning Nishida: Reflections on Three Critics

FUNDAMENTAL IDEAS OF NISHIDA'S THOUGHT

MY AIM in this short essay is to take up two or three of the more cogent criticisms directed against Nishida philosophy and to scrutinize a few questions that can serve as a common forum for Nishida and his critics. By "Nishida philosophy" I mean the current state of his thought,[1] which centers on the notion of the dialectical universal. By way of preparation, it seems best to begin by recalling some of the fundamental ideas behind his thought.

THE SELF-DETERMINATION OF THE WORLD

We begin with what may be the most basic idea in Nishida's philosophy. A comparison with Hegel's idea of the "cunning of reason" should help to remove some of the difficulty surrounding it.

Hegel's notion is well known: when a great personality in history fixes on a particular goal and pursues it with passion, the will of the World Spirit is at work within that passion. This will—the creative dynamism of world history—constitutes the basic stuff (*das Substantielle*) of the particular goal that is being pursued. When one devotes one's entire life to the pursuit of a particular goal, what happens is that the World Reason has taken over one's passions for its own aims, sacrificing the individual in order to actualize itself. As soon as the aim in question is satisfied, the individual falls to the ground like an empty shell left behind by a ripened seed. As Hegel puts it:

---

1. These lines were written in 1936 and thus do not reflect later developments in Nishida's thought.

The special interest of passion is thus inseparable from the active development of a general principle: for it is from the special and determinate and from its negation, that the universal results.[2]

Hegel's approach implies a sense of the world determining itself. In Nishida's terminology, the self-actualization of the World Spirit through the actions of individuals means that the individual's acting *is* the world determining itself. (Later we will come to see the difference between their ideas.)

The principal importance of this way of thinking is that it posits the world as primary and looks at things from there, and in particular that it looks at the individual self in the light of the self-determination of the world. As long as we maintain the primacy of the self rather than the world, we cannot escape mere abstract conceptuality because we have no way to get an adequate grasp of the various kinds of objectivity. Remarking on the difficulty of emancipating ourselves from the primacy of the self, Nishida comments at the start of his preface to *Fundamental Problems of Philosophy II*:

> In my last book, *I and the World*, my standpoint was largely one of looking at the world from the self. As a result, the work failed to give an adequate account of objective determination. Our individual selves are no more than thoughts born of individual determinations of a world that determines itself.[3]

Seeing things from the world — and seeing "the self" from the world — does not mean merely positing the world as a subject matter to be thought about in a purely objective fashion, and from there looking at the self. Neither does it mean leaving self and subjectivity out of the picture. If anything, seeing from the world provides the finest illustration of just how deeply rooted the idea of the primacy of the self is. The moment we look at the world in some merely objective fashion, we assume the attitude of a self that looks at the world by standing outside of it (the standpoint of the intellectual self), and the world is in fact changed into the world

---

2. G. W. F. Hegel, *The Philosophy of History*, trans. J. Sibree (New York, 1944), 32.

3. The work appears in vol. 7 of his *Collected Works*, but this preface has been omitted.

insofar as it is seen by the self. It ceases to be the true world and becomes the visual, notional world — a mere concept. This is why materialism and realism, in the attempt to break free of idealism, fall into what we might call an undercover idealism. It also accounts for the failure of this standpoint to deduce or explain things like self and consciousness. For empirical sciences like physics and economics, the attitude of seeing the world in a merely objective fashion is permissible as part of an overall positivist approach. But for the thoroughly reflective enterprise of philosophy, clinging unreflectively to the seeing self entails a self-contradiction.

If all attempts to view the world as a purely objective matter directly incite a subjective and idealistic viewpoint and collapse into intellectualism, a view of the world as it truly is must embrace both the objective world that forms the subject matter of thought and the self. The world must be simultaneously subjective and objective, simultaneously inside and outside. Nothing less can count as true reality.

Needless to say, in contrast to mere objectivism, Hegel's approach clearly contains the element of the subjectivity of the world. At the same time, his notion of the cunning of reason clearly reduces the autonomy and freedom of the individual to inner necessity. The universal is affirmed through the negation of the individual, a universal will that manipulates the individual and to that extent is something merely transcendent to it. The universal alone predominates in this negation-in-affirmation, and yet at the same time it directly infiltrates the individual will as its "basic stuff." A manipulating will must be immediately immanent to what is being manipulated.

Hegel's dialectic here, therefore, joins together the mere transcendence of the universal and its mere immanence, the former demonstrating its predominance, the latter its purposefulness. The universal will forms the kernel of the individual will, through whose efforts it ripens and eventually realizes itself in the act of negating the individual, casting it aside like a discarded husk. Hegel's idea of the cunning of reason shows the same predominance of purposefulness and the universal that distinguish his philosophy as a whole. Clearly the two go hand in hand. A view that gives the primacy to the world, must, unlike Hegel, be able to bring about the free autonomy of the individual and make the most of it.

THE SELF-DETERMINATION OF THE INDIVIDUAL

Important to the foregoing is Nishida's idea of the self-determination of the individual, according to which the individual is absolutely independent and self-initiating, and possesses an inner unity within itself. Hegel's process dialectic ended up rejecting this view of the individual because in spite of its firm grip on negation, a continuity of the activity of the universal lies spread beneath it. This accounts for the predominance and purposefulness of the universal mentioned above. In any event, only by breaking through the realm of the continuity underpinning the process dialectic and cutting off its internal bonds with the universal can the individual become a truly free and autonomous, self-determining and discontinuous individual.

Conversely, in order for the universal to include such individuals, it cannot remain merely the universal of a process dialectic. It, too, must transcend the process dialectic by moving in a direction opposite to that of the individual, to become a universal of "place" instead of a universal of process. In so doing, the world for the first time becomes a self-determining independent world. In other words, it goes beyond being a mere notion immanent in the individual and loses its meaning as something seen from the self to become the truly objective world spoken of above.

Unlike Hegel's view, which sees transcendence as the obverse of the universal becoming one with the immanent, for Nishida the world is something "located" absolutely in itself. World and individual are entirely independent of each other. They are not thought of as separate from each other, but rather as joined by an inner correlation deeper than the mere union of immanence with transcendence. This correlation of absolutely independent elements is expressed by the copulative *soku*. Thus Nishida speaks of the self-determination of the world *soku* the self-determination of the individual, and vice versa. The same device is used to join the immanent and the transcendent in the formula "immanence-in-transcendence, transcendence-in-immanence."

But this does not yet go far enough. One way or the other, the individual's becoming absolutely independent entails a confrontation with other individuals. I detach myself absolutely from every Thou by possessing an inner unity within myself, just as every Thou comes to an inner unity in detaching itself absolutely from me. I can be an I only confronted with a Thou, and the Thou can be a Thou only confronted with an I. On the one hand, the individual can be an independent, discontinuous individual only as part of a mutually negating, mutually determining relationship between individuals; on the other, the individual forms a connective continuity in its very individuality. This is what Nishida means by the "continuity of discontinuity."

To clarify this relationship further, Nishida has recently introduced the concept of "that one." In becoming a "he" or a "she" — that is, in becoming an objective third person singular, "that one" — both I and Thou can enter into an absolute separation-in-union. This is also what Nishida has in mind by seeing the world as a codetermination of "countless" individuals.

THE CODETERMINATION OF INDIVIDUALS

For Nishida, the codetermination of individuals signals a relationship of one-in-many, many-in-one. Individuals are many in their absolute separation from one another, and in that very separation are united as one. As this one, the world in its self-determination now turns out to be a universal of place (*basho*) that mediates this union. Place is not a mere location that has been added to individuals and their unifying connections from outside. By means of the *soku* relationship described above, the universal is at once completely independent of them and woven into the interiority of their existence and their subsistence. Only by virtue of being located in such a world as this can individuals be absolutely independent and at the same time directly united with each other in the world and through its mediation.

This is the sense in which the codetermination of individuals entails the self-determination of the world. Concretely speaking, a cycle is set up wherein the self-determination of the world is entailed *in* the codetermination of individuals, which in turn is entailed *in* the self-determination of the individual, and vice versa.

This is the concrete significance of the formula, "the one in the many, the many in the one." The self-determination of the world simultaneously entails a principle of the absolute separation of individuals and a principle of the union of individuals. This is why the world is described in Nishida's philosophy as "a universal of the continuity of discontinuity," "a universal of the mediation of no-mediation," and "a dialectical universal." But the picture is still incomplete.

INDIVIDUAL DETERMINATION-IN-UNIVERSAL DETERMINATION,
UNIVERSAL DETERMINATION-IN-INDIVIDUAL DETERMINATION

One way or another, the absolutely independent individual possessed of an inner unity confronts not only other egos, each possessed of its own inner unity, but also the outside, that is, the objective world as a subject matter of thought. But now, the outer that confronts the inner signifies a mere universal that negates individual determination. If the self-determination of the individual is taken as a temporal, linear determination, then the outer world is a spatial, circular one. What is outer affirms itself only by negating what is inner, and conversely what is inner affirms itself only by negating what is outer. This mutually negating codetermination of inner-in-outer, outer-in-inner—or of subjective-in-objective, objective-in-subjective—appears as an acting intuition which sees things in the work of formation whereby the self determines things and things determine the self. Because this is the most concrete regulation of the self-determination of the dialectical universal or dialectical world, the dialectical universal is not simply an external universal that opposes individuals one to another but also a universal that effects a negation-in-affirmation of absolutely independent individuals from the ground up. It is a universal that dialectically unifies and embraces individuals and the "mere universal" that opposes them.

THESE FOUR NOTIONS make up the fundamental concepts that form the system of the dialectical universal. They represent the sort of standpoint from which Nishida's philosophy provides profound insight into a variety of concrete questions. Of its abundant deliverances, no less impressive than its fundamental ideas, nothing further shall be said at this point lest we stray from the topic that concerns us.

THE CRITIQUE OF YAMANOUCHI TOKURYŪ

YAMANOUCHI TOKURYŪ'S criticism of Nishida's philosophy appears in an essay entitled "The Departure of Philosophy," from his work *System and Development*.[4] Let us begin with a résumé of the position from which he lodges his criticisms.

At first, it may seem that a philosophical system and a phenomenology of being are incompatible. The philosophical system functions from the standpoint of the whole, where philosophy's departure and its arrival look to be identical, and hence where individual things are seen in terms of the completed whole that embraces them all. For the phenomenology of being, in contrast, philosophy's departure qua departure already has a meaning of its own; and individual items are not mere instances of a whole but are possessed of their own particular existence that resists definition by the whole. In short, this standpoint views entities in terms of their becoming, not their completion.

Given these differences, the two standpoints need to be reconciled. Hegel's phenomenology of spirit represents an attempt in this direction. Take, for example, the idea that sensation is sensation and perception is perception; each is a unique phenomenon in its own right, and yet both are manifestations of the spirit. Thus system is introduced into the picture. What makes it possible to connect these two standpoints is the process-dialectical character of Hegel's work. Dialectics is a standpoint of system and totality, and at the same time its process aspect can preserve a phenomenological standpoint.

The next step is to ask what enabled this sort of process dialectic to come about. The answer lies in the conversion of that which connects one phenomenon with another from a "medium" into a

---

4. Yamanouchi Tokuryū, who taught philosophy at Kyoto University, was one of the earliest proponents of phenomenology in Japan. He was strongly influenced in his mature work by Husserl and also drew upon the Western mystical tradition.

QUESTIONING NISHIDA / 199

"means." A medium is like a being, whereas a means is less like a being than a device by which being is made to be being. A means is the work of mediating one thing to another so that it can be what it is in the mediation. System and totality are conceived of in terms of this work of mediation and not in terms of something existing outside of things. This is what Hegel means by seeing the Idea in each phenomenon. Thus he employs the notion of "means" to describe each being phenomenologically and at the same time to try to find the system. Therein lies his true dialectic.

On the basis of this reading of Hegel, Yamanouchi offers his threefold critique of Nishida's thought.

First, a standpoint centered on the "medium" is a standpoint of a systematic totality. It sees the world, Yamanouchi says,

> as the place where concrete things are made to exist. . . . Place is something based on a synchronic spatiality, where everything exists in "once and for all" total completion. . . . Philosophers in quest of a system, however finely honed their idea of development and however key the role they give to movement, are still thinking of system in terms of spatial modes of completeness.[5]

Second, the relationship between the "medium" and each of the facts in it,

> comes down in the end to nothing more than a relationship between the universal and its particular instances (*Beispiele*), as Hegel had thought. . . . Being is a play (*Spiel*) in the universal, and things have their being as *Beispiele* of this *Spiel* in the medium of the universal. . . . Things are only located there, without any necessity for them to be there. . . . They are contingent in that they can easily be replaced by other instances.[6]

Third, therefore, the concept of system is better associated with that of means than with that of medium and is to be sought in the development of a process along the lines of the working of mediation (*Vermitteln*).

---

5. 体系と展相 [System and Development] (Tokyo, 1937), 6–7.
6. System and Development, 7.

The concept of system should be rid of any sense of place. . . . "Place" remains spatial, no matter how deeply it can be led into the world of nothingness, . . . and presupposes that all things are brought to perfection once and for all. . . . [But] can dialectics come about at all if we neglect the development of a process? Of course individual phenomena exist in a single medium something like a place. But this does not help us to understand how one phenomenon develops into another so as to constitute present existence together.[7]

In particular, an adequate account of historical fact is impossible.

These three points, in broad outline, make up the brunt of Yamanouchi's critique.

Yamanouchi's characterization of process — in particular, his consideration of the concept of means — contains a fine insight that should not be passed over lightly. We can only hope to hear more about this in the future. But I cannot refrain from voicing a question about his notion of the process dialectic.

We may, I think, distinguish three forms of Hegel's process dialectic: that of the *History of Philosophy*, which is conceived in terms of historical facts; that of the *Phenomenology of Spirit*, which has to do with phenomena of the spirit; and that which is concerned with the concept (*Begriff*), as we find it for example in his *Philosophy of Right*. How the three are related to one another and united is a difficult question. Each unfolds in its own environment and expresses in its own dimension what Yamanouchi calls "a unity of phenomenal facts with a principle of wholeness." If this is so, why the need to turn to the *Phenomenology of Spirit* to treat the process dialectic? This strategy only seems to close off the way for the dialectic to historical facticity on the one hand and to logicality on the other. Indeed, this must be the reason that Hegel himself did not stop at the position he had developed in his *Phenomenology of Spirit*.

One may suppose that, in order to avoid the difficulties involved in the first and third positions, Yamanouchi has deliberately set out to pursue a standpoint of the phenomenology of spirit through to the end, and from there to embrace the two approaches

---

7. *System and Development*, 14–15.

of historicity and logicality, but I find this strategy impossible. Similarly, were we provisionally to eliminate the dialectic of the "concept," we would hardly do away with the difference between historical facts, where "before precedes after temporally," and the "phenomenon of spirit," which is "a single spiritual phenomenon wherein sensation is sensation and perception is perception."

But now Yamanouchi claims that inasmuch as the dialectic is by nature systematic and at the same time involves process, the standpoint of the phenomenal has been preserved. If by phenomenal he understands mental phenomena like sensation, the term would of course take into account the phenomenology of the spirit. The problem is that historicity then becomes inconceivable. If, on the contrary, the phenomenal is meant to point to historical phenomena, then the process dialectic, by virtue of its systematic character, would end up doing away with individual freedom and moral praxis and, by virtue of its character as mere process, would lead to a teleological theory of history. Yet Yamanouchi talks about phenomena like sensation and perception in order to show that the process dialectic is capable of uniting phenomena into a system, whereas he treats historical facts as phenomena and cites Hegel's *Philosophy of History* in order to show that the process dialectic is possessed of actuality.

I am not entirely clear on this view of process dialectic, which Yamanouchi describes as a unity of the standpoints of phenomena and system. When we add the dialectic of the concept, the difficulties only seem to multiply. If, as Yamanouchi himself insists, it does not have to do with "logic but with the phenomenology of spirit,"[8] then this actually points to a limitation in the standpoint of the phenomenology of spirit. Hegel's philosophy itself had already split into two directions, the logical and the historical.

Nishida's philosophy, meantime, comes from a position every bit as comprehensive as Hegel's but aims to sidestep the pitfalls into which Hegel's dialectic lands because of its view of process and continuity. I am afraid the standpoint from which Yamanouchi undertakes his critique of Nishida does not itself stand up to criticism very well.

---

8. *System and Development*, 10.

To continue, however, let us look at each of the criticisms seriatim. In the first place, for Yamanouchi place is "based on a synchronic spatiality, where everything exists in 'once and for all' total completion." To be sure, the dialectics of *basho* or world in Nishida's philosophy includes a kind of synchronic spatiality that may be described in terms like "the self-determination of the eternal now." (I will go into the reasons for this later.) But this synchronic spatiality is always conceived in terms of a *soku* relationship with temporality. The multiplicity of individuals determining themselves in terms of temporality comes about as a self-determination of the world, where the world is imagined as something infinitely creative. This multiplicity is not a simple numerical "many," but a "many-in-one." The multiplicity of individuals comes into being as individuals only when they are joined as one while at the same time remaining absolutely independent of one another—that is, only when they are mediated by the universal of unmediated mediation (or world as place). This is why the world as place maintains its self-identity in the midst of its infinite creative dynamism. It is this self-identity that makes creation possible, and vice versa.

The synchronic spatiality of place that Yamanouchi talks about can be seen as one aspect of "motion-in-stillness, stillness-in-motion." So to include the notion of place does not mean the static wholeness of a "once and for all total completion." Such an obvious misunderstanding derives from viewing place as something fixed and objective, which goes quite against the sense of *basho* in Nishida's philosophy. *Basho* means not simply place, but a self-determining place; and world is not simply an objective object-world, but something that pronounces a negation-in-affirmation at the ground of our self. This is why we can speak of it as temporal-in-spatial and spatial-in-temporal, and why we can say that a "synchronic spatiality" comes about in direct conjunction with the present's determining itself.

Yamanouchi's second objection, that the relationship between place and the things located in it is purely contingent and in no sense necessary, seems also to derive from an interpretation of place as something fixed. It is hard to accuse a standpoint that views the individual as radically self-determining—that is, as free and independent—of treating individuals as mere instances at play within a universal, or as "contingent in the sense that they can readily be replaced by other instances." Indeed, it was because the irreplaceable individual became an issue that the need arose to think in terms of the self-determination of the individual and the world and to bind them together in the *soku* relationship of negation-in-affirmation—in order to avoid the mere immanence of the universal and the damage it would inflict on the uniqueness of the individual.

Obviously such a relationship between world and individual is not a matter of necessity in the Hegelian sense. On the contrary, the *soku* relationship was devised as a way to overcome Hegel's view of continuity between the universal and the particular, which is the source of the relationship of necessity itself. Unlike necessity in the Hegelian sense, the *soku* relationship includes a sense of contingency writ large and at the same time has the quality of opposing mere contingency with a sort of necessity beyond Hegelian necessity.

Finally, we come to the view that forms the basis of Yamanouchi's critique: that the concept of *basho* is part of a wider motivation on Nishida's part to found a philosophical system. At least insofar as the theory of the dialectical universal is concerned, there are ample grounds for questioning this interpretation.

The basic motivation behind the theory of the dialectical universal—as is apparent from the fact that it represents the maturation of a standpoint of fact (*Tat-Sache*)—seems to consist in the desire to conform to the world of the actual and the real (albeit a world where subject and object are intimately related) and to comprehend that world as deeply as possible. In other words, the theory aims to carry out the spirit of what is called "seeing what is right underfoot." Lacking that spirit, the world would be viewed simply from within, in terms of the self, and hence become merely something objective, something intellectual and conceptual. The actual world in which the inner and the outer are joined as correlatives would be inconceivable, as would concrete activity that determines things and is determined by them. Not even Hegel's dialectic is immune from this sort of difficulty. Therefore, to repeat what was stated earlier, does not the process dialectic that Yamanouchi offers as an alternative to Nishida's dialectic of place fail

204 / NISHIDA'S THOUGHT

to persuade insofar as it misses the weighty significance of the idea that place determines itself?

For all my misgivings about Yamanouchi's attempts to substitute a dialectic of process for a dialectic of place, I have to admit that his criticisms touch on a problematic element in Nishida's thought. For Nishida's philosophy has not yet found a way to assess the importance of the process dialectic and make adequate use of it even as it goes beyond it. In other words, the dialectic of place has not reached the point where it can confront the dialectic of process through a negation-in-affirmation.

In his *Basic Problems of Philosophy II*, for example, Nishida notes that the system of the dialectical universal is only a "postulate of intellection" where living things are concerned, but actual reality and not a mere postulate of intellection where the world of acting personal egos is concerned. In the sense that philosophy aims at a fundamental grasp of phenomena by delving into ultimate essences, it follows as a matter of course that a higher stage of reality becomes a postulate of intellection by which to account for lower stages of reality: that we look at the lower from the higher, as it were. We must not forget that in so doing we have driven a wedge between the reality of such lower stages and the postulates of intellection. Looking at things from above tends to reduce this distinction to a quantitative difference between the perfect and the imperfect; but there is a qualitative difference that should not be overlooked. What is seen as an imperfection or a defect can, by an inversion of viewpoint, be seen as an act of resistance, a revolt against perfection.

For example, things like desire and abstract discriminative knowledge lock us into them and keep the whole of the spirit working there, thus preventing us from advancing higher. This amounts to a revolt against the postulates that run through all the stages of spirit, a qualitative counterposition against what is highest. From this perspective, even discriminative knowledge is already a kind of absolute behind the scenes, if only because it postures against absolute knowledge as a nonabsolute. That is to say, it possesses a positive significance and a reality distinctively its own. From the perspective of the higher stage, this same positive meaning may be mere empty illusion, an untruth reflected in an "imperfect way of seeing," but it does not therefore belong any less to the real world than what actually exists there.

The next step would be to say that there is no desire without an attachment to desire, and no discriminative knowledge without attachment to knowing discriminatively. However that may be, in order to see the positive significance of such things in general, we need to conform to *their* standpoint and to follow them in their development to the point where they exhibit the self-contradiction stemming from their nonabsolute absoluteness and then negate themselves.

In short, we need to look up at things from below. In so doing, a standpoint that seems imperfect when viewed from above turns out to be a perspective possessed of a positive significance. This seems to be the significance of Hegel's phenomenology of spirit and its dialectic of process. Meanwhile, a perspective that views things from above must also be able to include the positive significance of the perspective from below. It must be able to affirm through negation. Philosophy must effect a real unity of these two perspectives. Admittedly, Nishida's philosophy in its present state does not give the same weight to the latter perspective as to the former. Therein lies the importance of Yamanouchi's critique and the point of contact between his critique from the dialectic of process and that of Takahashi Satomi, which stresses the peculiar nature of the standpoint of nonabsoluteness and finitude.

THE CRITIQUE OF TAKAHASHI SATOMI

IN THE PREFACE to his *Standpoint of the Whole*, Takahashi introduces the two perspectives that guide his critique of Nishida:

> On the matter of absolute infinity, I find myself dissatisfied with Hegel's absolute spirit, as well as with the Buddhist theory of nothingness and even Nishida's "self-awareness of absolute nothingness" in pursuit of absolute infinity; as for the finite individual, not even Heidegger's way of thinking will do.[9]

9. The passage appears in the *Collected Works of Takahashi Satomi* (hereafter, CWTS) 高橋里美全集(Tokyo, 1973), 7:256. Takahashi Satomi (1868–1964), professor and later

Without straying from the limits of our problematic here, a look at Takahashi's recent essay, "Elemental Potential and Systematic Potential," should give us some idea of the contours of his thinking.

Takahashi's idea of the whole is a kind of high-dimensional static totality and system of all beings that is at once orientated towards development and away from it. A distinction is drawn here between, on the one hand, an elemental potential for development in a given direction and, on the other, a systematic potential that underpins the system in all its facets, a kind of "absolutely unbiased, neutral" locus that embraces development and counterdevelopment and allows them to occur. When these possibilities are "universalized and purified as far as they will go," they generate notions of a "primary elemental potential" and a "primary systematic potential" reminiscent of Aristotle's idea of prime matter. Takahashi describes the two possibilities as "elemental nothingness" and "systematic nothingness" respectively. He goes on:

> Elemental nothingness and systematic nothingness both verge on the identical nothingness (absolute nothingness), each in its own way. Absolute nothingness is the terminus ad quem of all kinds of nothingness, or perhaps we should rather say a Great Nothingness that embraces every form of nothingness.[10]

The reason why potentiality can be seen simultaneously as nothingness may be that while potentiality conforms to being, it also negates being. In other words, within the system of beings as a whole, the very "negative elemental nothingness" that as an elemental potential for development "appears as something that belongs to being, at the same time takes a positive stance against being." Hence, elemental potential and elemental nothingness are two sides of the same coin. What is more, when the system itself is comprehended within absolute nothingness, systematic potential, too, may be regarded as systematic nothingness. This interlacing

---

president of Tōhoku University, began his philosophical career under the influence of Nishida and the neo-Kantians but later broke away to develop a view of absolute nothingness as love that would transcend the dialectics of Hegel, Marx, Nishida, Tanabe, and even Buddhism itself.

10. CWTS 1:232.

of being and nothingness reaches all the way to absolute nothingness. In other words, even in the transition from systematic nothingness to absolute nothingness one can suppose the tension of "a
unifier that embraces the whole" or "a pure One encompassing all
beings from beyond." Accordingly, "the state in which the One loses
itself in acquiring its original self" is seen as absolute nothingness.

While the system of beings as a whole remains a relative
whole, absolute nothingness represents a truly absolute whole. In
an essay published in the same collection, entitled "Freedom and
Being," Takahashi says that in systematic being as "the most concrete all-in-one" (hen kai pan),

> absolute nothingness has to be seen as the outermost limit of a pro-
> cess of self-tension through which the One embraces all things from
> beyond. All things revert to the One, and the One reverts to noth-
> ingness.[11]

Put the other way around, "the aspect of the system's contact with
absolute nothingness" is systematic nothingness, whereas systematic nothingness in all its aspects constitutes the summation of the
manifold of elemental nothingness that conforms to its various developments.

But what are we to make of the transition from systematic
nothingness to elemental nothingness, from the system as a static
totality to a generative being undergoing development? What is
required in such transitions is that from the manifold of elemental
nothingness that makes up systematic nothingness, "one elemental
nothingness is selected." The choice is not itself a standpoint of
systematic nothingness. It is rather as if a kind of downfall occurs
that is described variously as a "fall into sin," a "radical contingency in the radical moment," "basic activity," and an "absolute
arbitrariness or freedom."

In "Freedom and Being" Takahashi suggests that, mediated
by this radical contingency, the "becoming" from "nothingness to
being" mellows into a basic mode of reality, giving us "history" in
the widest sense of the word.[12] Such becoming has nothing to do

---

11. CWTS 1:187.
12. CWTS 1:193.

with the dialectical unity of being and nothingness, as "many, including Hegel," tend to think, nor with any perfect systematic unity of being and nothingness that posits the two as opposite but equal. It is rather the unity of a transition from nothingness to being, a unity that maintains a permanent continuity by being based on process, is permeated by radical contingency, and admits of degrees as something relative. As the radical side of reality, this becoming is "a freedom to become," that is, it is always a relative freedom, not an absolute one. For this reason it is just as incorrect to see only necessity at work in history and moral practice as it is to see only absolute freedom there. This leads Takahashi to speak of the primary systematic potential referred to above (namely, matter) as a "prime-material flux or becoming" on which all natural phenomena and historical events float and which he even goes so far as to call a "cosmic destiny" or a "time of destiny."[13]

This is only a rough and partial résumé of what in the original is an extremely complex analysis, but it provides the standpoint from which Takahashi directs his critique against Nishida's philosophy. We may single out two main points here.

First of all, Takahashi finds Nishida's absolute nothingness insufficiently absolute:

Metaphorically, one might speak of being as the self-determination of nothingness, as does Nishida's dialectics of the individual and nothingness, but the original meaning is just the opposite: that being determines nothingness. . . .

People cannot refrain from asking how the relative emerges from the absolute. . . . But when it comes to absolute nothingness, we must be resolute in disallowing this irrepressible question. Absolute nothingness is not something that defines itself in terms of being. Any nothingness so conceived would not be *absolute* nothingness but only a nothingness confronting being *relatively*. What determines absolute nothingness is rather systematic being, which comprehends relative being and relative nothingness qua being. And there you have truly the greatest stumbling block that philosophy has ever had to contend with.[14]

---

13. CWTS 1:199.
14. CWTS 1:236–37.

Takahashi's second criticism stems from the emphasis he places on finite being. In this light, for example, freedom is not in reality absolute freedom but the freedom of becoming. As such, it is always relative and susceptible of degrees: "The same holds true even for decisions made on the basis of absolute nothingness." To think of absolute freedom as present in moral praxis is an error "arising from the fact that one draws becoming over to the side of potentiality rather than trying to place oneself in the standpoint of becoming itself."[15]

Or again, concerning time, he sees elemental time as a "time of destiny" that is continuous and flowing, as the temporality of becoming. "Thus, time is basically not a 'dialectical unity of being and nothingness.' "[16] In this sense time is merely the temporal form that volitional decisions take in special situations.

> It is not that we die and resurrect in each instant, but that we *become* at each instant. . . . If we were forever dying and resurrecting, there would be no particular need for us to discuss life and death as such momentous matters.[17]

On the subject of self-awareness, he writes:

> One cannot think of it as a flash of lightning that leads to a sort of "self-in-other, other-in-self." The process of human concrete self-awareness that occurs in us humans begins by thinking about the other and then flips around to think about the self. . . . In their opposition, self and other are not immediately identical. When we see the other, we have entered into the other to some degree oblivious of ourselves.[18]

This is why concrete self-awareness takes place mainly "from other to self and from self to other, not discontinuously but continuously, and at the fringes."[19]

---

15. CWTS 1:194.

16. This and the following quotations are from an essay entitled "The Finitude of Human Existence as the Foundational Concept to a View of the Human." CWTS 5:112.

17. CWTS 5:112–13.

18. CWTS 5:114.

19. CWTS 5:115.

His criticism concerning the first point about absolute nothingness is contained in toto in the sentence already quoted above:

Absolute nothingness is not something that defines itself in terms of being. Any nothingness so conceived would not be *absolute* nothingness but finally only a nothingness confronting being *relatively*. What determines absolute nothingness is rather systematic being, which comprehends relative and nothingness qua being.

I question whether this characterization of absolute nothingness as "defining itself in terms of being" can do justice to what Nishida calls the dialectical universal or universal of nothingness. Judging from this passage, it seems to me that Takahashi begins by positing a universal of nothingness by itself, apart from acting individuals (and thus again, as something both fixed and representational as well as intellectual and idealistic), and then goes on to conceive of beings as arising out of the self-determination of this universal in ongoing emanation. If this were what Nishida were saying, it would amount to the very question that Takahashi has correctly rejected: "How does the relative emerge from the absolute?" Elsewhere he portrays Nishida's philosophy as holding that "nothingness determines being," thus separating nothingness and being so that nothingness can then determine being. If this is so, nothingness and being can only be related in a direct and continuous manner.

The simultaneous appearance of these two descriptions in Takahashi's interpretation seems to suggest that he has mixed everything up and kneaded it into a single dough. If his point is to argue for continuity, it follows as a matter of course that nothingness is "finally only a nothingness confronting being *relatively*." There is no getting around the fact that Nishida's concept of the dialectical universal, in which all things are connected through the dialectical relation of *soku*, is in general far removed from such an idea of continuity. For Nishida, the self-determination of the universal of nothingness exists in (*soku*) the mutual determination of individuals (and vice versa), and this in turn exists in the self-determination of the individual (and vice versa). This circularity of mutual determination cannot be accounted for simply in terms of the idea of nothingness determining being.

I would also take issue with Takahashi's claim that "being determines nothingness." In speaking of the absoluteness of absolute nothingness he argues that "the unity of systematic being and absolute nothingness is itself established within absolute nothingness." If the relation of systematic being and absolute nothingness is one of relativity insofar as the two are "unified," then the absolute nothingness that embraces this relationship and unites the two sides would in fact be relative to this relativity; this relative absolute nothingness could not be true absolute nothingness. Furthermore, the whole scheme requires a "third absolute nothingness" to embrace this second relativity, and so leads to an infinite regress.

This kind of confusion seems to stem from thinking in terms of continuity and analytical logic instead of the dialectical logic that is called for. The option for continuity already appears in Takahashi's claim that nothingness and being are present on the same dimension, intertwined with one another like the warp and woof of a single cloth, while on a different dimension there is a "connectivity" between one being and another, between one nothingness and another. It also shows up in his attempt to use the notion of matter to conceptualize nothingness — an argument we find in Plotinus. Similarly, Takahashi describes elemental nothingness in terms of elemental matter and systematic nothingness in terms of systematic matter. Whereas the nothingness of Plotinus is mere privation, Takahashi sees it as something concrete that embraces particular beings. But they are agreed in seeing nothingness as the point at which being vanishes. If we suppose, with Takahashi, that "all nothingness is connected with absolute nothingness" and that "systematic nothingness is at bottom absolute nothingness," we have to see absolute nothingness as matter, or at least to approach it in terms of matter. Such remarks as "being determines nothingness" and "systematic being qualifies absolute nothingness" clearly demonstrate this material nature of absolute nothingness. Despite his claim that absolute nothingness comprehends both relative being and relative nothingness in its very nothingness, is not his view of nothingness (matter) as opposed to being (form) after all too one-sided to be more than a relative absoluteness?

To go a step further, this conclusion seems to stem from a neglect of subjectivity in Takahashi's thinking. In Nishida's dialectical universal, all types of material things come about in an "individual determination-in-universal determination" as a movement in which the universal determination negates particular individuals and individual determinations are eliminated from the universal determination to which they correspond. And yet no universal determination exists without a *soku* relationship to individual determination. That is to say, form and matter (if one may borrow those terms here) constitute a dialectical unity in the sense that they represent the self-determination of the dialectical universal, and this is where one can begin to speak of actual reality.

Thus, if one were to conceive of a dialectical universal (D) in which the determinative role of the individual (I) or noetic subject was altogether lacking, there would be no more left of it than a simple universal (U). In Nishida's diagram, if one removes I from the formula $\frac{I}{U}D$, D disappears and U becomes a universal of absolute nothingness. In that case, absolute nothingness may be approached in terms of matter. This way of thinking by abstracting from individuals belongs, as I explained earlier, to the intellectual self. It is an idealistic standpoint that eliminates praxis completely from the picture.

In other words, a standpoint that looks for continuity and adopts analytical logic as its philosophical method represents a destruction and a reduction to the abstract of the dialectical system resulting from a failure to consider the noetic and subjective nature of the individual (the self-determination of the individual). It also overlooks the primacy of praxis, which plays the role of providing access to the absolute. This remark seems to be valid to some extent when applied to Takahashi's theory, where the subjective viewpoint is comparatively weak. His concept of absolute nothingness is too meager in its implication of subjectivity to give due consideration to the practical characteristics of the subject. It is only conceived as the outer limit that is reached when being, seen as the absolute whole inclusive of beings, is taken away. Is this not merely carrying the viewpoint of looking at things from above to an extreme of abstraction?

Regarding Takahashi's second point, which is concerned with seeing becoming from the standpoint of becoming itself, that is, with emphasizing the special significance of the finite, I can only express profound agreement. At the same time, I doubt somewhat whether the point is adequately supported by his approach.

To begin with, he claims that actual freedom is always relative and a matter of degree. As plausible as this sounds, when we speak of freedom, can we really think in terms of *degrees* of freedom? Even without appealing to the insights of Kant and Fichte, is it not clear that freedom is by nature infinite or unlimited and that we are able to speak of freedom confined to actuality as freedom only because, while confined in its realization, it remains total in its confinement and infinite in its finiteness? In other words, freedom is purely freedom and necessity is purely necessity, and there is no conflating the two. What we have to see is that actual freedom arises as something finite in its infinitude and scaled by degrees in its absoluteness only by way of a negation of negation: necessity negating freedom, and freedom negating that negation.

It might be objected that something like "infinite freedom" is a mere possibility, not an actuality. But the question is whether we can find a connection between the possibility of freedom and its reality by distinguishing them as two "things," or whether we would do better to think of possibility as belonging to reality or lying beneath it—that is, as the possibility *of reality*. In this latter approach, possibility is also the possibility of something real. It is the subjective force of actuality. Although Takahashi remarks in "Freedom and Existence" that actual freedom also contains at its root the "pure possibility" of freedom, he does not seem to have developed this idea sufficiently from the subjective viewpoint. Indeed, his idea of freedom as a matter of degree seems to involve the same slighting of the subjective viewpoint.

In a word, we cannot conceive of finite freedom without recourse to the notion of a finiteness-in-infinity mentioned above—a state of affairs that recurs again and again in everyday life. For example, can one who has maliciously harmed another plead innocence by appealing to the fact that actual human freedom is a matter of degree? The reason we do not put up with such an excuse is that we attribute to the perpetrator of the act the potential freedom *not* to have done what was in fact done. In criticizing others, and particularly in criticizing ourselves, we always work backwards from actuality to potentiality.

Hence finding freedom in praxis is not, as Takahashi holds, the result of a philosophical "*consideration* of real becoming by bringing it back to the realm of possibility." Where freedom is concerned, the return of reality to possibility is rather a matter of necessity belonging to events themselves. Is not his reducing it to a matter of studied consideration a further result of a standpoint of reflection and abstraction removed from subjectivity? Are we not more concrete in thinking of action and freedom as arising from a dialectical unity that brings together the mutually negating determinations of the self-determining individual and the objective world, that is to say, from the self-determination of the dialectical universal? Nor can becoming or the relative freedom of becoming be conceived of on their own. To see becoming from the perspective of becoming itself already entails viewing becoming in terms of its relation to something beyond it. In other words, the need arises for a unity of what we spoke of earlier as a way of looking at things from above and a way of looking at things from below.

It is the same with time, a thorny question into the thick of which I do not wish to enter here. Although I agree wholeheartedly with Takahashi's attempt to delve into the "time of destiny" by considering how "illustrious men of deeds and ordinary men of no distinction get old and die when their time comes," I cannot help wondering whether this does justice to the idea. Such a view of the time of destiny would also include, for example, the world of plants and animals. But while plants and animals exist in this time, time does not exist in them. Only in the human being are the two sides present such that we can speak of inside-in-outside and outside-in-inside. It seems to me that the cosmic character of the time of destiny needs to be looked at in these concrete terms, and thus that the self-determination of the "world" in Nishida's sense must in one way or another be brought into the picture. (On this point, Heidegger's standpoint of "being-in-the-world" is inadequate.)

It is the same with destiny, which becomes concrete only when one sees oneself in destiny and destiny in oneself. Or again, in the matter of life-and-death, it is only of the human being that we can speak of life-and-death in the true and concrete sense. When all these things are taken to be only something outside the self, this "outside" takes on an abstract meaning. It becomes merely what is viewed as outside by one who does the seeing from a position outside the outside. To see oneself as also inside that outside—and hence as completely belonging to the time of destiny and life-and-death—one has also to see things from a perspective of inside-in-outside and outside-in-inside. Only then can one grasp the outside concretely.

Regarding self-awareness, Takahashi holds that it is not a question of "a self-in-other and other-in-self that comes out like a sudden flash of lightning" but of first "seeing into the other" and then turning back to see oneself. As far as the psychological process goes, this seems true enough, but there is more to it. No matter how far the self enters into the other, even to the point of forgetting itself, one cannot speak even in a psychological sense of the other seeing itself. The very psychological process of seeing into the other rests on the foundations of a *soku* relationship wherein self is self and other is other in absolute independence from one another but in which a connection is also established between the two. Obviously this is not merely a process taking place at the psychological level, and therefore it is hardly proper to speak of it occurring like a "flash of lightning."

To summarize, Takahashi's second point—both the criticism and the assertions he makes from the standpoint of finitude—amounts to a complete abstraction of the way of seeing things from below, while the critique and claims of his first point proceeded by way of a complete abstraction of the way of seeing from above. Both these points rest on the failure to give the standpoint of subjectivity its due. Yamanouchi tries to force the way of looking at things from above and the way of looking at things from below into a tight unity and as a result risks erasing the very traits that distinguish them: their logical character and actuality. Meanwhile, Takahashi pursues these two ways of seeing to the end but does not develop their interpenetration adequately, and as a result he risks reducing both ways of seeing to the level of abstraction.

Earlier I touched on the positive significance of Takahashi's criticism and noted that, whereas Nishida's current philosophical position represents a concrete standpoint that identifies the finite correlatively with the infinite, he tends to view this correlation from the perspective of the infinite and to neglect the perspective of the finite that views it from below. Takahashi's critique points out this tendency in Nishida's philosophy. Indeed it sometimes looks as if the "dialectical universal" and "place" are posited immediately rather than as negative mediations of finite opposites. For a position drawn to a scale that embraces logic as well as life or historical reality, and at the same time uses a radically dialectic logic to make great strides towards the concrete unity of the ways of looking at things from above and from below, we may turn to the sharp and closely argued critique of Tanabe Hajime.

THE CRITIQUE OF TANABE HAJIME

IN HIS RECENTLY PUBLISHED "The Logic of Species and the World Scheme," Tanabe describes his standpoint as one of "absolute mediation." In contrast to abstract rationalism, which begins by abstracting a logic from the immediate things of life and then turns around to deduce actual existence logically, he offers a standpoint of absolute negation, which begins by acknowledging the logic-defying irrationality of life, imports the irrational as its own element of negation, and then negates it again to arrive at a sublated reaffirmation of life. Such logic is not the mere imposition of a rationality that erases life or distorts it, but neither is life itself posited as a pure irrationality standing apart from and indifferent to the mediating activity of logic, as it is in the so-called *Lebensphilosophie*. Life's every assertion of its own irrationality rather makes it mediate the way to logic as the negation of logic, and leads it to set up a logic of absolute mediation in this negation of negation. This is why Tanabe can claim that "merely from a standpoint of the irrationality of life, we cannot even say that life is irrational," and at the same time, that a life-negating logic

> cannot truly negate life in its immediacy as its own negation without sublating it by making it a mediating element of logic itself, negating it in affirming it as that which lies behind absolute negation — the negation of negation.[20]

In the end, Tanabe continues,

---

20. *Collected Works of Tanabe Hajime* (hereafter, CWTH), 6:176.

Life and logic do not exist apart from each other. It is only their correlative identity that exists concretely. When we focus on the aspect of immediacy, we speak of life, and when we focus on the aspect of mediation, we call it logic. Just as there is no logic apart from life, there can be no life of philosophical self-awareness apart from logic. Logic is the logic of life, and the self-awareness of life is the self-awareness of logic.[21]

This enables him to claim further that "dialectic itself is the logic of life mediated through the negation of dialectic" and "a logic that is a truly absolute rationalism."

Such a self-awareness of life through affirmation-in-negation provides the setting for the emergence of a subjective center to life and of a spontaneous, volitional ego. (This ego has a body. For when life enters into the mediating work of logic, it is objectified as the ratiocination of logic and is negated in its immediacy. This objectified life we call physical nature. Hence, when the subjective ego is mediated by negation and emerges in the concreteness of a negation-in-affirmation, it is mediated by the limitations of physical nature — that is, by the body.)

In the self thus viewed as the negating unity of life, unity and the negation of unity go hand in hand. The negation aimed at the unity of the self is both a Thou that is an alter ego as well as an immediate life that provides a common mediation between I and Thou. The immediate life that works to negate the individual now appears as "species." Tanabe notes that since the opposition between I and Thou

> can only be an opposition within the unity of one and the same life — as a negation-in-affirmation on the one hand and as the negation of that unity on the other — mutually related individuals constitute an opposition between affirmation and negation, with the common content of life as the mediating element. The continuous life that provides this common mediation for individuals set in opposition to one another is none other than the species.[22]

---

21. CWTH 6:180.
22. CWTH 6:193.

Species here represents a continuous substratum of discontinuous individual subjects that arise in the act of mutual negation, functioning in a negative mediating role. Just as an individual comes into being by negatively opposing another individual with the common substratum of species providing the negative mediation, so, too, the mutual relationship between individuals and the species is "not an immediate relationship of colorless, indifferent conformity but rather one of mutually negating opposition."

Furthermore, one species cannot avoid opposition with another. The unity of genus arises here as a universal mediating these opposing species negatively. The unity provided by the genus frees individuals by liberating them from the compulsion of species and at the same time universalizes the species to bring it into accord with the individual, thus sublating the opposition characteristic of the species:

> The absolute mediation of the genus as a whole is realized when every opposition between species and individual, between one individual and another, and between one species and another is brought to unity through negation and enters into complete mediation. Indeed genus is simply the concrete universal in and for itself.[23]

The immediate unity of species appears concretely in history as racial *Gemeinschaft*. The species is the substratum of history. When individuals opposed through mutual negation rupture this specific unity and join themselves in a contract for their mutual benefit, they form a *Gesellschaft*. At the same time, the essential structure of the nation is said to consist in a unity through negation in which the individual coincides with the species, the particular with the universal—a unity of substratum-in-subject and continuity-in-discontinuity.[24] On the one hand this unity is based on the substratum of a specific community which it affirms through negation, sublating it into the standpoint of humanity. On the other, it gives full rein to the free initiative of individual

23. CWTH 6:218.
24. For details concerning the notions of substratum-in-subject and continuity-in-discontinuity, Nishitani refers the reader to CWTH 5:292–329 and CWTH 6:264–98.

subjects and to the underlying desire for autonomy. This unity represents the mutually negating unity of the spatiality of the specific substratum and the temporality of the individual subject. By seeing this correlative equivalence of time and space as the world-character of the structure of being, Tanabe erects a world schematic to replace Kant's temporal one. Beginning with the nation as an absolute unity in the sense of what is particular-in-universal, he sets out to formulate an ontology of the world's existence as an actualization of the logic of absolute mediation by structuring all of nature, history, morality, society, and individuality as modalities of the world.

The kind of unity through absolute negation in which the logic of absolute mediation is driven to its outer limits in the form of a self-awareness of logic and of life, is neither mere ideal nor fait accompli. Nor, obviously, is it posited directly and without mediation. As a fact in the making and at the same time a task to be carried out practically, it is rather a unity of "absolute negative nothingness," which surpasses all movement in the process of becoming and yet conforms to it. It is here that "a faith pervading the dialectic from within" becomes possible. This faith "differs essentially from a faith in Other-power, which encompasses faith in a direct and unmediated mode from outside the dialectic itself." It is "an immediate self-evidence of both the realization of the absolute negation at work in the self and the guarantee of an absolute unity in the practical negative mediation." It is also "a trust in the affirmative quality of the absolute negation that forms the bedrock of the infinity of the self." It is, in short, a matter of "self-evidence-in-trust" and only in that sense also of "self-power-in-Other-power."

Tanabe's thought is too rich and overwhelming to succumb to the simple sketch I have just made of it, which has been tailored to the purposes of this brief essay. In any case, the above account puts us in a position to lay out Tanabe's criticisms of Nishida's philosophy.

First, Nishida's "concept of the *place* of nothingness" refers simply to an absolute wholeness posited in a direct and unmediated manner. As a "place that erases being," it is ultimately the product of a nondialectical logic of identity. Consequently, the logic of nothingness, which Nishida tried to present as dialectical by seeing the place of nothingness as bringing about a continuity of discontinuity or a mediation of nonmediation between individuals, falls short of being a true dialectic in that the mediator is itself unmediated. In Tanabe's terms, "it is a logic, but not really a logic."

The above shortcoming arises, Tanabe argues, because of a second lack in Nishida's philosophy: the omission of "species." While Nishida ends up in a self-identity of place by setting up the agent that mediates between individuals as itself unmediated, Tanabe tries to see that mediator as subject to a further mediation, thus leading to an absolute mediation in which everything mediates, and is mediated by, everything else. In place of Nishida's universal of nothingness we are presented with a continuous substratum that mediates individuals negatively—that is, with species. It can therefore no longer be a question of a continuity of discontinuity but only of a discontinuity-in-continuity or a "subject-in-substratum."

Moreover, since the individual is only really an individual in manifesting its "egoity" in a mutually negating opposition to other individuals who are no less involved in the negative mediation of the specific substratum, Tanabe says of the individual that is not mediated by this species: "The individual without negative opposition is an individual, but not really an individual."

And since true genus is only conceivable by sublating the opposition between one species and another negatively by correlating it with the individual, it too fails to appear in the idea of the universal of place. Put the other way around, Nishida's philosophy replaces true specific mediation with a generic universal (in the sense that the term has in a subsumptive logic) and replaces true genus with a sort of extreme extension of species in the direction of the universal. In short, a merely "colorless, indifferent" mediator itself is made into the universal of nothingness and thus also set up against individuals in a direct and unmediated fashion.

Third and finally, it follows from what has been said that Nishida's approach leaves out social existence, and in particular nations and history. "Without the substratum of species," Tanabe writes, "history is history, but not really history." Even where Nishida speaks of shifts in the determination of nothingness from one epoch to another, his is "a religious contemplation pondering history from the standpoint of nothingness." These I take to be the main points of Tanabe's critique.

SPECIES

It seems clear enough that the second point, dealing with species, is absent in Nishida's thought or at least has not been fully developed. In this regard, Tanabe's view of dialectic as "the logic of philosophy," whose logical nature is a finely-sculpted model of clarity in providing a logic of absolute mediation where the mediator is itself mediated, points to a similar lacuna in Nishida's thinking. In its current form, Nishida's philosophy holds that logic clarifies the basic structure of reality itself and represents the logos-structure of reality such that all of reality is logical,[25] but it awaits further development on matters such as the relationship between the "real" and the "logical" that emerges in the structure of the dialectic qua logic and the logos-structure of reality, as well as the status of "philosophy" in his system as a whole.

These points are philosophically serious, and their gravity only increases the more one considers, as I shall do presently, how the self-determination of the dialectical universal in Nishida's thought at times reaches beyond the pale of Tanabe's logic of absolute mediation. But inasmuch as they touch on matters like reality and idea, life and logic, praxis and knowledge, which harbor at their roots the problem of the "philosophy of philosophy," I am confident that Nishida's struggles with these questions will eventually bring new developments to bear on his philosophy. Meanwhile, there is no denying the fact that Tanabe's logic of absolute mediation ranks with Nishida's idea of the dialectical universal as having opened up a new and unprecedented perspective in philosophical thinking and addresses questions that Nishida has overlooked.

The problem is rather with the first of Tanabe's points referred to above, namely his critique of Nishida's concept of the

---

25. Nishitani refers the reader to the concluding sections of Nishida's essay on "The Standpoint of Acting Intuition" (CW 8:107–218).

universal of place, a consideration of which must begin with a question about the logic of absolute mediation. Tanabe claims that this logic is a dialectic that both includes the irrationality of life as a negative element and mediates the negation of the dialectic. I have no problem with the validity of this idea as such, and I have noted above that it represents a thorough attempt to pursue the dialectic as a logic of philosophy. My problem is with the meaning of "life" in this connection.

Life must both negate logic and be negated by it. In negating logic, life is in an immediate mode; whereas in being negated by logic, life passes through the mediation of logic to be sublated, in an absolute negation, into absolute rationality and to become self-aware. If either of these senses of life is missing, no logic of absolute mediation is possible. What qualifies life to negate logic turns around at once to qualify it for being mediated by logic. Without the former, the latter would be impossible; without the latter, there would be no logic of absolute mediation to mediate irrationality. Although this logic is concrete and thorough, it is not entirely above suspicion.

From what has been said so far, does not the fact that the logic of absolute mediation is capable of mediating life in its immediacy mean, conversely, that life in its immediacy constitutes a logic of absolute mediation? Naturally, this logic is not so ineffective as to give the in-itself character of immediate life free rein. Without the power of the logic of absolute rationality, the in-itself character of life could not be taken into this logic through absolute negation and tied into the mediating activity that transforms it into something in-and-for-itself. If, however, the in-itself is taken to be totally transformed into an in-and-for-itself, all that remains is an Eleatic completeness without any trace of a negative element left — yet another reduction to the abstract of the logic of absolute mediation.

The in-itself quality must therefore remain within this logic and maintain ties with the mediating activity that transforms it into an in-and-for-itself, while at the same time remaining within this mediating activity as something that resists it. But this resistance inherent in direct life cannot be derived from logic itself (unless we resort to the approach of the Eleatics). Hence even in its relationship to absolute mediation, life must be inside and at the same time outside. Viewed from the logic of absolute mediation, of course, what is outside can for that very reason be seen as inside, and yet always inside qua outside (the negative element). For a logic whose essence is mediation, this assertion holds true, making it possible, as I noted earlier, to recognize the resultant logic of absolute mediation as a thoroughly concrete logic.

The very fact that all of this can take place means that what for logic is inside in being outside, for life is rather the inside seen from the outside of logic. In other words, only by virtue of its position outside and opposed to the logic of absolute mediation can life bring that logic about and yet maintain its significance as the negative aspect of that logic, that is as its outside on the inside. This negative aspect is rooted outside logic and for that very reason can be within it and yet always outside it. Hence to regard life as the negation of logic from within logic, is still to see it one-sidedly, from the side of logic, and seems to imply further that life is being understood with a certain negativism, even when it is sublated into a negation-in-affirmation. This is the gist of the doubt I wish to raise.

Simply put, life is not related to logic merely as something outside in being inside; it is also inside in being outside. This is a matter not of tautological reversal but of a conversion of perspective, of a relationship in which each element needs the other in order to exist. Obviously Tanabe has engaged himself deeply in this question. A logic affirming life in its immediacy and yet negating it requires "first, that all affirmation must be mediated by negation" and second, "that all negation must mediate affirmation as the negation of affirmation." He continues:

> While the first requirement is clearly a necessary deduction from the essence of logic and hence conditioned, the second appears at first glance to be a free and unconditioned demand that renders the logic possible. In a sense, therefore, the latter imposes limits on logic, and its free recognition is nothing other than the realization of logic. To this extent, it is a matter of *direct self-evidence*. But since it is simply the actual self-awareness of logic, it can hardly be something that conditions logic from the outside; it must rather be the

condition of the possibility of logic *immanent to logic*. . . . Not to recognize this condition means nothing less than to give up logic itself.
The opposition of the mode of immediacy to the logic that it negates is itself something required by logic for its realization. But the
negation of logic is not something unrelated to logic and opposed
to it from the outside. The negation of logic *is brought to self-awareness by means of* logic. Something that opposes logic is recognized as
an opposition to logic within logic.[26]

The foregoing passage is a model of lucidity in setting forth
the concrete and positive sense of the standpoint of logic. From
this perspective the claim that the mode of immediacy is "immanent to logic as the condition of its possibility" no doubt stands up.
But at the same time, it seems to me that the spontaneity of the
"free recognition" that logic grants to the second requirement,
namely that the negation of life through logic mediates an
affirmation of life, must be identified with passivity in the sense
that this recognition is *forced upon it* by life. Could this compulsion
be present without a relationship of inside-in-outside and outside-
in-inside?

It is therefore not enough to argue that life is "the limitation
or negation of logic itself" merely by appealing to the immanence
of life in logic as the condition of its possibility. We have also to
bring an externality to bear on this immanence as its correlative,
so that "possibility" is seen as something that depends on a conversion of the two perspectives, from outside in and from inside out.
To say that logic becomes possible with life as its negative element
can directly be turned around to mean that life makes logic possible. A correlative equivalence between the two (life-in-logic, logic-
in-life) is inconceivable unless the mode of immediacy limits logic
from the outside.

Furthermore, the claim that "the negation of logic is brought
to self-awareness by means of logic" is valid from the standpoint of
logic. But when the logical recognition of the limits imposed on
logic are referred to as a "self-evident immediacy," does not immediate self-evidence imply, as the phrase itself suggests, some-

---

26. CWTH 6:173–74.

thing that cannot be exhausted simply by a "self-awareness through logic"? In other words, the implication is that the activity of self-awareness *through* logic can only take place in correlative equivalence with the passivity that appears in logic in the form of a compulsion — namely, the demands imposed on logical thinking. If this were not the case, we could not speak of a state such as we find in self-evident immediacy in which the negating function of logic is reduced to a bare minimum or the work of mediation is all but unmediated. In short, the immanence of life cannot be seen as a negative element without the externality of life or what we might call the immediate *self*-affirmation of life vis-à-vis logic.

In the foregoing I have tried to approach life in terms of the in-itself substratum of logic, but we could as well approach life in terms of the in-and-for-itself self-awareness of logic. Actually, Tanabe speaks of "the faith that permeates the dialectic from within" as a "self-power-in-Other-power," which is

> none other than an *immediate self-evidence* for the realization of absolute negation in the workings of the self and for the guarantee of absolute unity in practical, negative mediation. The "other" here does not imply belief in what is other to the self but rather a *trust in the affirmation* of the absolute negation that forms the infinite basis of the self.[27]

I admire the profundity of the moral sentiment that animates these words. But can we not repeat here what was said above regarding the term "immediate self-evidence"? Does not talk of "the realization of absolute negation in the workings of the self" and "the affirmation of the absolute negation that forms the infinite basis of the self" rather imply a *self*-realization of absolute negation in the working of the self and a *self*-affirmative character of absolute negation? (Naturally, the sense of "absolute negation" would have to be adjusted accordingly.) In the same way, the element of self would seem to belong to the constitution of things like faith, guarantee, and promise.

Tanabe rejects such an idea because it seems to place the immediate mode of life outside and separated from logic. Although

---

27. CWTH 6:223.

placing life outside logic does make life unmediated, it does not necessarily imply that life has no relationship to logic at all. The relationship is not one of mediation but rather of a "mediation of nonmediation." If what is outside enters into relation through the mediation of logic, since mediation is the essence of logic, a logic of absolute mediation arises in which what is outside is seen as such to be inside.

Here "outside" means only outside logic. The question is whether we can speak of a mediation of nonmediation that surpasses the full breadth and depth of the realm delineated by the activity of logic—going, that is, beyond the pale of absolute mediation—and relates to it through a kind of exit-in-entry and entry-in-exit, to effect a negative mediation and a vital connection between the things that arise within the realm of logic (the individual, the species, relations between individuals, between the individual and the species, between one species and another, and so forth) and logic itself.

On this line of thought, Nishida's idea of the universal of the mediation of nonmediation seems to be fundamentally sound, despite the variety of difficulties that Tanabe has rightly pointed out. Of course, what Nishida calls "the self-determination of the dialectical universal" inverts Tanabe's idea of "the realization of absolute negation" at work in the ego to make it a *self*-realization of absolute negation. In Nishida, the two are related in a correlative equivalence. There the self-determination of the universal—a determining without a determining agent—is the self-determination of the individual. Behind the self-affirmation-*in*-self-negation of individuals he sees the self-determination of the world effecting a relationship of negation-in-affirmation.

But a problem still remains in relating Nishida's idea of the universal of the mediation of nonmediation to a logic whose essence is mediation, since that idea implies that something also stands outside the logic of absolute mediation. The difficulties entailed in working this idea directly into a system of logic are considerable, as Tanabe has indicated. We may need to look for a new way of thinking in order to escape the criticism that "it is a logic, but not really a logic."

SOCIAL EXISTENCE

It has been noted above regarding questions of the state, history, and so forth that the lack of a concept of species in Nishida's thought has landed it in a variety of difficulties. But here again, Nishida's notion of world relates to Tanabe's idea of the state in much the same way that the dialectical universal relates to the logic of absolute mediation. Hegel theorized that the racial spirit of the state would ultimately actualize itself in world history as a universal world spirit. This view requires a conception of the world as related to the state in terms of place or *basho*. Tanabe acknowledges the standpoint of humanity only in line with his idea of the state, which excludes the abstract concept of humanity. For him, it is not a mere abstract universal, but rather a universal in the sense of being particular-in-universal. This approach is manifestly valid as far as it goes, but Tanabe's idea of particular-in-universal seems to come more to life when viewed in terms of Nishida's standpoint of particular-in-universal, universal-in-particular, that is, when the positive aspect of the world implied in the idea of self-determination of the world is recognized.

Further, when history is conceived without attention to its substratum of species, the results are not sufficiently concrete. Nishida's idea of the self-determination of the world as movement-in-stillness contains the possibility of unlimited development from one epoch to another and at the same time conceives of all the ages of history as synchronic self-determinations of an eternal now. As ahistorical as it may appear at first, the idea of synchronicity is in fact indispensable to reflection on culture in history. Philosophy, the arts, morality, religion, and the like are unimaginable without some idea of the past surviving in the present. This is one of the reasons that Nishida chose to reflect on synchronicity.

THE PHILOSOPHY OF PHILOSOPHY

Finally, I must touch on a question that I have deliberately postponed until now. The reason Tanabe lays his foundations by discounting whatever stands outside logic and mediation is that to take them into account would lead to a negation of philosophy. If philosophy needs to have a logic, the conclusion would seem foregone. I have only a simple comment to add. What is meant here by the negation of philosophy is a reversal from a standpoint that views philosophy in terms of its own special logic — that is, from within — to one that views philosophy in terms of life — that is, from without. Thus philosophy is seen as a historical reality, not as a system whose theory encompasses the totality of cultural forms but as one form of culture among others, as one of the many branches of life. In its vital interchange with other cultural forms, philosophy is a *Weltanschauung* in Dilthey's sense of the term. But when philosophy is seen as a *Weltanschauung*, the distinctive standpoint of philosophy in the original sense of the term disappears. This is why Dilthey's idea of the *Weltanschauung* was criticized by those who took seriously the need for academic rigor in philosophy.

Indeed, only when we view philosophy both from without (from the perspective of life) and from within (from the perspective of logic), and then sublate the two perspectives by having them negate each another, can we speak of having arrived at the standpoint of "the philosophy of philosophy." Dilthey, it will be recalled, labored in his final years to contribute to this question but could not find a way to work the perspective of logic into his position and hence failed to reach a satisfactory solution. Even if the standpoint of "the philosophy of philosophy" were accepted in the provisional form that has been presented here, it still needs a logical system in order to be a philosophy. In a word, what this standpoint calls for is a new logic.

TO RECAPITULATE, the criticisms of Nishida's philosophy by Tanabe from the standpoint of the logic of species, by Takahashi from the perspective of finitude and becoming, and by Yamanouchi from the claims of a process dialectic, have all pointed to problems in Nishida's philosophy as it has developed so far. Each of these standpoints (including Tanabe's) shows a tendency to counter Nishida's position with its own distinctive "philosophy from below." At the same time, the idea of the self-determination of the world — the pillar of Nishida's philosophy — seems to me to reach deeply into the ground of historical reality, and for that reason I am less than fully persuaded by what these others have to say in this regard. As for the question of a "philosophy of philosophy" that might synthesize "philosophy from below" and "philosophy from above," we can only await further developments from Nishida and the other philosophers treated above.

In philosophy, as in other disciplines, problems represent a common substratum and criticisms a common process of formation. The purpose of this essay has been to describe a cross section of the current state of this common substratum and its formation as seen in the process of these thinkers' development.

Index